STRATEGIC METEOROLOGY

ROLE OF WEATHER IN WARS

Strategic Meteorology

Role of Weather in Wars

Ajey Lele

Vij Books India Pvt Ltd

New Delhi (India)

Published by

Vij Books India Pvt Ltd
(Publishers, Distributors & Importers)
2/19, Ansari Road
Delhi – 110 002
Phone: 91-11-43596460
Mobile: 98110 94883
e-mail: contact@vijpublishing.com
www.vijbooks.in

ISBN: 978-93-93499-82-0 (Paperback)

Contents

Preface		vii
Prologue		1
Chapter 1	Understanding the Science of Meteorology	12
Chapter 2	History of Weather Impacting Wars	48
Chapter 3	21st Century Warfare and Meteorological Requirements	76
Chapter 4	War and Weather: Case Studies	98
Chapter 5	Weaponising the Weather	139
Chapter 6	Weather Modification Efforts: China and other States	163
Chapter 7	Space Weather and Space Warfare	178
Chapter 8	Geoengineering, Environmental and Legal Aspects	200
Epilogue		213
Index		221

Preface

Since the beginning of history, humans have been affected by weather, occasionally to a shocking extent. From shaping the outcome of wars to indiscriminate destruction of lives and property, at times, weather affects human lives in an adverse manner. Obviously, there is a great attraction towards the science of weather. As a professional aviation weather forecaster, who was required to study, analyse and predict the weather for tactical military requirements, there was always a curiosity about how the expanse of the science of meteorology has contributed at a larger strategic level. This book is an attempt to understand the strategic dimension of meteorology.

I owe my sincere gratitude to the Manohar Parrikar-Institute for Defence Studies and Analyses (MP-IDSA), New Delhi and its Director General Amb. Sujan R. Chinoy for allowing me to undertake this work. I also thank Mr Mukesh Kumar Jha from the MP-IDSA library for his useful assistance.

There have been various Indian Air Force officers, who have been my 'friends, philosophers and guide' for all these years and have taught me the nuances of meteorology; I owe a great sense of gratitude towards them.

Last but not the least, my gratitude to my wife Pramada and my son Nipun for always being there. The views in this manuscript are my own.

New Delhi
September 2022

Ajey Lele

Prologue

S trategy could be viewed as an overall plan to realise the individual or organisational goals under the settings of uncertainty. It involves identifying and fixing goals and priorities and building on mechanisms to achieve them. Strategy also gets viewed as a concept for relating means and ends. There could be various types of strategies: nation's strategy, defence strategy, military strategy or grand defence. They all could be deduced from the character of the means and ends[1]. Strategy is formulated based on objectives and aims of the organisation. For this, the correct formulation of the vision is necessary. Many times, the process of building of organisational mechanisms gets identified as a strategic proposal, which is nothing but a long-term plan. The word strategic, which often gets recognised as a synonym to strategy has wider connotations. The Oxford dictionary identifies the word strategic as something 'relating to the identification of long-term or overall aims and interests and the means of achieving them'[2]. Actually, the meaning of word strategic would depend on the context it has been used. At present, the word strategic gets very frequently used in the business domain too, besides the military domain. In military framework, the meaning of world strategic broadly amounts to the actions undertaken for gaining overall or long-term military advantage.

Possibly, the earliest-known debate on strategy is found in the Old Testament of the Bible. About 3,500 years ago, Moses could be said to have faced a major management challenge after leading his fellow Hebrews out of enslavement in Egypt. At that time, he was the lone strategist at the helm of a nation that may have exceeded one million people. For ease of administration, he began delegating authority to other leaders, each of whom oversaw a group of people. This ordered delegation of authority shaped a command structure that freed Moses to concentrate on the

---

1   Carl H. Builder, "The Army in the Strategic Planning Process", April 1987, https://www.rand.org/content/dam/rand/pubs/reports/2006/R3513.pdf, accessed on Jun 04, 2021

2   https://www.lexico.com/en/definition/strategic, accessed on May 18, 2021

biggest decisions and helped him implement his strategies[3]. Now, for many centuries such structures are found getting employed in social, political, military and business systems worldwide.

History is replete with examples about the use of the word strategy/strategic in the military context. One of the most famous examples of strategy in ancient times revolves around the Trojan horse. According to legend, Trojan horse[4], a huge hollow wooden horse was built by the Greeks to gain entrance into Troy during the Trojan War. The Greeks, offered the horse as a gift, an offering to Athena (goddess of war) that would make Troy impregnable. Actually, there were soldiers hiding inside the horse. As night arrived, these hidden soldiers opened the gates for their army, leading to a Greek victory. Presently, the term Trojan horse gets referred to as treason introduced from the outside. In recent times this term is famous in computing, where a Trojan horse is known to be any malware that misleads users of its true intent.

In the military domain, the word strategic is found getting prefixed for range of actions from goals to objectives to interests to weapon systems to technologies. While in business domain, foreign policy and some other domains the word is found getting used as strategic alliance, strategic planning, strategic management, and strategic disinvestment. Simplistically speaking, the strategic investments is all about the investments made based on some (mainly, long-term) strategy.

A conventional way to understand the meaning of the word strategic in military domain amounts to linking it with the state's plans to ensure security. It is connected with the state's overall long-term military planning for offensive and defensive purposes for achieving success in any conflict. Historically, it has been observed that the development of militaries in particular and warfare in general follows a technological logic. Technology innovation during the Second World War (WWII) and Cold War period was dictated by military requirements and innovations, which used to first happen in military field and subsequently used to find utility in the civilian domain. Computers, Internet and GPS are best examples of such technologies. However, today mainly owing to factors like globalisation

---

3 1.4 The History of Strategic Management – Mastering Strategic Management (umn. edu), accessed on May 19, 2021

4 https://opentextbc.ca/strategicmanagement/chapter/the-history-of-strategic-management/ and https://www.britannica.com/topic/Trojan-horse, accessed on May 19, 2021. In a cyber age, Trojan horse or Trojan is a malware that helps to gain access to users' computer systems illegitimately.

and market economics, new technologies are mostly found first getting first developed in civilian domain. All this is known to be impact the process of strategy building, for the military organisations' world over in some form or other.

In this age of Industry 4.0[5], some major technological developments are getting witnessed. In the year 2003, scientists have succeeded in sequencing the entire genetic code of a human being, to an accuracy of 99.999 per cent. In 2012, scientists confirmed the detection of the long-sought Higgs boson, also known by its nickname the "God particle". Major progress in development quantum computers is getting witnessed and during 2019 Google has officially announced that they achieved quantum supremacy. During April 2021, the National Aeronautics and Space Administration (NASA, the US agency responsible for the civilian space program), lived a 21st century Wright Brothers moment on Mars, when its miniature robot helicopter Ingenuity undertook the first powered controlled flight of an aircraft on another planet. All such technological developments could have long-term impact on the process of strategy building in case of both industry and military.

In the post-Cold War period/post 1991 Gulf War phase, there has been much of talk about the importance of Strategic Technologies for the militaries. When a technology is judged for its long-term relevance in military domain, for its effectiveness to challenge the enemy's military preparedness, then it could be considered as a strategic technology. In the era of Industry 4.0, various new and emerging technologies are found bringing major changes in the military structures. There are some technologies, which are disruptive in nature and are found impacting the process of military doctrine making. Man-machine interphase, Artificial Intelligence (AI), Robotics, Drones, Blockchain, Next-generation genomics, Additive Manufacturing (3D Printing) and some other technologies, which gets viewed as disruptive technologies essentially for military domain are expected to dictate the future of warfare.

There are various debates happening on different aspects of Strategic Technologies. However, there are hardly any reference to the terminology called Strategic Science. At times, there are some passing references to the concept of strategic science and technology (S & T). Here obviously, science and technology are getting clubbed together and finally, the debate tends

---

5   The forth industrial revolution which is normally known to have begun around the year 2000.

more towards deliberating the aspects of technologies, possibly because there is a direct connect between applications and technology.

Much public debate about science and technology policy is normally found dominated by a 'pipeline' model of the innovation process. Here new technological ideas emerge as a result of new discoveries in science and move through a progression from applied research, design, manufacturing and, finally, commercialisation and marketing. Mainly, this model corresponds to the known success stories of World War II, such as the atomic bomb, radar, development of transistor, lasers and computers[6]. The recent examples could be nanotechnology, biotechnology (say the discovery of recombinant DNA techniques) and artificial intelligence (AI).

Broadly, science could be demarcated as the systematic study of the structure and behaviour of the physical and natural world through observation and experiment. While technology is the application of scientific knowledge for practical purposes. There are various branches of sciences, which have been instrumental towards developing an array of technologies which are getting used for the conduct of various activities for survival and progress of human race. Such branches of sciences include astronomy, mathematics, physics, chemistry, biology, zoology, environmental science, earth sciences to engineering sciences and computer sciences[7].

Sciences like mathematics, physics, chemistry and biology are recognised as basics sciences and they help us to understand (to know) more about the universe. We study science owing to the curiosity and the quest for inquiry. For example, we study the scientific discipline called astronomy, because we want to know about the planets and galaxies. Geology is a science that deals with understanding the physical structure and substance of the earth. Depending on the applicability, purpose and the context of the science, one could identify the strategic nature or relevance of that particular science. Tentatively, one can use the terminology Strategic Science, with a purpose to close the gap between knowledge and policy. This could help complement the traditional scientific inquiry by soliciting input from change agents, when a scientist is crafting the research questions[8]. Basic sciences are all pervasive. While the scientific

---

6   Harvey Brooks, "The relationship between science and technology", *Research Policy* 23 (1994) p. 477

7   https://www.oxfordreference.com/page/scienceandtech/science-and-technology, accessed on Jun 01, 2021

8   Christina A. Roberto, "Closing the Scholarship-Policy Gap with Strategic Science", 22

disciplines like astronomy, geology, nano science, info science and few others could be viewed as disciplines, with narrow and specific focus. Meteorology is one more branch of science, which could be said have a narrow and specific focus.

There are various sub-branches of meteorology like climatology, synoptic meteorology, dynamic meteorology, aviation meteorology, oceanography, space meteorology and few others. All these sub-branches have specific purposes. Meteorological information has much of a relevance for various social and business sectors like agriculture, energy, aviation, tourism, disaster management and few others. It is only science of meteorology, which could help to know and address issues related to climate change. Wide canvass of weather information is necessary to understand and to undertake the prognosis of weather. Weather information all over the world, gets collected and catalogued in structured formats of current weather observations (information on temperature, pressure, wind, cloud condition and few other parameters) and medium and long-term weather patterns. Weather forecasting could be viewed as one the most important sub product of the science of meteorology. For any query on weather, first it is necessary to understand the patterns in climate changes and the reasons for weather behaving in a particular fashion. Also, understating atmospheric chemistry and understating the reason behind weather events happening over land, in air and in the oceans is essential. Space weather also has some relevance to understand the future of weather over the earth.

For centuries, it has been observed that the knowledge of meteorological conditions is extremely essential during warfighting. Weather is known to have played a critical role in the outcome of various military conflicts. Weather has always been a challenge for commutation networks in general and even today these challenges continue. To a limited extent, humans have also mastered the art of modifying weather for their own benefit. Unfortunately, there have been some attempts to artificially manipulate the weather systems for gaining military advantage. Today, the concept of space warfare is fast becoming a reality. Obviously, there would be a requirement for having a specific focus on the aspects of space meteorology. All this indicates that there is a need to have an absorbed look at the science of meteorology, exclusively from the perspective of

August, 2017, https://ldi.upenn.edu/healthpolicysense/closing-scholarship-policy-gap-strategic-science-0#:~:text=Strategic%20Science%20is%20meant%20to,or%20advo-cate%20for%20a%20position, accessed on May 27, 2021

modern-era warfare. There have been some important attempts in the past, reviewing the impact of meteorology on various military campaigns. Also, for long military meteorologists are known to be forecasting weather for battlefield needs. Now, with a new paradigm of warfare, there is a necessity to expand on such efforts further, by exploring the strategic applications of meteorology in the context modern warfare.

From a military perspective, at tactical level, weather could have a major impact on the approach and tactics of any military engagement. This could depend on the prevailing (actual) weather conditions (in and around the warfighting area, the so-called tactical battleground) during the phase of combat. The modern-day warfare is mostly not getting fought as a proximity warfare alone, where both the waring forces are expected to be close to each other. Modern-day warfighting platforms can be positioned at much farther distance from the targets and hence it is also important to cater for the enroute weather conditions, before launching any attack. The geographical expanse for the issue of weather forecast has significantly changed than the past. It is also important to note that the weather conditions would impact both sides in a battle, but not necessary in the same ways. So, the military meteorologists are required to be watchful about weather in different sectors, where activities related to war are happening.

Globally, weather is known to have played an important part in human history. Events like floods and famines have always remained the civilisations that humans are at the mercy of weather events. Natural disasters bring more misery of human life. It is important to recognise the fact that from military perspective, weather information has strategic relevance. But since weather systems do not cater for political boundaries, hence long back nation-states have realised that there is a need to proactively share the information of weather with each other. More than 100 years ago the international community decided that in the larger interest of humanity, it is important to share weather related information and technologies, for everyone to prepare for and tackle the potential risks caused by adverse weather situations. Even during the most frigid. years of the Cold War, the Soviet Union and the US used to report weather patterns to each other and to the rest of the world. This is a notable example of continued international cooperation for the greater good, in the interest of taking correct decisions about public safety, agriculture, civilian safety, transport and insurance[9].

---

9   Algirde Pipikaite and Haiyan Song, "What Do Hurricanes and Cybersecurity Have

Globally as scientific understanding started developing, efforts started happening to understand the behaviour of weather. Fascinatingly, wars have played an important role towards enhancing this understanding. For example, we came to know about the phenomenon of Jet Stream when military aircrafts started flying. On various occasions, militaries have experienced that weather has been responsible either partially or fully to change the course of the battle itself. Particularly, during the 20th century, as military technology started making progress, there was a realisation that vagaries of weather impact the performance of the various fighting platforms like ships, tanks and aircrafts. During the Second World War there was a realisation that adverse weather conditions significantly impact the performance of the bombers and other types of aircrafts like transport flights and helicopters. From air, target acquiescence becomes difficult during snowfall, rain, storm or fogy conditions/low clouds situations. Land offensives also requires knowledge of ambient weather conditions and predictions for near future. Knowledge of sea conditions is much essential for any maritime battle, both operations of ships and submarines.

All this pushed the scientific community to invest more towards developing a better understating of the atmosphere and attempting to start estimating the possible behaviour of the weather for the near future.

Planning is the most critical aspect for the militaries to remain war ready. Obviously, there is a need to know in advance the possible weather conditions around the battleground for long-term planning. This could be known from the climate data. Historically, it has been found that the states do undertake the climatic information in consideration in their military planning. Meteorological understanding over the years have improved significantly owing to various technological developments. Also, defence industry developing some of the modern-day military platforms as all-weather systems, however the experience shows that still they have some limitations. Likewise, the nature of warfare and approach towards warfighting is found changing continuously. Issues of human rights are getting much prominence than the past and military leaders are required to keep these aspects in mind, while planning and preparing for war. During the actual war, there are constant efforts to limit the collateral damage and damage to civilian lives and infrastructure. For achieving greater accuracy in bombing operations various factors need more critical examination and weather is one such factor. Cold War period had witnessed instances of

in Common?", October 29, 2019, https://blogs.scientificamerican.com/observations/what-do-hurricanes-and-cybersecurity-have-in-common/, accessed on July 09, 2022

states artificially modifying the weather for the gains in the war. There exists a possibility that such efforts could be done in the future too. Hence, the accurate knowledge of various weather elements in essential, both during peacetime and wartime. There is a need to expand on the earlier lessons learnt about the impact of weather on warfare, in the present context.

War planners always try to prepare for future wars by considering the lessons learnt from pervious wars. Simultaneously, they are required to take into consideration the new technologies adopted by the armed forces and doctrinal changes happening over a period of time, while undertaking the planning process. Knowledge of the past is essential but needs to be deciphered with a comprehension of the context prevalent then. War learnings indicate that, the military leadership involved in the process of strategic planning for addressing current and futuristic challenges need to factor in various dimensions of weather (from a warfare perspective) in their planning process. This it is not to argue that militaries are not factoring weather in their planning processes for all these years. In fact, globally many military setups have established specific agencies to advise them for the weather. However, it is important to note that, the nature of warfare is evolving itself continuously and expected to witness some radical changes in this present era of Industry 4.0. In this era the world as such is found moving from automatic systems to autonomous systems. Quantum technologies and other technologies like Artificial Intelligence, 3D printing and few others have capacities to implode existing military setups. Simultaneously, modern instrumentation is allowing to expand the weather observation base and is also bringing in more accuracy in weather observations and climate/weather modelling.

The relevance of meteorology could be different for different fighting arms. The weather information could have different connections for the army operations, maritime operations and air operations. Like, the sea state could be important for navy, while the information about the prevailing and forecasted upper air wind and temperatures profiles, would be a major requirement for military aviation. For ground forces, nature of specific military maneuvers could have its own requirements, like armoured vehicles and tanks involved in desert operations would depend on particular weather inputs, while air defence artillery could require a different set of weather information. All this indicates that there are short-term, mid-term and long-term requirements of weather inputs for making of policy and strategy. With space emerging as a major theatre for future warfare, there is an additional requirement to evaluate the space meteorology from a warfare perspective.

Hence, any high-order vision of warfare needs to factor in the various climate and weather-related information with more rigour than the past to assist the forces to operate in changing operational environment. Today, major militaries in the world are required to remain prepared for various forms of warfare, which include conventional warfare, asymmetric warfare, nuclear warfare, network-centric warfare, cyber warfare and space warfare. Future operational environments are expected to be more complex than the past. The correct and timely meteorological inputs are likely to enhance the fighting capabilities of the armed forces. Also, there is a possibility that few states could intentionally tamper the weather to fulfil the nation's objectives. Legally such acts are not acceptable. It has been observed that the notion of 'Just War' remains a figment of imagination in the present era. There is a need to put the science of meteorology in the context of warfare bit differently than the past owing to modern-day challenges. From the warfare viewpoint, there would a need to enhance the meteorological assessment process of interpreting and communicating scientific evidence to defence agencies and the state's leadership. Apart from providing the weather information in real time, there could be a requirement of weather forecast for the entire area of operations and some specific military missions related forecasts. Hence, this work attempts to present the warfighting related aspects of science of meteorology as 'Strategic' Meteorology. It is not the author's intention to claim that the weather could be the most important cause to decide on the outcome of the future battles or wars. Nevertheless, importance of weather in the context of modern wars, just cannot be disregarded and there is a need to explore the weather from strategic perspective.

Regrettably, in regards to various military campaigns, it has been observed that the war historians have not given adequate prominence to the significance of the impact of meteorological events in the progress of wars and also on the outcomes of wars. Still in passing some references to the weather and climate specific information are found in been made. If one reads between the lines then some important conclusions could be drawn on. Luckily, some systematic studies have been carried out in recent past (mainly by the military meteorologists) to develop a context of climate and weather in military campaigns. Various historical evidences demonstrate that at least on some occasions, weather has been an important component in the progress (or regression) of the battles, campaigns and wars.

It has been famously said by the strategic thinker Carl von Clausewitz[10] that "War is the realm of uncertainty; three quarters of the factors on which action in war is based are wrapped in a fog of greater or lesser certainty. A sensitive and discriminating judgement is called for; a skilled intelligence to scent out the truth". On various occasions, the climatic conditions and prevailing weather patterns have been found in the 'realm of uncertainty'. Historically, it has been observed that some weather events have extremely impacted the course of battles/wars. A careful examination of the relationship between topography and terrain features of the battlefield and adjoining areas indicates that topography does impact the formation of local weather systems. Hence, it is important to factor in the terrain aspects, while issuing the weather forecasts for tactical battlefields. There are occasions when the prevailing weather conditions had left a remarkable impact on the wars. Both aggressor and defender are required to study the weather before launch of any operation or while offering a response to an incoming attack.

Unfortunately, very less discussion is found happening on the role played by weather in deciding the outcomes of conflicts. Modern-day wars are not found getting fought in isolation, for most of the wars amongst to nation-states, there are power groups backing (covertly or overtly) the warring factions, like in the 2022 conflict, Ukraine has the backing of the European Union (EU) and the North Atlantic Treaty Organization (NATO). The 1991 Gulf War and India-Pakistan War of Kargil (1999) are the initial examples demonstrating the role particularly, the electronic media can play towards framing the public opinion. Now present-day wars are happening in full glare of print, electronic and social media. The presence of various states agencies, UN organisations and media is making lot of information about the actual battlefield scenario out in the open domain. Such information includes terrain and weather-related inputs too. Then again, owing to digitisation of the battlefield more amount of data is available in respect of various aspects of the war. In addition, there has been significant addition to the meteorological data owing to the presence of automatic weather stations, radars, satellites and aircraft/drone observations. For modern-day military meteorologist, it is important to collect the data inputs, not only from the conventional sources alone, but also from the non-conventional sources too and also, when possible, some deductions should be done from the actual data available (strictly, not for the weather information purposes, but for other reasons) from

---

10 He was Prussian general and military theorist (1780-1831), refer Clausewitz, Carl von, *On War*, Princeton University Press, Princeton, 1976, p. 101

the battlefield and adjoining areas. This would help the meteorologists to better understand the weather situation on the ground. All this demands the modern-day meteorologist to raise his/her awareness much beyond the science of meteorology. They need to continuously upgrade their knowledge about the new and emerging military technologies, the changing nature of warfare and more importantly, educate themselves to pick the requisite information by analysing the actual happenings on the battlefield based on the various reports received. Possibly, some weather sensors needs to be added in the systems, which undertake battlefield damage assessment.

There is a view that modern-day fighting platforms and weaponry are state-of-art in nature and are known to be all-weather systems. Definitely, there is a certain amount of change in military thinking since all-weather warfighting systems are available. However, this does not mean that the importance of weather, while planning for military operations has disappeared. It has been observed that even with modern technology, still specific weather inputs are much required. Weather knowledge is important, for the perforce of men (women) and machine. Weather observations are required to be fed to all modern fighting platforms for assisting the platform software towards mission planning.

At the backdrop of all this, it is important to carry out qualitative and quantitative assessment of the impact of weather on war waging. Various climatic assessments and weather models developed would help to prepare for the future wars. The time has come to critically dwell on the 'strategic' dimension of meteorology, the science of weather.

Chapter 1

Understanding the Science of Meteorology

Brief History of Meteorology

The science of meteorology has a long history. It belongs to a branch of natural science called physical science. This science attempts to explain and predict nature's behaviour based on empirical evidence, collected by observing weather and collecting the information acquired by the instruments specifically designed to further the knowledge about the weather phenomenon. Normally, as the name suggests, the science of Meteorology could get erroneously associated with the study of meteors. However, that is not the case. In the Greek language, 'metéōros' is the terminology used for 'things in the air', like temperature, air pressure and water vapour[1]. Hence, the term Meteorology.

Meteorology is one of the oldest atmospheric sciences. The early development of meteorology can be traced back to 350 BC, when the Greek philosopher Aristotle debated about the weather phenomenon and water evaporation in his work Meteorologica. There have been some references to the weather events during the period of the Indus Valley, one of the earliest human civilisations. In a document called the Upanishads (composed around 800 BC to 500 BC), which are available in Sanskrit, a classical language of India, there are references to different seasons, cloud formation and rain. In general, various ancient civilisations are known to have valued the meteorological seasons and events. There are references in ancient Egyptian and Chinese literature giving indications about the knowledge of weather phenomena. The understanding of what we can today, the science of Meteorology, was very limited then. For many centuries, the progress of this science was slow, and it was viewed that this science has fewer practical

---

1   Tiffany Means, "What is Meteorology?" ThoughtCo, Aug 25, 2020, thoughtco.com/what-is-meteorology-3444439, accessed on Jun 06, 2021

applications than other branches of science. Some centuries back, the knowledge available was more in the form of observations/information. Humans had developed some understating about the formation of clouds, possible direction of movements of storms and a few other weather-related phenomena. Also, in those times, humans had developed an understating that the winds are caused by heat, rainfall happens owing to the cooling of moist air, and lightning is a form of electricity[2]. Then these were mostly observational facts, and it took time to understand the science behind the occurrence of such phenomenon.

Aristotle is acknowledged as the first meteorologist. However, his approach was to study weather based on observations, and there was no attempt to discover any scientific understanding behind happenings in the atmosphere. He made many observations, but they lacked the scientific focus and possibly there was no attempt made towards extrapolating the knowledge for weather predictions. But Aristotle is known to have enthused some earliest meteorologists. A contribution towards the science of weather forecasting has been made by his own pupil Theophrastus (372 BC-287 BC). He presided over the Peripatetic School in Athens as successor to Aristotle for 35 years. He had interests in various fields associated with the natural phenomenon. He had great knowledge about the theory of the winds. He presented new theories for advection and for the causes of the horizontal motion of the winds. His famous work called De Ventis (On Winds) is built on a highly accurate observational base. It also contains perceptive comments on climate change, and on local climatic peculiarities[3].

Some four and a half billion years ago, two ancient planets collided and merged into one to become the earth. During the gigantic meeting of these two planets, proto-Earth and Theia – a small rocky mass spun off to become earth's moon[4]. Researchers have concluded that the first human ancestors appeared between five million and seven million years ago, perhaps when some ape-like creatures in Africa started to walk habitually on two legs. They were flaking crude stone tools some 2.5 million years ago. Then some of them spread from Africa into Asia and Europe and

2   "Meteorological Science" in Scientific American 20, 24, 378-379 (June 1869)

3   V. Coutant and V. Eichenlaub, "the De Venus ol Theophraslus: its contributions to me theory of winds", Bulletin American Meteorological Society, Vol. 55, No. 12, December 1974, p. 1454

4   https://www.bbc.com/future/article/20210820-the-subtle-influence-of-the-moon-on-earths-weather, accessed on July 15, 2022

possibly around two million years ago, the earth got inhabited by the human species. Many scientists claim that people who look somewhat like present day humans evolved at least 130,000 years ago from ancestors who had remained in Africa. However, based on some recently made available evidence, for much of the last century, archaeologists have predicted that modern behaviour flowered relatively recently, some 40,000 years ago[5].

The human race possibly started to understand weather patterns when agricultural practices began. These practices are known to have begun 12,000 years ago. Actually, agriculture triggered such a change in society and the way in which people lived that its development has been dubbed the 'Neolithic Revolution'. Traditional hunter-gatherer routines were swept aside in favour of permanent settlements and a reliable food supply. Out of agriculture, cities and civilisations grew. In different parts of the world people took up to farming for different reasons. Like in some parts of the world, climatic changes at the end of the last ice age brought seasonal conditions that favoured annual plants like wild cereals[6]. Directly or indirectly the understating of weather phenomenon became important for cultivating seasonal crops.

During the sixteenth century, meteorology developed on two different levels: a purely theoretical overview based on the work of Meteorologica and atmospheric predictions based on astronomical events. There was good popularity for astrological predictions. There were almanacs and calendars, which presented new compilations regarding signs of weather. The Krakow Academy professor Marcin Biem, is known to have systematically observed the weather conditions during the period of 1502 to 1540[7]. There were some myths associated with occurrence of some weather phenomenon. During the seventeenth century, the so-called divine warnings, punishments and bad omens started getting challenged by a few intellectuals[8]. These were

---

5   John Noble Wilford, "When Humans Became Human", Feb. 26, 2002, https://www.ny-times.com/2002/02/26/science/when-humans-became-human.html#:~:text=The%20first%20human%20ancestors%20appeared,after%20two%20million%20years%20ago, accessed on July 16, 2022

6   "The Development of Agriculture", https://www.nationalgeographic.org/article/development-agriculture/, accessed on Jun 12, 2021

7   The Kraków School of Mathematics and Astrology was an influential 15th century group of mathematicians and astrologers at the University of Kraków (later Jagiellonian University, Poland). Marcin Biemthe (1470- 1540 was a Polish astrologer, astronomer and theologian.

8   Neves, Gustavo & Gallardo, Nuria & Vecchia, Francisco, "A Short Critical History on the Development of Meteorology and Climatology", Climate, 2017, Volume 5, pp. 1-23

times when continental travels started happening, but it was found that mostly the people were reluctant to leave the areas where they were staying. Hence, not much of knowledge about the weather got shared across the continents. Obviously, the belief that the severe weather phenomenon are the signs of divine was difficult to reject. Surprisingly, even today such beliefs are present in some parts of the world.

Weather Observations and Weather Predication

A revolution in predicting weather could actually be said to have happened with the invention of instruments like the barometer and the thermometer. Actually, the process of using instruments for understanding weather phenomenon is known to have begun many centuries back. Weathervanes were invented by the Greek astronomer Andronicus in 48 B.C. to determine the direction of the wind. Italian inventor and architect Leon Battista Alberti gets credited for the designing of Anemometer. This instrument to measure wind speed has been in existence since 1450. The invention of the Rain Gauge happened in Korea during the 1440s. The mercury barometer was invented by the Italian physicist Evangelista Torricelli in 1643. While Daniel Gabriel Fahrenheit, a German physicist invented the alcohol thermometer in 1709 and the mercury thermometer in 1714. The process of undertaking routine and time-bound weather observations began on ships, which used to operate in high seas during the 18th, 19th, and late 20th centuries A.D.

Anne Lawrence-Mathers, a historian at the University of Reading whose work Medieval Meteorology demonstrates that the roots of scientific forecasting are much deeper than is usually recognised. She has shown that comprehensive weather observations and intricate astronomical and mathematical calculations were occurring as early as the ninth century. Arab philosopher Al-Kindi (c. 801 to c.873) put forward the idea that heat was the fundamental driving force for the weather, with heated air expanding into zones where cooler air had contracted, thus determining the strength and direction of the wind. There have been various historical evidence available in respect of issues related to weather in various periods of history. Some of the earliest examples of weather observations have been found in the margins of a calendar from 1269/1270 belonging to English philosopher Roger Bacon (c. 1219/20 to c. 1292). By the 14th century, weather observations were studied together with planetary data to produce 'rules' for weather forecasting. Weather prognoses became popular by the

16th century and weather terminology, such as 'overcast' and 'unsettled', entered the normal language around the same time[9].

Meteorological understating and the aspects of weather forecasting witnessed a major improvement with the advent of the telegraph. Which got established around 1830/40s, and the chief architect behind this development was Samuel Morse (1791-1872). Telegraph transformed long-distance communication. This allowed the weather observations from different locations to be swiftly collected, plotted and analysed. Pattern analysis possibly got easier due to this. By the time telegraph came into being, some process of systematic representation of weather information had already begun. In fact, the earliest known systematic weather observations in the United States (U.S.) were taken by John Campanius Holm along the Delaware River during 1640s. Interestingly, some of the U.S. presidents around that time were also were avid weather observers. The third U.S. president, Mr Thomas Jefferson (1801 to 1809) had purchased weather observational equipment like thermometer and barometer and is known to have maintained an almost unbroken record of weather observations until 1816. While the first president, Mr George Washington (1789 to 1797) also took regular weather observations; the last weather entry in his diary was made the day before he died on 14 December 1799.

The establishment of weather networks is known to have begun during the early and mid-1800's and started expanding across the U.S. The medical fraternity of the U.S. Army realised the importance of weather knowledge towards health management. They issued a directive to Army surgeons in 1818 to record the weather and everything of importance relating to the medical topography in their respective stations. They collected information on climate and diseases prevalent in the vicinity of their area of operations. The idea was to try to find the correlation between weather and disease. It was an attempt to find the cause-and-effect relationship between climate and the soldiers' health and determine whether any change in a given district's climate impacts the health situation over there. In the years following the Civil War (the American civil war: 12 April 1861 to 9 April 1865), the necessity to warn mariners of imminent storms led the U.S. Congress in 1870 to authorise the Secretary of War to take observations at military stations and to warn of storms on the Great Lakes and on the Atlantic and Gulf Coasts. This service was extended in 1872 throughout

---

9   https://www.theguardian.com/news/2021/feb/27/weatherwatch-how-forecasts-emerged-in-medieval-times, accessed on Aug 11, 2021 and Anne Lawrence-Mathers, Medieval Meteorology, Cambridge University Press, Cambridge: 2019

the entire U.S., not for the purposes of war, but for the benefit of commerce and agriculture. The weather agency which got born under the Army's Signal Service then in later years got recognised as the Weather Bureau and at present is known as NOAA's National Weather Service[10]. The National Oceanic and Atmospheric Administration (NOAA) is the U.S. scientific agency within the U.S. Department of Commerce dealing with various atmospheric aspects and was formed on 3 October 1970.

The weather observations gathered over centuries and general scientific understating about the reasons behind the presence of seasons and occurrence of different weapon phenomenon has led to conveying the science of meteorology in a concentrating manner. This is a field, which studies the atmosphere of the planet on which humans are living; its structure, composition, and properties; the physical processes closely related to the earth's surface, water and air; various weather phenomena; weather and climate; and the future state of the atmosphere. The earth's atmosphere is a gaseous envelope gravitationally bound to the planet. To know the status of this atmosphere and its behaviour at a given time, it is important to note the observations at different locations, both on the earth's surface as well as at certain heights above the sea level. In addition, some special observations are taken for monitoring of certain electrical, optical and sound phenomenon, turbulence in the atmosphere and some specific physical processes happening in the clouds[11].

It is not the purpose over here to present a detailed account of the evolution of the science of meteorology since the period of Aristotle till the 21st century. However, it felt necessary to present some important happenings in this process of progression of the science. The purpose is to develop a realisation that meteorology is not a science say like physics or any such natural sciences which made a progression by conducting various experiments in the laboratories. For this science, the laboratory for observation and experimentation is the actual nature and the natural phenomena happening over there, some with regular intervals and some happening unannounced. It is obvious that the strategic (long-term) relevance of this science has been evident for centuries.

---

10 Jay Lawrimore, "Thomas Jefferson and the telegraph: highlights of the U.S. weather observer program", May 17, 2018, https://www.climate.gov/news-features/blogs/beyond-data/thomas-jefferson-and-telegraph-highlights-us-weather-observer, accessed on Jun 12, 2021

11 Vlado Spiridonov and Mladjen Curic, *Fundamentals of Meteorology*, Springer, Switzerland, 2021, p.4

From Galilei Galileo (1564-1642), the father of observational astronomy to astronomer Johannes Kepler (1571-1630) to Edmund Halley (1656-1742) after whom Halley's Comet is named to French mathematician, mechanical engineer and scientist Gaspard-Gustave Coriolis (1792-1843) who by profession were not meteorologists, but are all known to have flirted with the science of meteorology directly or indirectly and are known to played important role towards increasing the understating of this science. Galileo's idea of a thermoscope helped to measure heat in air and provided quantitative meteorological information for the first time ever. While Kepler is known to have believed that the earth's atmosphere was susceptible to planetary influences; for instance the conjunction of Saturn and the Sun would produce cold weather. Halley was responsible to publish a map of the world that showed the prevailing winds over the oceans-possibly, the first meteorological chart. Coriolis described a force, which has an effect of motion on a rotating body. This force is known by his name and is of foremost importance to meteorology and oceanography[12].

Around the period 1659/62, Robert Boyle articulated his famous pressure law pV =constant, when temperature is kept constant (there is an inverse relationship between volume of gas and its pressure). This was followed by the Charles' Law, relating volume and temperature of gas at constant pressure. Combination of Boyle's Law and Charles' Law leads to the well-known equation of state p alpha = R.T. Halley (1686) presented a detailed and methodical account of the trade winds as observed in the tropical oceanic regions. Hadley (1735) accepted the idea of Halley (1686) that solar heating maximum at the equator would lead to horizontal convergence of Northerlies and Southerlies and vertical upward motion near the equator, but he rejected Halley's idea that motion towards warmer region would lead to a net motion also from east to west. He suggested that the absolute velocity of the earth's surface from west towards east is highest at the equator. All this helped in explaining the occurrence of north-easterly and south-easterly trade winds in the tropics[13].

---

12 "Kepler and Weather Prediction", http://www.sites.hps.cam.ac.uk/starry/keplerweather. html and Tim Sharp, "Edmond Halley: An Extraordinary Scientist and the Second Astronomer Royal", December 12, 2018, https://www.space.com/24682-edmond-halley-biography.html, and "Gaspard-Gustave de Coriolis", May 21, 2015, https://physicstoday. scitation.org/do/10.1063/PT.5.030970/full/, accessed on Jun 13, 2021

13 G C Asnasi, Tropical Meteorology, Published by G. C. Asnani, c/o Indian Institute of Tropical Meteorology (IITM): Pune, 1993. p. 1.3 and https://www.intechopen.com/ chapters/71295, accessed on Aug 24, 2021

Normally, there are mainly five basic laws[14] which are known to assist the meteorologists to understand the evolution of larger scale atmospheric flow patterns. They include:

1. Ideal Gas Law (Equation of State): Expresses the relationship of the pressure a gas exerts to the volume it occupies and its temperature. (The product of the pressure a gas exerts and the volume the gas occupies is directly proportional to the temperature of the gas).

2. First Law of Thermodynamics: The total energy of a system includes internal, kinetic, potential and chemical energy. These are related, respectively, to air parcel's temperature, characteristics of the three dimensional wind field, and to the molecular properties of air. This law tells us how the air parcel's temperature changes. It changes either by direct addition of "heat" (such temperature changes are called "diabatic" or "sensible" and examples include conductional warming or cooling, latent head addition etc.) and/or by contractional heating/expansional cooling (such temperature changes are termed "adiabatic")

3. Newton's Second Law of Motion: It states that the acceleration experienced by an object is due to the sum of the forces acting on the object. (An object at rest will be accelerated in proportion to the forces that act on the object)

4. Hydrostatic Law (Obtained from the Equation of Vertical Motion): The upwards directed pressure gradient acceleration acting on an air parcel is balanced by the acceleration of gravity.

5. Conservation of Mass Applied to the Atmosphere (Equation of Continuity): The fractional rate of increase experienced by an air parcel (or air column, following its motion), is equal to the convergence (negative divergence). For stationary air columns or parcels, this simply means that net convergence of air into the column results in increases in density and vice versa.

Apart from the natural forces owing to the variations in factors like the pressure, temperature etc, there is a major impact of topography and terrain characterises on the formation and movement of weather systems. In addition, the oceans are known to play an important role in shaping the climate and weather patterns. Nearly three-fourths of the earth's surface

---

14 http://tornado.sfsu.edu/Geosciences/classes/e260/PrimtiveEquations/Primitive_Equations.htm, accessed on Aug 12, 2021

is covered with water. Approximately, 8000 years ago, humans are known to have started using boats from travelling in waters. Egyptians were among the earliest ship builders possibly around 6000 years back. Over the centuries, it has been mankind's incredible, sea-born drive towards global discovery and interconnection. The voyage, which is known to have begun during prehistoric times and is continuing till date. It is said that 'the very seas' that separates different civilisations actually serves as a liquid bridge, both between neighbouring islands and also amongst the continents and hemispheres. The oceans continue to be the biggest thoroughfare for global commerce. More importantly beyond commerce, for centuries, naval strength is continuing to play a critical part in the international balance of power[15].

Since the human activities in and around the vicinity of oceans had begun, there was much a realisation about the importance of navigation and knowing about the weather. Many centuries back it became clear that weather information is much necessary for supporting various marine and coastal activities. There are many references from the 18th/19th century, where the maritime forces, say the Royal Navy and other Navies, had started collecting weather information and undertaking forecasting of the weather. In 1805, the Irish hydrographer Francis Beaufort, a Royal Navy officer had formulated an empirical measure (the Beaufort scale) that relates wind speed to observed conditions at sea or on land. During 1817, the first global temperature map was published by Prussian polymath Alexander von Humboldt[16]. This was first ever detailed climate report indicating detailed information. With the increased emphasis about pressure, temperature, currents and magnetism, the journey towards modern meteorology had begun.

Around the mid of 18th century some noteworthy efforts were done to form some sort of international network of weather-watchers, they achieved limited success. Actually, there are references to the formation of networks for collecting weather-data during the middle of the seventeenth century in Italy. During 1723, the then Secretary of the Royal Society James Jurin had trained observers to collect timely observations from the equipment made available to them and submit them to the Royal

---

15 Aram Bakshian Jr., "Waterworld: How Oceans Help Shape Human Civilization", Oct 20, 2019, https://nationalinterest.org/feature/waterworld-how-oceans-help-shape-human-civilization-89221, accessed on Jun 14, 2021

16 Sebastian Vincent Grevsmühl, "Images, imagination and the global environment: towards an interdisciplinary research agenda on global environmental images", *Geo: Geography and Environment*, Volume 3, Issue 2, 2016, pp. 1-14

Society. The observers were provided with a thermometer, barometer, wind instruments and knowledge about how to measure the amount of rain or snow collected and decide on the appearance of the sky. All this information was published annually in the Philosophical Transactions journal. The major boost to data collections was given by the Societas Meteorologica Palatina (Meteorological Society of Mannheim) which was set up in Germany in 1781 to coordinate observations of the weather on an international scale. It had requested major universities, colleges and scientific academies for cooperation in data collection. For this purpose, they were given the necessary standardised instruments at no cost. There was a good response to this idea and thirty companies and fifty-seven institutions had accepted the task and received an initial kit containing properly calibrated instruments like barometer, thermometer, hygrometer, electrometer, windsock, rain gauge, and compass. Also, a notebook with instructions was provided, which included requirements like the time of observations to be made at 07, 14, and 21 h. Owing to funding problems, this activity continued only till 1792[17].

The success behind the evolution of the science of weather and atmospheres (in early phase the word Meteorology was not directly associated with such events) is the result of having a sophisticated instruments-based weather observation facility and an attempt to correlate huge data with the weather patterns. Still, forecasting the weather has always been challenging for the forecasters and even today some challenges do exist.

It is important to note that along with the instrument based observations, visual observations have also played (is playing) a major role towards the science of weather. During Dec 1802, Luke Howard[18] (1772-1864, some call him father of meteorology), a manufacturing chemist and amateur meteorologist, in an essay entitled 'On the modifications of clouds', which he read to the Askesian Society where he presented the first practical classification of clouds. The most commonly used classification to various types of clouds, which is based on height and patterns/thickness/size and are known as cirrus, cumulus, stratus, cirro-cumulus, cirro-stratus etc was provided by him.

The late 19th century was the commencement of the creation of most meteorological services, subsequent to the world's first International

---

17 P. P. Aspaas and T. Hansen, "The Role of the Societas Meteorologica Palatina (1781–1792) in the History of Auroral Research", *Acta Borealia*, Vol 29, 2012, pp.157-176

18 D. E. Pedgley, "Luke Howard and his clouds", *Weather*, Volume 58, feb 2003, p. 51

Meteorological Conference in 1853. By the start of the 20th century, most countries in the developed world had established societies specifically dedicated to the study of weather patterns and local climate conditions. The U.K.'s Met Office was the first in 1854. The U.S. Weather Bureau during 1890 got established as a division of the Department of Agriculture. International organisations got established quickly with the International Meteorological Organization beginning in Vienna in 1873. It continued until the 1950s and got subsequently replaced with the World Meteorological Organization (WMO)[19].

The British Royal Navy officer named Robert FitzRoy gets recognised as the father of modern-day forecasting. However, Vice Admiral Robert FitzRoy story is a very tragic story. Since 1831, he was involved into charting coastlines around South America, the South Pacific and the Indian Ocean. During 1854, he established a new weather department within the Board of Trade, the forerunner to the modern U.K. Met Office. He designed a new type of barometer, gave regular storm warnings to ports, and issued the first daily weather forecasts to newspapers. Like modern meteorologists and climatologists, he also faced intense scrutiny. Obviously, during those times there was a lack in precision for forecasting and some forecasts did go totally wrong. This led to some ridiculing his often laughably inaccurate predictions. He was being ridiculed publicly in the newspapers in the most derisive and humorous terms. He undertook acute stress of predicting the weather and finally on 30 April, 1865 he committed suicide[20].

During August 1861, the London-based newspaper The Times published the world's first 'daily weather forecast'. It was Robert FitzRoy, who had invented this term. He wanted to distance his work from astrological 'prognostications'. There was a general understanding then that weather forecasting was an entirely modern phenomenon and that in earlier periods only quackery or folklore-based weather signs were available. However, subsequent research demonstrates that astronomers and astrologers in the medieval Islamic world drew widely on Greek, Indian, Persian, and Roman knowledge to create a new science termed astrometeorology. There was a push for astrometeorological forecasting. This led to the development of records of precise observations. Such records mainly kept by Europeans during the 13th century, have been very

---

19 https://www.environmentalscience.org/meteorology, accessed on May 30, 2021

20 Jeremy Deaton "The tragic story of the founder of weather forecasting in Victorian England", Apr 25, 2021, https://www.washingtonpost.com/weather/2021/04/25/robert-fitzroy-meteorology-weather-forecasting/, accessed on Jun 20, 2021

useful in correlating with astronomical data. All this paved the way for the data-driven forecasts produced by FitzRoy[21].

In 1917 the Norwegian physicist Vilhelm Bjerknes presented his theory describing the formation of wave cyclones on the polar front and laid the basis for modern approaches of weather forecasting. In 1922, L. F. Richardson professed the basis for the mathematical prediction of atmospheric circulation. During 1938 C. G. Rossby made additional mathematical contributions. Assessment of some such theoretical postulations became possible with the introduction of high-speed electronic computers. This machine was first used for weather forecasting in the late 1940s by J. G. Charney and John Von Neumann. By 1955, computer-based operational forecasting became a reality[22]. Another big and positive change in forecasting techniques happened with the availability of satellite imagery and data during 1959. Radar technology has also played a very dominant role towards improving the understating of the weather.

Over a period of time, there is a general realisation that weather forecasting is an imperfect science. It offers us probabilities of a particular outcome, not a conclusive prediction. Weather predictions can go wrong for various reasons and Chaos Theory offers a definitive explanation for that. This theory argues that conditions can change wildly based on minor fluctuations in conditions. In fact, much before the formulation of this theory in his 1814 treatise, "A philosophical essay on probabilities," the French mathematician Pierre Laplace (1749-1827) argued that any need to invoke probability in nature stemmed from ignorance, including uncertainty in weather forecasts. Sooner or later, he suggested, weather forecasts would be perfectly accurate, as predictable as the orbits of planets, with nothing left to chance. Yet even if it weren't for quantum phenomena like Heisenberg's uncertainty principle, this wouldn't be the case. No matter how well you know the initial conditions, determinism doesn't rule the Universe. Prof Edward Lorenz (1917-2008), the father of Chaos Theory who had worked as a meteorologist during the Second World War and subsequently at MIT (dynamic meteorology and forecasting) had argued that long-term forecasting is not feasible. He argued that chaos theory proves that weather and climate cannot be predicted beyond the very short term and that even with modern state-of-the-art observing systems and

---

21 Anne Lawrence-Mathers, "Medieval weather prediction", *Physics Today*,74, 4, 38 (2021)

22 "Meteorology: Modern Meteorological Science and Technology", https://www.info-please.com/encyclopedia/earth/weather/concepts/meteorology/modern-meteorologi-cal-science-and-technology, accessed on Jun 06, 2021

models, weather/climate, it still cannot be predicted beyond 2 to 3 weeks in advance[23]. He believed that long-term climate forecasting is impossible.

The art (and science) of forecasting as mentioned above has a long history. For forecasting it is important to first understand the normal composition of the atmosphere around us and then take into account the specific changes happening before and then take into account the deviations from the normal pattern. It is the atmosphere, which is a critical part of the water cycle. It moderates earth's temperature and weather takes place in the atmosphere. Atmospheric pressure, air temperature, humidity, wind profile (direction and speed), nature of clouds present, and precipitation are all atmospheric characteristics of the transitory states what we call as a weather. Atmosphere could also be identified with the thin layer of gases surrounding the earth. It holds the planet earth by the force of gravity. For any student of meteorology, it is important to have a good knowledge about the structure of atmosphere.

Structure of Atmosphere

The earth's outermost atmosphere is a region of extremely low density. Near mean sea level (MSL), the quantity of atoms and molecules present in a cubic centimetre (cc) of air is about $2x10^{19}$, while at altitude around 600 km the amount is about $2x10^7$. At sea level, an atom or molecule on the average move about 7x10-6 cm distance before colliding with another particle. While at the 600 km level this distance (called as the 'mean free path') is about 10 km. Broadly, near sea level, an atom or molecule undergoes about $7x10^9$ collisions each second, whereas near 600 km, this it is about 1 each minute. It is important to note that both pressure and temperature change with the altitude. The atmosphere can be divided into four different regions. The diagram[24] below shows these regions along with the altitude and temperature profile.

---

23 https://archive.org/details/philosophicaless00lapliala/page/n5/mode/2up and Paul Halpern, "Chaos Theory, The Butterfly Effect, And The Computer Glitch That Started It All", Feb 13, 2018, https://www.forbes.com/sites/startswithabang/2018/02/13/chaos-theory-the-butterfly-effect-and-the-computer-glitch-that-started-it-all/?sh=1c25727469f6 and http://www.lavoisier.com.au/articles/climate-policy/science-and-policy/chaos-theory-and-weather-prediction.pdf accessed on Jun 21, 2021 and "The Bulletin Interviews: Prof Edward N. Lorenz", WMO Bulletin, Volume 45, No 2, Apr 1996

24 http://sir-ray.com/Chapte6.jpg, accessed on April 16, 2021

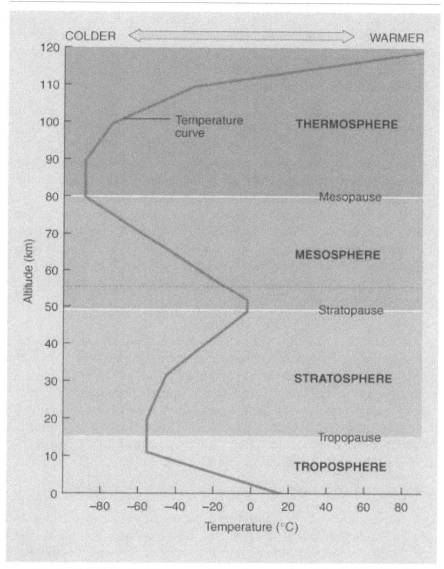

As depicted in the diagram above, 'troposphere' is the bottom layer, where temperature decreases with altitude and is present till around 12 km. Most of the weather phenomenon happen in the troposphere. The top of the troposphere is the tropopause, above which lies the stratosphere. This layer is stratified with the denser, cooler air below the warmer, lighter air. Here an increase in temperature with height is noticed. This layer extends till about 45-48 km. The stratospheric region has less turbulence and is frequented by aviation activities. It has been found that the temperature increases with height till about 48 km altitude, where it reaches to about 10°C. Owing to the presence of ozone in the stratosphere, rise in temperature with the altitude happens. Here ultraviolet light interacting with the ozone causes the temperature increase. The boundary between the stratosphere and the next layer is called the stratopause.

The temperature again starts decreasing with altitude above the stratopause, and this layer is called the mesosphere. This layer extends till about 80 km and temperature there almost drops to about negative 90°C. In the above mesosphere, the mesopause is located. Beyond mesopause is the layer called thermosphere, which starts and extends well beyond 120 km. Here again the temperature starts rising with height drastically. Above the thermosphere lies the exosphere, where the molecules have enough kinetic energy to escape the earth's gravity and therefore fly off into space. This is the region where helium disappears. The outer part of the mesosphere and the thermosphere also gets identified as the ionosphere. The thermosphere thus constitutes the larger part of the ionosphere. Broadly, ionosphere lies from about 80-400 km in height.

The ionosphere is electrically charged as short-wave solar radiation ionises the gas molecules. The electrical structure of the atmosphere is not uniform and is arranged into three layers: D, E and F. Since the production of charged particles requires solar radiation, the thickness of each layer, particularly the D and E layers, changes from night to day. The layers weaken and vanish at night and reappear during the daytime. The F layer is present during, both day and night. Above stratosphere (mostly), no weather activity takes place. But, the change in the height of the various electrically charged layers affect radio signals[25].

Classification of Meteorology

A broad scan of available literature on atmospheric sciences and weather prediction indicate that the classification of meteorology has been attempted differently by different agencies/scientific groups. The following paragraphs present a normally accepted organisation of the science of meteorology. The categories identified are from the point of view of general understanding of the subject and no intricate process of classification has been followed.

---

25 For the discussion above on atmosphere, please refer http://www.ux1.eiu. edu/~cfjps/1400/atmos_struct.html, accessed on Jun 24, 2021

Earth encompasses of gas (atmosphere), liquid (hydrosphere) and solid (lithosphere). Normally, all these three components are studied together under the branch of science called geophysics. Important sub-branches of geophysics include earth physics and oceanography. Since, there is a significant amount of impact of sun on the weather, studying the physics of sun is also important for the overall understating. Presently, for deeper understating of weather and climate, scientists are known to study both the layer of atmosphere in the shallow vertical space up to a height of 20 km and also the upper part of the atmosphere. Aeronomy is a branch of science, which studies the upper parts of the atmosphere. Hence, to develop correct understanding of meteorology, it important to factor in the nuances of all such branches of sciences.

Classification of meteorology could be done into various sub-branches that study fundamental principles of science of physics in general and meteorology in particular. Also, the classification is done based on the geographical regions/areas where typical weather conditions are observed. In addition, there are various types of meteorology which are identified with the scale of processes. They include micro (horizontal dimensions 1 km or less) and mesoscale (horizontal dimensions 5 km to several hundred km) meteorology, syntonic scale (horizontal length scale, 1000 km or more) meteorology and global (planetary scale) meteorology. Following table offers details about the scales of atmospheric motion systems[26]:

Type of motion	Horizontal scale (meter)
Molecular mean free path	10^{-7}
Minute turbulent eddies	$10^{-2} - 10^{-1}$
Small eddies	$10^{-1} - 1$
Dust devils	$1-10$
Gusts	$10 - 10^2$
Tornadoes	10^2
Thunderclouds	10^3
Fronts, squall lines	$10^4 - 10^5$
Hurricanes	10^5
Synoptic Cyclones	10^6
Planetary waves	10^7
Atmospheric tides	10^7
Mean zonal wind	10^7

26 James R. Holton, *An Introduction to Dynamic Meteorology*, Elsevier Academic Press, London, 2004 (fourth edition), p.5

There are three basic branches of meteorology, which study the fundamental principles. They are dynamic meteorology, physical meteorology and applied meteorology.

Dynamic meteorology is the study of those motions of the atmosphere that are associated with weather and climate. Here the movements in atmosphere are studied using laws of dynamics and thermodynamics of the atmosphere. Physical meteorology deals with the study of optical, electrical, acoustical, and thermodynamic phenomena in the atmosphere including the physics of clouds, aerosols and precipitation. It elucidates the physical processes in atmosphere like solar radiation, absorption, reflection and scattering and, ongoing terrestrial radiation. While applied meteorology is an arena of study, where interpretation and analysis of weather data is carried out. It essentially deals with weather and climate predictions and putting them to practical use. Here a connection between the science of meteorology and fields like transportation, agriculture, health, water etc. are, is made. The sub branches of applied meteorology include synoptic meteorology, climatology, aviation meteorology, hydrometeorology, radar and satellite meteorology and some more[27].

Technology used for Observations and Analysis

Earlier in this chapter, some mentions have been made about few inventions like the Anemometer, Rain-gauge and few other metrological observational equipment. The process for the development of the instruments was possibly happening at various laboratories. In literature there are references which mention that the air thermometer was invented in 1600, perhaps by Galileo. His acolyte Castelli standardised a rain-gauge in 1639. Another understudy working with Galileo, knows as Torricelli, invented the barometer in 1644. By that time, different forms of hygrometer and anemometer also made their appearance[28]. These are very basic equipment, but they have survived the test of the time and are still in use in some modified form.

---

27 James R. Holton, *An Introduction to Dynamic Meteorology*, Elsevier Academic Press, London, 2004 (fourth edition) and B. J. Retallack, *Physical Meteorology*, Secretariat of the World Meteorological Oranization, 1973 and Vlado Spiridonov and Mladjen Curic, *Fundamentals of Meteorology*, Springer, Switzerland, 2021, pp.4-11 and https://www.dictionary.com/browse/ physical-meteorology# :~:text=the%20branch%20of% 20me-teorology%20dealing,physics% 20of%20clouds% 20and%20precipitation, accessed on Aug 02, 2021

28 G C Asnasi, *Tropical Meteorology*, Published by G. C. Asnani, c/o Indian Institute of Tropical Meteorology (IITM): Pune, 1993. p. 1.3

A barometer, thermometer, wind vane and a few other equipments helped collecting useful information about various weather parameters. Presently, in order to increase the data availability various automatic weather stations are located at far-flung places, which provide continuous observations. Weather balloons were the rudimentary tool then for getting knowledge of wind patterns in upper atmosphere (primary source of data above the ground). At present, balloons are still is use duly supported by modern technologies and are tracked by radars. A gadget called a radiosonde is attached to these balloons to measure pressure, temperature and relative humidity, as it climbs up into the atmosphere.

Initially, immediately after the Second World War, various important breakthroughs were found happening in arena of weather prediction. This could be said to have happened, because much technological upgradation had happened during this war. There was a realisation that military platforms could also be used obtaining weather observations. The radar technology and weather observations taken form the aircrafts/ships ended up increasing the accuracy and range of the observations. There was increase in knowledge about the impact of terrain on local weather situation. Eventually, all this had led to increasing the accuracy in the forecasting.

The British began using microwave radar in the late 1930s to monitor enemy aircraft. It was observed that the radar give excellent returns from raindrops at certain wavelengths (5 to 10 centimetres). Radars were found useful to track and study the evolution of individual showers or thunderstorms. They also helped to provide some advance 'knowledge' about the precipitation structure of bigger (super) storms. Today, with meteorology specific developments in technology, radar have grown as a major forecaster's tool and play an important role in the storm forecasting. Radar observation of the growth, motion, and characteristics of such storms provide clues as to their severity. Contemporary radar systems use the Doppler principle (Doppler radars) of frequency shift associated with movement toward or away from the radar transmitter/receiver to determine wind speeds as well as storm motions. There are other types of radars too, which have meteorological observation utility. Some of them are getting used for continuous detection of wind (otherwise upper wind observations are taken only twice a day). These wind-profiling radar systems essentially pick up signals' reflected' by clear air and so can function even when no clouds or rains are present.

Satellite technology is another technology, which offer great advantages for knowing the exact weather patterns. Around since 1959, satellites are providing cloud imagery, which is helping in predicting various weather phenomena. These images are of a great help to understand and predict the behaviour of hurricanes, cyclonic storms, tornados, cloud bursts and monsoon rains. For some years now, there are specifically designed meteorological satellites. The infrared (I.R.) sensors on such satellites gives observations of the vertical temperature structure of the atmosphere, which greatly help in weather forecasting[29]. Computers, particularly the supercomputers are of great help in climate modelling and makes numerical weather prediction easier. Moreover, there are various modern information processing systems available, which generates graphics and hazardous weather warnings.

Supercomputers are in use for accurate weather and climate-change forecasting. Japan's Fujitsu Laboratories used the world's most powerful supercomputer, Fugaku, to develop an A.I. based model to predict tsunami flooding. While Hewlett Packard Enterprise is known to be developing a supercomputer, which are meant for use at the NCAR-Wyoming Supercomputing Centre[30] in the U.S., to help study climate change and cases of severe weather occurrences. In February 2020, the U.K. government had announced funding of £1.2 billion to develop this supercomputer, which is expected to be one of the top 25 supercomputers in the world. This system is likely to be operational by 2022/2023 and is expected to provide accurate warnings on severe weather and help protect from impact of increasingly extreme storms, floods and snow in the U.K[31].

Presently many states in the world are known to using supercomputers for weather forecasting. For example, the National Weather Service (NWS) of the U.S. uses supercomputers around the clock to accurately produce forecasts, watches, warnings and a whole host of data for the public. This

---

29 The information on radar and satellites is referred from https://www.environmental-science.org/meteorology and "Meteorology: Modern Meteorological Science and Technology", https://www.infoplease.com/encyclopedia/earth/weather/concepts/meteorology/modern-meteorological-science-hand-technology and https://www.britannica.com/science/weather-forecasting/Progress-during-the-early-20th-century accessed on Jan 06, 2021

30 Is a high-performance computing and data archival facility located in Cheyenne, Wyoming that provides advanced computing services to researchers in the Earth system sciences

31 Ishan Patra, "World's most powerful weather, climate-change forecasting supercomputer to be built in UK", Apr 26, 2021, *The Hindu*

system is recognised as the most powerful weather-predicting systems in the world. These supercomputers run sophisticated numerical models of predicting weather changes in atmosphere, ocean, and even for space. These supercomputers make use of virtually all observational data that the NWS collects. Finally, the forecasts are issued for various kind of weather hazards including hurricanes, tornadoes, extreme heat, and even space weather. The NWS has been using supercomputers for many decades now. The latest major update to the computer systems was done during 2018. At present, the combined processing power of NWS supercomputers is 8.4 petaflops, which is more than 10,000 times faster than the average desktop computer[32].

Weather Forecasting

The science of Meteorology has direct applicability to human life. For conduct of various activities on land, water, air and space knowledge of weather and the possible trajectory of the behaviour of the weather is essential. Weather warnings/alerts and weather forecasts plays a major role in the conduct of various activities by the humans. For weather forecasting, the basic necessity is the availability of timely and reliable data. Also, is important to have the data covering large geographical extent, both at the horizontal scale and vertical scale. For this purpose, globally the data gets collected in form of surface weather observations and upper-air weather observations.

The fundamental data is in form of surface weather observations. They include information in respect of atmospheric pressure, temperature, wind speed and direction, humidity and precipitations like rain and snow. Also, the present atmospheric condition like rain, thunderstorm, fog, dust storm etc is taken into consideration. In addition, the visual observations about low, medium and high clouds (if any) are taken. Such observations are taken either manually or they are received from the automatic weather stations. The upper-air weather observations are collected by using various means. They include wind (direction & speed) and temperature data at various altitudes. Mainly weather balloons, radiosonde and dropsondes apparatus are used for this purpose. Some data is also collected from observations taken by mostly the commercial aircrafts flying on standard routes and ships at sea. Military aircrafts also share such observations with their agencies. Radar observations add to the kitty of observations. In addition, based on cloud movements, satellite-derived winds are made

---

32   https://www.weather.gov/about/supercomputers#, accessed on Aug 12, 2021

available at uniform intervals. Numerical weather model algorithms help in providing (creating) inferred data, which subsequently becomes an input for model forecasting.

Meteorological observations taken around the world have specific patters for representation on the metrological charts. They are plotted in a specific fashion. The data gets further formatted and presented with in grid and graph form and also in a diagrammatic format. There could be differing data-access and data presentation policies in the case of a few countries, however, broadly the similar pattern for data presentations is followed globally. The data gets collected at specific intervals globally (mainly at, 0000 and 1200 UTC). It is further transmitted on the Global Telecommunications System (GTS) of the World Meteorological Organization (WMO) to regional and global centers. There the data inputs are collated, redistributed back across the GTS, and used in various numerical forecast models. Present-day forecasters use interactive computer systems, which are very important to manage the huge mass of available data[33].

Climatologists and meteorologists are known to be focussing on two basic types of forecasting: deterministic and probabilistic, both of which have multiple subsets. A deterministic forecast predicts a specific event that will occur at a precise location and place, like providing the location for landfall of tropical cyclone/hurricane or a tornado. Probabilistic forecasting leads to suggesting the outlook of weather events that may occur in a certain region during a set period, for example, a storm that may last for few days.

Some of the specific forecasting methods include[34]:

1. **Climatology Method:** It offers a simple technique for generating a weather forecast. This is based on the weather statistics, which is calculated by using the weather data for several years in the past.

2. **Analog Method:** Here the forecasters look for comparable type of meteorological conditions in the past and offers a forecast on the lines the weather conditions had developed then.

---

33   George Huffm, "Weather Forecasting", https://www.scholastic.com/teachers/articles/teaching-content/weather-forecasting/, accessed on Aug 06, 2021

34   Laurie Brenner, "Four Types of Forecasting", November 22, 2019, https://sciencing.com/four-types-forecasting-8155139.html, accessed on Aug 06, 2021

3. **Persistence and Trends Method:** The forecast issued is based on the past trends.

4. **Numerical Weather Prediction:** These are algorithm-based forecasts. Here software forecasting models undertakes into consideration multiple inputs about the atmospheric conditions like temperatures, wind speed, high- and low-pressure systems, rainfall, snowfall and other conditions.

There are few other methods (mostly from 19th century), which are also put in use even today (in a limited sense) and they include the Use of Barometer, Looking at Sky and Ensemble Methods. Forecasters do get reasonably good indications from the variations in the barometric pressure and the pressure tendency. The larger the change in pressure (say more than 2.54 mmHg), the larger the change in weather is likely. If the pressure drop is rapid, expect the approach of a low-pressure system with increased chances of rain. Rapid pressure rise normally leads to clear sky conditions. Looking at sky allows to observe the variations taking place in cloud cover. Thick and heavy cloud increases the possibility of rain, mainly in hilly areas. The presence of morning fog indicates that the weather would become clear since there is an absence of wind and cloud. The aim of ensemble forecasting is to give an indication of the range of possible future states of the atmosphere[35]. Ensemble forecasting involves the making of many forecasts in order to reflect the uncertainty into the initial state of the atmosphere[36]. Say, in case of tropical cyclone forecasting, different methods of forecasting could be (like Persistence, Analog and other Mathematical methods) used and the outputs received as taken together and averaged out. Also, greater number of runs of the forecast model are undertaken and the best fit is found using the law of averages. They also could be viewed as probability forecasts, which indicates that the probability of the event occurrence, like say there is 70% of changes of the fog appearance.

Meteorologists are required to issue short-range, medium-range and long-range forecasts. Very short-range forecasting is known as Nowcasting, which is a forecast for a period of less than six-hours. Normally, visual, satellite and radar observations studied at the backdrop of the forecast for the day, helps for issuing such very short-range forecasts. Weather

---

35 https://www.stratumfive.com/climate/extended-range-forecasting-making-sense-of-chaos/, accessed on Aug 09, 2021

36 Iseh A J and Woma T Y, "Weather Forecasting Models, Methods and Applications", *International Journal of Engineering Research & Technology* (IJERT), Vol. 2 Issue 12, December 2013, pp.1953-54

warnings are issued for various requirements. It could be possible to give a notice a day or two/three in advance about the possibility of heavy rains, floods, snowstorms or some other weather phenomenon, which could lead to very adverse weather conditions. On the other hand, particularly in the case of military aviation, the weather warnings are given only few hours in advance say, for one or two hours. Such warnings belong to the category of forecasting called Nowcasting.

Short-range weather forecasts are generally issued for a period of six to twelve hours. On occasions such forecasts could be issued even for period of 48 hours. Medium-range forecast is normally issued for 6 to 10 day period. While the extended-range and long-range weather forecasts are issued for a period of month or more. Various meteorological events have their own lifecycles and the forecaster needs to issue the forecast accordingly. The following table give indications about the type of meteorological events happening in the different parts of the world and their duration[37]:

Phenomena	Geographical occurrence	Temporal /Spatial scale
Madden Julian Oscillation (MJO)	Tropical	30 – 40 days
Planetary waves	Mid latitudes	10 – 20 days
Baroclinic waves	Mid latitudes, subtropics	3 days
Tropical Cyclones	Tropical	7 days
Easterly waves	Tropical	7 days
Thunderstorms	Anywhere	5 hours
Fog/Haze	Anywhere	Hours/days
Droughts	Anywhere	Days/Months
Heat /Cold waves	Except Equatorial regions	Days/Weeks
South West Monsoon	Tropical & Equatorial regions (mainly Indian region)	Four months

37 http://www.wamis.org/agm/meetings/walcs10/S3-Mukhopadhyay.pdf and https://www.britannica.com/science/weather-forecasting/Progress-during-the-early-20th-century, accessed on Jun 24, 2021 and A James Wanger, "Medium and Long-range Forecasting", Weather and Forecasting, Vol 4, Issue 3, Sept 1989, pp. 413-426

As per one definition, an extended-range forecast, provides an overview of the forecast for the coming 46 days, focusing mainly on the week-to-week changes in the weather. Similar to the medium-range forecasts, the extended-range forecasts too include information like the possibility of the occurrence of the tropical cyclone/hurricane activity during the period of forecast. A significant source of predictability on the monthly time scale, is the Madden-Julian Oscillation (MJO), which is characterised by an eastward propagation of convection in the tropics, characteristically started over the Indian Ocean[38].

When such forecasts, which are issued one and half months in advance, gets stretched to three months, then they are known as long-range forecasts. These forecasts provide information about expected future atmospheric and oceanic conditions. Different types of numerical forecasting models are used for issuing medium-range, extended- range and the long-range forecasts. Long-term predictions rely on aspects of Earth system variability, which have long time scales (months to years) and are, to a certain extent, predictable. The most important of these is the ENSO (El Nino Southern Oscillation) cycle. Although ENSO is a coupled ocean-atmosphere phenomenon centred over the tropical Pacific, the influence of its fluctuations extends around the world[39]. Various other causes of predictability are also inputted in the model. For example, for the prediction of the intensity of South West Monsoon (Indian Monsson), parameters like the European Snow Cover and the Southern Oscillation (the difference in pressure over Tahiti and Darwin) are also taken into account by some models.

The following table[40] gives the forecasting ranges indicating how early the forecasts for some weather phenomenon could be issued and what is the normal area coverage for such forecasts:

---

38 https://www.ecmwf.int/en/forecasts/documentation-and-support/extended-range-forecasts, accessed on Jun 23, 2021

39 https://www.ecmwf.int/en/forecasts/documentation-and-support/long-range, accessed on Jun 23, 2021

40 http://www.wamis.org/agm/meetings/walcs10/S3-Mukhopadhyay.pdf, accessed on Aug 02, 2021

Range	Time	Methods	Phenomena	Utility
Nowcasting	6 hrs	Radars etc	Hailstorms, Squalls with high accuracy	Severe Weather Warnings (500 m to 1 km)
Short Range	2-3 days	Atmospheric Models	Synoptic scale weather systems	Conventional Forecasting resolution (3-25 km)
Medium Range	7-10 days	Global Atmospheric Models	Synoptic scale weather systems	Conventional Forecasting resolution (25 – 50 km)
Extended Range	10–30 days	Climate Model	Persistent systems • Blocking Highs • MJO • ITCZ	Droughts and Heat / Cold Waves

Numerical Weather Prediction

Presently, Numerical Weather Predication (NWP) is the comely used technique for weather predication, almost universally. NWP employs a set of equations that describe the flow of fluids. These equations are translated into computer code and use governing equations, numerical methods, and parameterisations of other physical processes combined with initial and boundary conditions before being run over a domain (geographic area). The entire process of NWP is a very complex method dealing with laws of nature and physical processes represented in mathematical equation forms.

Almost every step in NWP includes omissions, estimations, approximations and compromises. Broadly, the governing equations include conservation of momentum (Newton's laws), conservation of mass, conservation of energy and Ideal gas law. While the numerical methods are created because computers can perform arithmetic, but not calculus. These methods are also used to convert spatial and temporal derivative into equations that computers can solve. It needs to be noted that the numerical methods directly affect model output, mostly at small scales. The physical process that cannot be directly predicted requires a parameterisation scheme based on reasonable physical or statistical representations. It is used to approximate the bulk effects of physical processes, which are too small, brief, complex or poorly understood to be explicitly represented by the governing equations and/or numerical methods[41].

---

41 https://www.weather.gov/media/ajk/brochures/NumericalWeatherPrediction.pdf, accessed on Aug 08, 2021

Actually, NWP is an old method, first attempt to predict the weather numerically was done by the British scientist L.F. Richardson (1881 –1953)[42] who was an English mathematician, physicist and meteorologist, His extraordinary book Weather Prediction by Numerical Process, was first published in 1922. He had successfully constructed a systematic mathematical method for predicting the weather and had demonstrated its application by carrying out a trial forecasts (all were not accurate). His innovative ideas were fundamentally sound and the methodology proposed by him is essentially the same that gets used in practical weather forecasting even today. However, in those days, the method devised by him was utterly impractical and the results of his trial forecast were very poor (possibly, the data input itself was poor). As a result, his ideas were eclipsed for decades.

Subsequently, the NWP gained prominence only around the Second World War. The interests for use of this technique grew then, mainly because of the availability of a good data network and the presence of computers. During 1948, J. G. Charney (1917-1981) an American meteorologist showed how the dynamical equations could be simplified using the geostrophic and hydrostatic approximations so that sound and gravity waves were filtered out (essentially the quasi-geostrophic model). A special case of his model, the equivalent barotropic model was used in 1950 to make the first numerical forecast[43].

Now, with more experience at hand, more accurate data collection platforms, ably supported by more powerful computers (supercomputers) and better modelling techniques, much growth in the NWP has taken place and the forecasting ability has also increased significantly. Some useful models, include Grid point models, Spectral models, Hydrostatic models and Non-hydrostatic models. Every model has got some limitations and NWP products at time do depict inaccuracy in their model outputs.

Even though the era of numerical weather prediction could be said to have begun in the 1950s, still it took good number of years to bring in perfection in the system. Numerical forecasts have improved steadily over the years. Computing power was one challenge and the other challenge was the data. For more accuracy in the forecasts, the availability of good and widespread data is a prerequisite. One global experiment carried out

---

42 Lewis Fry Richardson, *Weather Prediction by Numerical Process*, Cambridge University Press, Cambridge: 2007

43 https://maths.ucd.ie/~plynch/Dream/Book/CHAP01.pdf and https://rams.atmos.colo-state.edu/at540/fall03/fall03Pt7.pdf, accessed on Aug 10, 2021

during the 1980s could be said to have highlighted the importance of data. WMO carried out the Global Weather Experiment[44], an experiment involving more than 140 countries in 1979. It was the most intense survey and study carried out for examining the atmosphere, the sea surface, and the upper layer of the world's oceans. The high-quality global observations gathered during this experiment, when were coupled with numerical modals, there was a realisation that the accuracy of the forecast increases significantly. This established the fact that availability required data is an extremely important factor for issuance of a better forecasts.

The major tool for carrying out NWP is a supercomputer. Actually, the process of operations in a supercomputer is somewhat analogous to the actual process of weather forecasting using numerical methods. A supercomputer takes very complex problems and breaks them down into parts that are worked on simultaneously by thousands of processors, instead of being worked on individually in a single system, like a regular computer. Owing to parallel processing, researchers and scientists can generate insight much faster than doing calculations on a normal computer. A supercomputer can solve complicated mathematical equations required for weather prediction and they also take into account the thousands of rapidly-changing variables. The mathematical weather models of the atmosphere consist of equations describing the state, the motion and the time evolution of various atmospheric parameters, such as wind and temperature. Such equations are solved numerically on supercomputers and hence these systems could be viewed as the heart of the NWP. It is important to note that only with the help of supercomputers, NWP can issue the early warnings for tsunamis and analyse the trajectory or impact of hurricanes or study patterns in climate change[45].

The U.S. is known to be running its numerical models for many years. The forecast-model activity in the U.S. is concentrated in the NWS's National Centers for Environmental Prediction (NCEP). Their state-of-the-art supercomputer runs four primary models. Two of the models focus on North America and surrounding waters. The other two models uniformly cover the entire globe. One model for each domain is comparatively simple, envisioned for a quick computation as an early update and the

44 R. J. Fleming, T. M. Kaneshige and W. E. McGovern, "The Global Weather Experiment", Bulletin American Meteorological Society, June 1979, Issue 55, pp.649-659

45 Hollyn Phelps, "How Will the Supercomputers of 2030 Transform Weather Forecasting?", Dec 17, 2019 https://news.lenovo.com/how-will-the-supercomputers-of-2030-transform-weather-forecasting/, accessed on July 30, 2021

other model for each domain is more complete, offering a better answer at greater expense. As per the requirement, mainly during the hurricane season additional models are run and the forecasted output is distributed to various concerned agencies.

Another significant weather modelling activity happens at the European Centre for Medium-Range Weather Forecasting (ECMWF) in U.K. It has additional sites in Bologna, Italy, and Bonn, Germany. This is a global model with more spatial detail and costlier approximations than any other model in existence at the time. Forecast results are sent to the member states of the consortium, and selected results are also broadcasted for the benefits of others. However, post Brexit, there is risk of losing the contract for the expansion of this programme. ECMWF has been based in Berkshire, UK (in town called Reading), but its future EU-funded activities are now the subject of an international battle. It is important to note that this body is also involved in climate-change research and is backed by 34 countries (22 are E.U. member states). It also operates two services from the E.U.'s Copernicus satellite Earth-observation programme, monitoring the atmosphere and the climate crisis[46]. The span of ECMWF is significant since it is one of the six members of the Co-ordinated Organisations, which also include the North Atlantic Treaty Organisation (NATO), the Council of Europe (CoE), the European Space Agency (ESA), the Organisation for Economic Co-operation and Development (OECD), and the European Organisation for the Exploitation of Meteorological Satellites (EUMETSAT). These six Coordinated Organisations represent 57 member countries[47]. There are few others states too like Canada, Australia, China, India and Russia, who also depend for weather forecasting, on global or reginal numerical models.

Meteorological Agencies

There are various meteorological agencies at global, regional and state level. In addition, there are private agencies, which undertake weather forecasting jobs. This section highlights few such agencies. However, before getting into the discussion on various such agencies it could be of

---

46 George Huffm, "Weather Forecasting", https://www.scholastic.com/teachers/articles/teaching-content/weather-forecasting/ and https://www.theguardian.com/politics/2020/sep/26/uk-risks-losing-contract-for-new-climate-weather-research-centre-due-to-brexit-ecmwf-reading, accessed on Aug 06, 2021

47 https://www.ecmwf.int/en/about/who-we-are#:~:text=The%20European%20Centre%20for%20Medium,predictions%20to%20its%20Member%20States and https://www.sirp-isrp.org/index.php?lang=en&Itemid=836, accessed on July 28, 2022

interest to recognise the nature of activities happening in the domain of meteorology during 18th and 19th century. Actually, this rich history of past including some collaborative research efforts has eventually led to the formation of various inter and intra-national meteorological agencies.

The Meteorological Society of Mannheim started in 1780 and established a network of 39 weather observing stations (14 in Germany, 4 in the U.S. and the rest in other countries). All these stations were equipped with comparable and calibrated instruments like a barometer, hygrometer, and rain-gauge and wind vane. Lavoisier, in 1783 and Dalton, in 1800 published their findings concerning the nature and composition of air. The genius Lavoisier, a chemist, who coined the word oxygen, fell victim to the French Revolution[48]. Based on the data collected, the first known systematic attempt at preparing a weather map was made by H.W. Brandes, in Leipzig (Germany), in 1820. Almost at the same time, W.C. Redfield of New York prepared the first series of charts showing the rotatory and translatory motions of the American hurricanes. On 14 August 1872, in Leipzig a number of leading meteorologists met. They arrived at an arrangement on standardised methods of observation, uniform set of weather symbols and methods of chart analysis. They prepared the ground for holding the First International Meteorological Congress in Vienna (1873). At Vienna, it was decided to set up a Permanent Committee to stimulate and organise voluntary international cooperation and uniformity in observations and analysis. Buys Ballot was the first President of this Committee. In a slightly modified form, the permanent Committee continues till today with the name of WMO'S Executive Committee[49].

WMO

One of the most important agencies, which is the torchbearer for the global weather assessment is the World Meteorological Organization (WMO), and was founded on 23 March 1950. This is an intergovernmental organisation with a membership of 193 Member States and Territories. WMO's 'DNA' is the International Meteorological Organization (IMO), which resulted from a process launched at the First International Meteorological Congress (Vienna, September 1873) to facilitate coordinated observations and instrument standardisation and was also

---

48 He was beheaded during the French Revolution's Reign of Terror on May 8, 1794 being an investor in a private tax collection company was also accused of selling watered-down tobacco

49 G C Asnasi, *Tropical Meteorology*, Published by G. C. Asnani, c/o Indian Institute of Tropical Meteorology (IITM): Pune, 1993. p. 1.3 to 1.5

responsible for the 1896 publishing of the first international cloud-atlas. The Second International Meteorological Congress (Rome, April 1879) led to the establishment of the International Meteorological Committee. These were the only two governmental meetings held to push the meteorological agenda in those days. Subsequently, it was decided that for more efficient functioning IMO should operate on a non-governmental basis. Furthermore, to its main role in the standardisation of observations, IMO made significant contributions to scientific research, especially by organising the first two International Polar Years, during the periods 1882-1883 and 1932-1933, on a scale that outdid the abilities of any single nation. Actually, IMO and WMO coexisted for a very short period, before the final IMO Conference of Directors took place in Paris from 15-17 March 1951. During this meeting it was formally declared that IMO ceased to exist and that WMO had taken its place. On 19 March 1951, the First WMO Congress opened in Paris and finally, on 20 December 1951, the United Nations General Assembly adopted its Resolution 531(VI) and WMO became a specialised agency of the United Nations System[50].

Presently, the WMO provides global leadership and expertise in international cooperation in the delivery and use of high-quality, authoritative weather, climate, hydrological and related environmental services by its Members, for the enhancement of the well-being of societies of all nations. This organisation works to facilitate global cooperation in the design and delivery of meteorological services, nurture the rapid exchange of meteorological information, advance the standardisation of meteorological data, shape cooperation between meteorological and hydrological services, inspire research and training in meteorology, and enlarge the use of meteorology to benefit additional sectors such as aviation, shipping, agriculture and water management[51].

Under the umbrella of the WMO World Weather Watch (WWW) programme got established in 1963, the World Weather Watch is the core of the WMO Programmes. It combines observing systems, telecommunication facilities and data-processing and forecasting centres which are operated by WMO member states. It makes available meteorological and related environmental information needed to provide

---

50 https://public.wmo.int/en/bulletin/60-years-service-your-safety-and-well-being, accessed on Aug 09, 2021

51 https://public.wmo.int/en/about-us and https://public.wmo.int/en, accessed on Aug 4, 2021

efficient services in all states[52]. In September 1966, the US White House had circulated a press release announcing, 'plans for U.S. participation in the World Weather Watch (WWW), one of the boldest and most complex scientific programmes ever attempted as an international effort'. It was mentioned that the U.S. President had directed eight federal agencies to engage in an international effort to establish a cooperative, worldwide weather service[53]. The scale of entire programme was such that no one nation could have undertaken it alone. The WWW network had created a gigantic structure for the collection of an unprecedented volume of environmental observations. For this purpose, a system was put in place consisting of meteorological satellites, weather buoys, automated weather stations, and hundreds of observer posts from across the globe[54].

Almost within ten years after the birth of WMO, considerable progress was made towards expanding and improving, both observational and telecommunications capabilities in various parts of the world. Efforts were made to improve the networks of land stations and systematic data collection started from merchant ships and civilian aircrafts. In addition, some special ocean weather vessels gave data inputs. This oceanic data collection was complemented in some areas by meteorological ocean buoys. Still large areas over which little meteorological information was required remained untapped. The WMO was quick to respond to arrival of satellite technology. There was a realisation that satellites are going dominate the future of meteorological observations (particularly, the cloud systems). The world's first dedicated weather satellite, the Television Infrared Observation Satellite (TIROS-1), was launched by the U.S. on 1 April 1960[55]. Similar such launches in future have effectively marked the beginning of a new era of observational data coverage for the whole globe. Today, meteorological satellites are making available significant amount of data required for weather assessment.

---

52 https://archive.unescwa.org/world-weather-watch-programme, accessed on Aug 10, 2021

53 Draft Press Release, 19 September, 1966, file: Meteorological Weather Link, box: 15 National Security File of Charles E. Johnson, Lyndon Johnson Presidential Library (hereafter, Johnson Papers).

54 Angelina Long Callahan, "Satellite Meteorology in the Cold War Era: Scientific Coalitions and International Leadership 1946-1964", a PhD Dissertation submitted to Georgia Institute of Technology, December 2013, https://smartech.gatech.edu/bitstream/handle/1853/50350/CALLAHAN-DISSERTATION-2013.pdf, accessed on July 13, 2022

55 https://public.wmo.int/en/programmes/world-weather-watch, accessed on Aug 02, 2021

The success of WMO lies in its global acceptability. This international cooperation even continued during the period of Cold War. The observational networks were extended to cover almost the entire globe and various traditional and non-traditional environmental parameters measurements are gathered. WMO has also been aware of the climate risks of possible nuclear war. On the other hand WMO has been quick to realise the possibility of the climate change. Their programmes like the World Climate Research Programme (WCRP) has provided the scientific foundation for the assessments of the Intergovernmental Panel on Climate Change (IPCC), which WMO and the United Nations Environment Programme (UNEP) have co-sponsored since 1988. Actually, the programmes like WCRP got established after the 1979 first Would Climate Conference, which was organised to debate the looming threat of climate change and its potential impacts. While the Second World Climate Conference (Geneva, November 1990) led to establishment of the Global Climate Observing System (GCOS). In addition, the Second World Climate Conference set in motion the process leading to the establishment of the United Nations Framework Convention on Climate Change (UNFCCC)[56]. WMO is an important partner of these agencies.

NOAA[57]

The U.S. agency that caters for the state's meteorological needs is the National Oceanic and Atmospheric Administration (NOAA). NOAA was officially formed on 3 October, 1970. Before establishment of this agency, there have been multiple agencies in the U.S., which were associated with various aspects of earth sciences and meteorology. Most of these agencies were established during the 19th century. For example, during 1807, the Coast Survey was founded, the oldest scientific agency dealing with weather related issues in the U.S. During 1965, just five years before the formation of NOAA, the Environmental Science Services Administration (ESSA) was formed. This agency was formed by merging various other agencies like the Coast and Geodetic Survey, the Weather Bureau and the uniformed Corps into it. Its mission was to combine and administer the meteorological, climatological, hydrographic, and geodetic operations of the United States.

---

56 https://public.wmo.int/en/bulletin/60-years-service-your-safety-and-well-being, accessed on Aug 09, 2021

57 http://chesneaumarineweather.com/?page_id=1756 and http://www.weather.gov/organization.php#support/_and https://www.noaa.gov/about/organization_and https://www.noaa.gov/about-our-agency and http://www.meteohistory.org/2006historyofmeteorology3/4white_noaa.pdf accessed on Aug 01, 2021

The basic mission of NOAA is to understand and predict changes in climate, weather, oceans, and coastlines, to share that knowledge and information with others, and to conserve and manage coastal and marine ecosystems and resources. Presently, the NOAA works toward its mission through six major line offices, the National Environmental Satellite, Data and Information Service (NESDIS), the National Marine Fisheries Service (NMFS), the National Ocean Service (NOS), the National Weather Service (NWS), the Office of Oceanic and Atmospheric Research (OAR) and the Office of Marine & Aviation Operations (OMAO). The largest sub-agency of NOAA is the National Weather Service (NWS) which provides weather, hydrologic, and climate forecasts and warnings for the United States, its territories, adjacent waters and ocean areas. The data and products form NWS form a national information database and infrastructure. Various government agencies, private sector and also many from the global community depend on the various serves provided by the NWS in particular and NOAA in general. Along with NOAA, there are few other agencies which deal with the issues of weather and they include Air Force Weather Agency and the Fleet Numerical Meteorology and Oceanography Center which are responsible within the U.S. Air Force and the U.S. Navy. While the National Aeronautics and Space Administration (NASA) is responsible for obtaining space weather inputs.

The U.K. Met Office

The Met Office in the United Kingdom (U.K.) was founded by Vice-Admiral Robert Fitzroy in 1854. The Met Office has a long history of defence (military) forecasting. The very first operational military forecast was issued on 24 October 1916. Probably, one of the most important forecasts in military history ever issued was for the D-Day landings in June 1944[58]. U.K. met also could be credited for formulating the idea of Numerical Weather Prediction (NWP). The father of NWP, was the U.K. Met Office scientist Lewis Fry Richardson, who had published his ground breaking work during 1922. However, only when the Met office purchased its first computer in 1959 some progress in NWP started happening. Finally, the operational weather forecasting, driven by NWP started happening since 2 November 1965. Since 1991, the U.K. Met office is working with their supercomputing systems, which are constantly getting upgraded. They have flood forecasting and space weather forecasting centres too[59].

---

58 Took place on June 6, 1944 and saw of tens of thousands of troops from the United States, the UK, France and Canada landing on five stretches of the Normandy coastline

59 https://www.metoffice.gov.uk/about-us/who/our-history, accessed on Aug 12, 2021

Few scientists in the U.K. had joined hands together to establish a British Meteorological Society. This society was formed on 3 April 1850. This society became The Meteorological Society in 1866. Subsequently, after it was incorporated by Royal Charter and it became the Royal Meteorological Society in 1883. This society works towards the advancement and extension of meteorological science by determining the laws of climate and of meteorological phenomena in general. This is a long-established institution that encourages academic and public engagement in weather and climate science. Its Quarterly Journal is one of the world's leading sources of original research in the atmospheric sciences[60].

The Bureau of Meteorology, Australia[61]

On 1 January 1908, Australia established its first national weather agency: the Bureau of Meteorology. It was created to consolidate the meteorological services of Australia's States, which had established extensive records of their regional weather during the 19th century. This Bureau was established in Melbourne through the Meteorology Act 1906. Amended in 1955, this Act and the Water Act 2007, form the Bureau's legal foundation. Over the years, this Bureau has grown into a world-class agency providing much-needed environmental intelligence to the community and industry.

The Bureau offers relevant information and forecasts in respect of drought, floods, fires, storms, tsunami and tropical cyclones. It gives information and advice to the government for the Australian region and Antarctic territory. It contributes to national social, economic, cultural and environmental goals by providing observational, meteorological, hydrological and oceanographic services and undertakes research into science and environment-related issues in support of its operations and services. It further collaborates with WMO and other meteorological agencies in neighbouring countries on vital atmospheric and oceanographic monitoring activities, as well as early-warning systems for extreme weather events, tsunamis, volcanic ash clouds and more.

---

60 "An interview with Professor Paul Hardaker, the new Chief Executive of the Royal Meteorological Society". Weather. Royal Meteorological Society. 61 (11): 299. 16 January 2007

61 https://media.bom.gov.au/social/blog/10/a-short-history-of-the-bureau-of-meteorology/ and http://www.bom.gov.au/inside/index.shtml?ref=hdr, accessed on Aug 11, 2021

India Meteorological Department (IMD)[62]

The commencements of meteorological understanding in India can be traced to ancient times. Early philosophical writings of the 3000 B.C. period, such as the Upanishads[63], contain thoughtful discussions about the processes of cloud formation and rain and the seasonal cycles caused by the movement of the earth round the sun. Varahamihira's[64] classical work, the Brihatsamhita, clearly demonstrates a deep knowledge of atmospheric processes. India is fortunate to have some of the oldest meteorological observatories of the world. The British East India Company established several such stations at Calcutta (1785) and Madras (1796) for studying the weather and climate of India. The Asiatic Society (Calcutta and Bombay) promoted scientific studies in meteorology in India. Captain Harry Piddington[65] at Calcutta published 40 papers during 1835-1855 in the Journal of the Asiatic Society dealing with tropical storms and is known to have coined the word 'cyclone'.

The formation India Meteorological Department (1875) probably happened as a consequence of the disastrous tropical cyclone, which struck Calcutta in 1864 and the failures of the monsoon rains in 1866 and 1871. Today, IMD has a major infrastructure for meteorological observations, communications, forecasting and weather services. One of the first few electronic computers introduced in India were at IMD. India was the first developing country in the world to have its own geostationary satellite, INSAT, for continuous weather monitoring of this part of the globe and particularly these systems were very useful for cyclone warning. India did face difficulties during the 1980s in importing supercomputers for IMD. This was because India was put under technology sanctions owing to its nuclear policies. Finally, during 1987, the U.S. and India reached an agreement to allow India to purchase a powerful computer for use in weather forecasting and monsoon prediction. However, the purchase of Cray Research Inc. single-processor XMP-14 was only permitted, when

---

62 https://mausam.imd.gov.in/imd_latest/contents/history.php and https://www.joc.com/maritime-news/us-india-reach-agreement-sale-supercomputer_19871012.html, accessed on Aug 12, 2021

63 The Upanishads are late Vedic Sanskrit texts of Hindu philosophy. It had major impact on the theological and religious expression in India

64 Varahamihira (505 AD-587 AD), an ancient Indian astrologer, astronomer and a sage.

65 Henry Piddington (7 January 1797 – 7 April 1858) was an English sea captain, who sailed in East India and China. He finally got settled in India (Bengal) where he worked as a curator of a geological museum and undertook pioneering studies in meteorology of tropical storms.

India was keen to have Cray's more powerful XMP-24 model. At present, India has its indigenously manufactured supercomputers and has very vibrant meteorological setup, which provides great assistance in tropical cyclones and monsoon predictions. IMD is offering services to agriculture sector and various other sectors.

Chapter 2

History of Weather Impacting Wars

The air surrounds the Earth and encompasses the region for many kilometres above the Earth's surface. This is what we call the atmosphere, a region for the presence of various gases, which surround the Earth and are responsible for the existence of life on the Earth's surface. The presence of oxygen in very important for the existence of life on Earth. Weather is the state of the atmosphere and is known to impact human life, both positively and negatively. It has been observed that most of the weather happens in the lowest part of the atmosphere called the troposphere. Climate is the average weather witnessed and experienced over a specific geographic area. Adequate sunshine and precipitation are required for the survival of all living things on the Earth's surface. Availability of water is mandatory for the existence of life. Broadly, the wind, temperature, pressure, moisture content/humidity and state of sky (cloudiness) are required to be maintained adequately so that different species can exist. Weather situations (or phenomenon) are known for reappearances after specific time intervals. These are known as weather patterns.

Human activities impact severely during unfavourable weather conditions. Normally, humans give less importance to weather activities as long as they are not impacting normal lives or if they can manage the unfriendly weather by taking certain precautions, like air-conditioners are used during hot climate. The real challenge comes up during the conduct of outdoor activities. Weather-related challenges emerge during heat and cold waves, heavy precipitations and stormy conditions. Historically, it has been witnessed that states have experienced various challenges owing to prevailing weather conditions even during the wars fought by humans. There have been some known incidences of wars been lost by superior powers owing to the weather difficulties faced by them. In most of such cases, it has been found that the agencies involved in warfighting were either overconfident of their capabilities to address the weather challenges or they failed to take into factor the weather or terrain features in their planning. This chapter discusses a few military campaigns that have experienced weather impact while undertaking military operations.

Weather, terrain, and time of day establish the basic environmental background for all military operations. These physical conditions impact operations, systems, and personnel and act as limitations on the available combat options[1]. Historically, it has been observed that weather does affect war. For that purpose, to know in advance the climate of a war zone is essential. The accurate knowledge about the possibility of occurrence of dust, cold, thick cloud cover, fog, heavy rains, hot and humid weather conditions, storms, difficult sea conditions and high winds is essential for military planners. Military operations, exercises and training is known to have got impacted by adverse weather conditions on various occasions, universally. Hence, it is very important to factor weather, while planning military campaigns. The examples discussed in this chapter clearly highlights this importance.

Backdrop

'When beggars die there are no comets seen; the heavens themselves blaze forth the death of princes': Name of Drama: Julius Caesar, Act 2 Scene 2, Calpurnia to Caesar. Calpurnia was the wife of Julius Caesar, the one to whom he was married at the time of his assassination. In this one of the celebrated plays of William Shakespeare, the appearance of comet has been associated with an omen foreshadowing Julius Caesar's impending assassination[2]. For long, comets, meteors, and eclipses have been both of interest and concern to human beings. Amongst them, comets have enticed the most attention. There have been references to historical incidences of the battles being stopped in mid-career, common people being thrown into panic, kings abdicated from their thrones, and possibly people dying owing to some known and most visible planet, comet or meteor or eclipse activity. Aristotle believed, three centuries before Christ, that comets caused severe winds and hot spells[3]. There have been various incidences in the history

---

1 http://www.bits.de/NRANEU/others/amd-us-archive/FM34-81-1%2892%29.pdf, accessed on Dec 02, 2021

2 Sarah Neville, "Why Shakespeare's Julius Caesar Makes Conservatives Mad", May. 7, 2020, https://thewalrus.ca/why-shakespeares-julius-caesar-makes-conservatives-mad/, accessed on Aug 25, 2021

3 Duane Koenig, "Comets, Superstitions, and History", Quarterly Journal of the Florida

when the activities associated with the celestial bodies have been correlated with the appearance of unfriendly weather conductions.

The most talked about incidences include the presence of Halley's Comet, held responsible for the fall of the Shang Dynasty in China. Interestingly, a solar eclipse frightened the Macedonian army enough at Pydna in 168 BC to ensure victory for the Romans. During the medieval period[4] and period before that there was very limited understanding of the solar system and the happenings about the various celestial phenomenon. There are various examples of humans relating warfare with the naturally occurring phenomenon. As the understanding of the universe grew, humans started realising about the confines of the perceived collaboration and the connection between nature and war.

The weather phenomenon and prevailing climate are known to have impacted warfare significantly in the past[5]. A massive rain storm turned the field of Agincourt[6] to mud in 1415 and gave Henry V his legendary victory. Other incidences include: the presence of fog which helped secure the throne of England for Edward IV at Barnet in 1471, wind and disease colluded to crash the Spanish Armada, snow aided to stop the American capture of Quebec in 1775 and confined the Revolution to the Thirteen Colonies, while extreme heat gave rise to the legend of Saladin at the Horns of Hattin in 1187[7].

Impacting Wars

Following as some historical incidences, in which weather is known to have impacted the military operations during the war.

The Second Punic War[8]

In the middle of the third century BC, Rome was a rising city-state, which had newly stretched its control over the other communities

Academy of Sciences, June, 1968, Vol. 31, No. 2 (June, 1968), pp. 81-92

4   The period in European history from the collapse of Roman civilization in the 5th century CE to the period of the Renaissance, say the commencement of 13/14th century

5   David R. Petriello, Tide of War, Skyhorse Publishing, New York, 2018, p.12

6   The Battle of Agincourt was an English victory in the Hundred Years' War. It happened on 25 October 1415 near Azincourt, in northern France

7   This battle was fought in summer when the grass was tinder-dry. Saladin's troops set fire to the grass, after cutting off the Crusaders' access to water in the Sea of Galilee (a freshwater lake in Israel)

8   https://www.historyextra.com/period/roman/how-hannibal-beat-the-alps-but-

of southern Italy. When Rome moved on to invade Sicily in 264 BC, it got a new enemy, Carthage, a city on the North African seaboard that already had a presence in Sicily. Carthage was the capital city of the ancient Carthaginian civilisation, the region now known as Tunisia. The First Punic War developed from Rome's illegal entry into Sicily and lasted from 264 to 241 BC. Carthage lost and had to evacuate Sicily and this led them to set off for Spain, where Carthage had a longstanding presence, with troops and war elephants. Subsequently, the control over Spain was an issue between Rome and Carthage. Almost for two decades, the problem in respect of control mainly over southern Spain continued. Rome was pushing Carthaginian forces not to cross river Ebro. Hannibal was the Carthaginian general and statesman in power then. He found Rome's interference in his territory unacceptable.

His forces had battled with the Romans in Spain. He made one of the most unexpected move, which was viewed as the militarily unconceivable mission. He marched his troops, including cavalry and African war elephants, across a high pass in the Alps to strike at Rome itself from the north of the Italian peninsula. The Alps are the highest and most extensive mountain range systems (around 1200 km) in Europe, with an approximate elevation of 4,810 m. The temperature normally remains below freezing level and can go down to around to negative 20 degrees centigrade during winters. He had a great faith on his 'elephant force' (the 'tanks' of classical warfare) which had a proven battle worthiness while fighting with the Roman forces in the north. This was the Second Punic War, which lasted from 218 to 201 BC.

Hannibal had assembled a massive army, including 90,000 infantry, 12,000 cavalry and 37-38 elephants. This force is known to have covered distance of some 1,600 km across the Rhone River and the snow-capped Alps to reach central Italy. Many of the animals of the Hannibal's force died of cold or disease in the following winter, but Hannibal fought his way down through Italy. However, he could not conquer Rome and it is said that finally he was left with one elephant that was his own. Historically this war is very famous since it demonstrates that having a superior and numerically stronger army does not guaranty a victory. It is always important for the generals to undertake the assessment of the topographic features and weather conditions before launching any military campaign.

---

couldnt-beat-rome/ and Philip Ball, "The truth about Hannibal's route across the Alps", Apr 03, 2016, https://www.theguardian.com/science/2016/apr/03/where-muck-hannibals-elephants-alps-italy-bill-mahaney-york-university-toronto and https://www.history.com/topics/ancient-history/hannibal, accessed on Aug 25, 2020

Typhoons Saved Japan's Invasion[9]

This particular case gets recognised as one of the earliest historical examples of atmospheric and oceanic conditions having a significant geopolitical impact.

Genghis Khan (c. 1158 – August 18, 1227) has been the most famous (infamous) Mongolian ruler who got together different tribes and ended up establishing a vast Mongol Empire. His grandson Kublai Khan conquered China and became the first emperor of its Yuan (Mongol) dynasty. He tried to invade Japan twice, once in 1274 and then in 1281, but he failed both times. The first invasion took place in the autumn of 1274. A very big force was employed for this job. The force comprised about 30,000 to 40,000 men (mostly ethnic Chinese and Koreans, except for the Mongolian officers) and an estimated 500 to 900 vessels. However, a typhoon struck as the ships lay at anchor in Hakata Bay, Kyushu, Japan, sinking about one-third of them, with the rest limping home; it is estimated that 13,000 of Kublai's men drowned.

The second, 1281 invasion was much larger. The attack was planned from two different directions. One force began the travel towards Japan from Masan (Korea), and the other undertook sailing from southern China. The overall military effort involved some 4,400 vessels and some 140,000 soldiers and sailors. The two fleets merged up near Hakata Bay, the main point of attack, on August 12, 1281. In comparison, the Japanese force defending the island had about 40,000 samurai and other fighting men. On August 15, to Kublai Khan's bad luck just before bingeing the assault, as a massive typhoon hit, smashing the Mongol fleet and once again blocking the invasion attempt. Major losses were suffered, both in case of maritime assets and the manpower. At least half of the Mongol fighters got drowned and similar fate was met by the hundreds of ships. Those soldiers who survived came under attack from Japanese samurai and only few managed to return home.

Japan understood that they were lucky that the nature came to their help and helped defeating such a major attack. It was 'kamikaze' meaning 'divine winds' which saved Japan. Since 1281 typhoon, this word is getting used in Japanese lexicon. It famously got used during the Second World

---

9 "Kamikaze of 1274 and 1281." Encyclopaedia Britannica, November 18, 2016. https://www.britannica.com/event/kamikaze-of-1274-and-1281, and Devin Powell, "Japan's Kamikaze Winds, the Stuff of Legend, May Have Been Real", Nov 05, 2014, https://www.nationalgeographic.com/science/article/141104-kamikaze-kublai-khan-winds-typhoon-japan-invasion, accessed on Aug 21, 2021

War to refer to the Japanese suicide pilots (kamikaze, divine winds that project Japan) who deliberately crashed their planes into enemy targets, usually ships.

The American War for Independence[10]

The French and English were rivalling for dominance of Europe since late 1600s, and they fought three major wars during 1689-1748. This conflict was happening in Europe, however, it did spill over to America. Where the French and England were at war, their colonies also went for a war. During 1754, the fourth struggle began. It was becoming difficult for the Americans to withstand the pressure of British rulers for greater control over their lives like taxation policy and some other issues. The War of American independence was fought by 13 colonies against the British Empire during 1775-1783. Till around 1778, the conflict was more of a civil war. Subsequently, it took an international course with France and Spain getting into the ring. While the Netherlands was fighting separately with Briton and had provided financial support to the United States. From the beginning, sea power was vital in determining the course of the war, but at the same time there were some important land campaigns too.

It is not the purpose of over to discuss individual campaigns during the eight-year period of war and the role played by weather in each campaign, however a broad assessment has been undertaken of the entire conflict. Largely, how the weather had ended up affecting the entire campaign has been viewed. It is important to mention that weather did not single-handedly decide the outcome of the war, but did impact various phases of the conflict. Some mentions have been made in following paragraphs about some specific campaigns, without giving any intricate details of the enter campaign.

Broadly, it was seen that the attacking army (the aggressor) met with the roads which were already in bad shape, also rain was abundant, and wet

---

10 Kenneth W. Noe, The Howling Storm: Weather, Climate, and the American Civil War, Louisiana State University Press, 2020 and book review of the same book by Lindsay R.S. Privette, May 26, 2021, https://www.civilwarmonitor.com/blog/noe-the-howling-storm-2020, and https://campussuite-storage.s3.amazonaws.com/prod/1471330/4ba60489-72e7-11e7-99ef-124f7febbf4a/1808973/527701d2-9984-11e8-b412-1236f486c430/file/chap04.pdf and https://www.britannica.com/event/American-Revolution/French-intervention-and-the-decisive-action-at-Virginia-Capes and Jonathan T. Engel, "The Force of Nature: The Impact of Weather on Armies during the American War of Independence, 1775-1781", a thesis submitted to Florida State University Libraries, 2011, https://fsu.digital.flvc.org/islandora/object/fsu:168711/datastream/PDF/view, accessed on Sept 06, 2021

red clay accurately promised immense problems for invading armies that had to bring men and supplies overland into an unacquainted environment.

This Civil War is known to have involved, at least five separate zones. The trans-Mississippi armies, western armies, and eastern armies all operated within a unique set of climate patterns. Besides, while Civil War armies and southern civilians often inhabited the same climate zones, most of the northern civilian population lived in a distinct zone. As a result, factors like food production, transportation, winter quarters, and combat varied between regions. For example, much of the "Hot-Humid" and "Mixed-Humid" climate zones that made up the southern United States were plagued by drought in 1862, 1863, and 1864. This undermined food production; consequences for northern farms were not much severe. Nevertheless, while each climate zone represented distinct patterns, seasonal changes had the potential to unify some experiences across the regions. The summer heat and dust plagued the soldiers on the battlefield at Manassas, caused the federal army's collapse outside of Wilson's Creek in Missouri, and slowed General Don Carlos Buell's march to Chattanooga.

Nature exerted a pervasive, inescapable influence that affected the strategy of British and American generals in this war, made various operations more or less challenging, determined victory or defeat in some battles, and fashioned the daily lives and activities of thousands of soldiers and officers. Occasionally the military leaderships tried to plan for the weather, sometimes they seemed to ignore it, but it was continually present, subtly but robustly affecting the conduct of the war

All in all, weather was often a greater threat to Civil War armies, than the opposing force. Exposure to extreme conditions deprived the soldiers of sleep, food, and water. It braked their advances, destabilised their retreats, and placed added burden on their bodies which were already under duress.

The French Invasion of Russia[11]

Napoleon Bonaparte (1769-1821) was the French military leader and a ruler. He conquered much of Europe in the early 19th century. He witnessed a major defeat when he invaded Russia during 1812. This Napoleon's military campaign is famously known as a Patriotic War of 1812

---

11 https://courses.lumenlearning.com/suny-hccc-worldhistory2/chapter/invasion-of-russia/, accessed on Aug 24, 2021 and Laura Lee, Blame It on the Rain, Harper Collins e-book, p.2 and a chapter titled "Napoleon's Invasion of Russia, 1812", refer Gompert, David C., Hans Binnendijk, and Bonny Lin, Blinders, Blunders, and Wars: What America and China Can Learn, Santa Monica, CA: RAND Corporation, 2014, pp-41-52

in Russia. This campaign began during June 1812, when Napoleon's Grande Army crossed the Niemen River to engage and defeat the Russian Army. Napoleon wanted to coerce Tsar Alexander I of Russia to cease trading with British merchants through proxies in an effort to pressure the United Kingdom to opt for peace. The approved political aim of the campaign was to free Poland from the threat of Russia. The Grande Army was famous for its professionalism and during 1804-1809 had won important military victories allowing Napoleon to take control of major parts of the Europe.

For this War, Napoleon had assembled the largest army Europe had ever seen. Possibly around six hundred thousand strong army was there and many of them were on horseback. He had a very bold plan for invasion and possibly had not given much of the thought about the winter weather in Russia. Apart from the climate battle there were issues concerning logistics and food supply in particular. Napoleon had thought that capturing Moscow would ensure him the victory and did not realise the vastness of Russian geography. Interestingly, the Russian army decided not to put much of direct resistance to Napoleon's army and withdrew in the interiors of the country. This pushed Grande Army to move inside the country. They lacked the apparatus to efficiently move so many troops across such large distances of hostile territory. Also, there was no exist strategy planned. The war had started in the period, when the soldiers were wearing summer uniform. They were forced to handle the harsh winter weather in the summer uniforms. Bad weather and food shortages were the main reasons for the suffering of the forces. His army got diminished by a third, many soldiers and horses died.

Napoleon's army faced temperatures, which fell to –40°C. The soldiers fell to frostbite and starvation. Most men and horses died from the cold. At the same time it is important to mention that some of the deaths had taken place before the setting up of the winter. Hence along with inclement weather, other logistical issues and flawed war tactics were also responsible for the massive defeat of the Grande Army. All in all, this war is a classic example of what happens when the militaries underestimate the power of climate.

Battle of Waterloo[12]

It appears that in some measure, weather has played an important role towards making of Napoleon's strategic planning and warfighting abilities

---

12 History.com Editors, "Battle of Waterloo", Nov 7, 2018, https://www.history.com/topics/british-history/battle-of-waterloo, accessed on Sept 01, 2021, Dennis Wheeler and Gas-

to a certain extent inconsequential. Few years after facing the harsh Russia winter, Napoleon again found weather conditions detrimental to the progress of his forces.

In 1812, Napoleon led a disastrous invasion of Russia. During 1813 what is known as the Battle of Leipzig, Napoleon's army got defeated by a coalition of Austrian, Prussian, Russian and Swedish troops. Subsequently, in March 1814, the coalition forces captured Paris. Napoleon was abducted, but he managed to escape during February 1815. Later he regrouped and raised a new army. During June 1815, his forces marched into Belgium. The Battle of Waterloo that took place in Belgium on June 18, 1815, marked the final defeat of Napoleon Bonaparte, who conquered much of Europe in the early 19th century.

On June 18, Napoleon led his army of about 72,000 troops against the 68,000-man British army. These forces met close to south of Brussels near the village of Waterloo. Napoleon delayed the attack until midday, because he waited to let the waterlogged ground dry after the previous night's rainstorm. This delay allowed the enemy to get additional troops.

Weather scientists and military analysts have carried out a detail assessment of the weather during the Battle of Waterloo. There is a realisation that it is not the weather alone which has been responsible for this defeat. Inadequate military planning and also incorrect reading of the weather events had led to the destructive consequences. At a broad climatic level, it needs to be mentioned that the decade 1810 to 1819 was the coldest, since the awful years of the 1690s. It is important to look at the localised weather-related challenges at the back of this climate reality. Changes in the weather pattern just before the beginning of the battle of Waterloo were evident. On June 16, 1815, thundering activity had begun. Some reports also suggest that the thunder was followed by the rain. The thunderstorm was clearly of monumental proportions. Possibly, there was heavy rain for two days before the start of the campaign making the ground wet and muddy.

Because of the weather conditions the performance of the warfighting equipment also got impacted. The soft ground hindered the deployment of cannon and there were other influences too. The cannon shots were found falling short of the target. In muddy conditions, vehicular traffic was problematic and this led to restricting the artillery fire. Horses too

---

ton Demarée, "The weather of the Waterloo Campaign 16 to 18 June 1815: did it change the course of history?", Weather, June 2005, Vol 60, no 6, pp.159-164

found the going difficult. Another weather influence on the battle was on visibility with prevalence of mist and smoke. The topographic and terrain conditions of the area were not helping for surface wind speed to increase. Bit stronger wind could have helped towards increasing visibility. All in all, a genuine 'fog of war' type situation was prevalent. All this had put the last nail on the ambition of Napoleon Bonaparte.

Crimean War[13]

The Crimean War (1854-56) was started with Russia's invasion of the Turkish Danubian principalities of Moldavia and Wallachia (now Romania). Britain and France, both wanted to prop up the ailing Ottoman Empire and resist Russian expansionism in the Near East. This war was fought by an alliance of Britain, France, Turkey and Sardinia against Russia. This war, which Russia lost eventually, was the only major European conflict, the Army engaged in, between 1816 and 1914. This war symbolised various faces and is also known to have ploughed the seeds for the First World War. For the British, this campaign embodied their military and logistical incompetence alongside the bravery and endurance of its soldiers. Overall, this war is famous for military and political incompetence and logistic failures. It is also known that disease accounted for a disproportionate number of casualties, the approximately 250,000 people lost by each side. Significant entrepreneurial and technological novelties are known to have emerged from the war. One less discussed aspect of the war is weather. On occasions, weather is known to have impacted the conduct of this war significantly.

In November 1854, in an early phase of the war, two meteorological events occurred that had substantial effects on the conduct of war. The first event (November 5 1854) was about the occurrence of an intense fog and the second incident (November 14 1854) was that of an unusually violent storm. The Russians launched their first major assault on the Allies in the early hours of the November 5, without realising that the fog formation has taken place. Forty thousand Russian troops attacked the Mt. Inkerman area of the Crimea, which were defended by a small British force of 3000. The fog greatly helped the Russians hide the start of the attack from the

---

13 Yakup Bektas, "The Crimean War as a technological enterprise", Feb 01, 2017, https://www.ncbi.nlm.nih.gov/pmc/articles/PMC5554787/ and S. Lindgrén and J. Neumann, "Great Historical Events That were Significantly Affected by the Weather: 5, Some Meteorological Events of the Crimean War and Their Consequences", Dec 01, 1980, Bulletin of the American Meteorological Society, Volume 61: Issue 12, https://journals.ametsoc.org/view/journals/bams/61/12/1520-0477_1980_061_1570_ghetws_2_0_co_2.xml and https://www.britannica.com/event/Crimean-War accessed on Sept 15, 2021

Allies, until they were at close range to the British. The lack of visibility twisted Inkerman into a series of close-quarter fights. British regiments marched near the sound of gunfire and engaged the enemy anywhere they found them. Nonetheless the fog 'assisted' the British, too, insofar as it made the Allies fail to appreciate the multitude of the Russian force. This failure helped the British keep up their aggressive morale (they were simply unaware about the massive scale of enemy force) a few hours later when reinforcements, mainly French, brought about a turn in the battle's tide. The excessive damages on both sides of the front led to a reduction in warlike operations for some time. On the November 14, an intense storm crossed the Black Sea-Crimea area leading to heavy losses and damage to the Allied navies and much misery to the troops on land. According to British ship reports, the wind touched force 11 on the Beaufort scale (103-120 km/h). The British lost 21 ships or vessels and additional ones were destroyed; the French lost 16, including the battleship Henri IV, the 'pride of the French Navy'; the Russians' losses were light. The great losses of the Allies (ammunition, warm clothing, food, fodder, etc., in the ships) and the suffering of their land forces resulted in a notable drop in fighting activities for some weeks. The loss of the battleship Henri IV prompted the French Minister of War to ask Le Verrier, the great French astronomer, to institute an inquiry to determine if the approach of the storm could have been predicted and the Navy warned in time.

This particular case is viewed as a unique example, which indicates that how only two bad weather days can impact the wars significantly and create damage of such a magnitude that even intense warfighting for many days cannot cause.

Operation Typhoon[14]

Hitler possibly had some sort of obsession for Soviet Union and was known to be always interested to invade it. During the Second World War he had launched Operation Barbarossa (German invasion of the Soviet Union) on June 22 1941 with an aim to triumph over the western Soviet Union. However, the first major setback came in August, when

---

14 https://www.history.com/this-day-in-history/operation-typhoon-is-launched, and David W. Rolfs, "The Treachery of the Climate: How German Meteorological Errors and the Rasputitsa Helped Defeat Hitler's Army at Moscow", September 30, 2010, https://www.tcc.fl.edu/media/divisions/library/citation-guide/turabianx2fchicago/Turabian-Sample-2012-Footnotes_ADA.pdf, accessed on Aug 31, 2021 and David Stahel, Operation Typhoon, Cambridge University Press, New York, 2013 and Rüssel H. S. Stolfi, "Chance in History: The Russian Winter of 1941-1942", History, 1980, Vol. 65, No. 214 (1980), pp. 214-228

the Red Army's tanks drove the Germans back from a strong position. Subsequently, during October 1941, Hitler launched Operation Typhoon, the German drive to capture Moscow and knock the Soviet Union out of the war. This was the period of the beginning of the winter season. Hitler was warned by the Generals about the possible difficulties of waging a war during that period. Also, the Germans were fully aware about that it was Russian winter, which had been one the important cause for Napoleon's defeat during 1812. Still Hitler pushed his forces in the battle and decided to capture Moscow before the onset of winter weather. Possibly, since the German forces had captured the city of Kiev by September and that could have given Hitler the confidence to launch an assault.

Operation Typhoon was a relatively simple plan. German tank groups were expected to rapidly surround and destroy the Russian armies deployed in front of Moscow and then proceed to encircle and besiege the enemy capital. Significant amount of force was involved in this operation. Also, for Germany air support from fighter and bomber aircrafts was available. Plan was to reach 200 miles just short of Moscow before the arrival of winter weather. Pre-war weather forecast was taken into consideration while planning. Unfortunately, some misreading about the Russian winter also happened from the side of German meteorologist too. Basically, there was less information available on Russia's climate. Hence, the forecast was issued based on deductive reasoning. It was reasoned that since the preceding three winters had been unusually cold in Russia and as per the available records, there had never been four consecutive cold winters in the 150 years and the 1941-42 winter would be mild. However, that winter happed to be one of the severest Russian winters.

Another problem was that probably the German meteorologists also disregarded or were unaware of the extensive local cultural and historical references to Russia's Rasputitsas[15]. German forecasters were in the possession of the meteorological data on western Russia's annual precipitation rates. However, they failed to analyse this data in a larger context. The data told them that western Russia received its greatest rainfall in August. Hence, German forecasters concluded that Russia's dirt based roads would be muddier and more difficult to negotiate in August than in October. However, during the month of August the evaporation rates are

---

15 Rasputitsa is a term used for the two seasons (spring and autumn) of the year when travel on unpaved roads or across country becomes difficult, owing to muddy conditions from rain or melting snow

much higher, it being the summer period. With rain/snow in the month of October, the mud season begins owing to drop in the ground temperatures.

Around the combat phase, there was a heavy snow fall during the night of October 6-7. This was followed by nearly a month of cold rain, mixed with snow, across the entire front. In addition, a seasonal shift in the regional storm track had begun pushing a series of Scandinavian Cyclones into the greater Moscow region, resulting into the deterioration in weather conditions. The intermittent snow and rain squalls were taking place driven by strong north-eastern winds. This impacted the air efforts of Germany significantly. Mud and low temperatures hampered the advance of the German motorised units, vehicles, troops and horses. It was an irony that the German troops were still clad in their lightweight summer uniforms. Obviously, there was much of suffering. Various types of illnesses including respiratory complaints and frostbites became common. It was said that even by Russian standards, the winter was brutal. It froze German tanks, weapons, other equipment and vehicles. It impacted air efforts significantly. The major sufferers were the soldiers on ground who were without any snow boots, winter caps and gloves and were just not in a position to fight a winter campaign.

The Second World War Period[16]

This section is bit different from other sections in this chapter. It is not about how the weather impacted a particular operation, but more about the efforts done by the Germans to keep a watch on weather during this long war by establishing various weather units. Their efforts give an indication that how much importance they were giving for the knowledge of weather for deciding on their warfighting strategies. This war saw very decided efforts being made for the collection of data for understanding and analysis the weather.

Meteorologists of the 1940s lacked modern devices as weather radars and satellite imagery. They were depending more on traditional forms of observation the equipment present then. Various cloud observations were taken by the naked eye and for other weather elements barometers, thermometers and wind vanes were used. Obviously, they were not in a

---

16 "The Weather War: How Both Sides Scrambled for Weather Data During WWII", Oct 05, 2020, https://nationalinterest.org/blog/reboot/weather-war-how-both-sides-scrambled-weather-data-during-wwii-170129 and https://totallyhistory.com/greenland-during-world-war-ii/ and Eric Niderost, "The Second Great War (and the Weather that Defined it)", https://warfarehistorynetwork.com/2018/12/11/the-second-great-war-and-the-weather-that-defined-it/, accessed on Aug 21, 2021

position to issue long-range weather forecasts. Still for Germany, the knowledge of likely weather situation over Europe was very important. Forecasting of European weather was a huge challenge, since noting was forming in situ and the prevailing weather systems used to approach form outside the Europe.

The air mass circulation provides the main key to Europe's climate. European weather originates in the Arctic regions of the Northern Hemisphere and drifts west to east. During 1939, when the war begun, the Germans found themselves at a disadvantage since no weather-related information (weather observations/ meteorological data) was available to them for undertaking the interpretation. The information was sparse since Germany had no colonies in the region that it could use them as reporting stations. Greenland, Jan Mayen Island, and the Svelbard Archipelago were cases of prime weather-reporting sites, but they were owned by then-neutral Denmark and Norway. Interestingly, during the early phase of war, Scandinavia's neutrality actually helped the Germans. In Greenland, the island's weather stations regularly transmitted information in plain international code. The meteorologists on Norway's Jan Mayen Island did the same. But that all changed when Hitler invaded Denmark and Norway on April 9, 1940. By the summer of 1940, the Germans found themselves on the horns of a dilemma. They had triumphed in Scandinavia, but that very success jeopardised future operations.

This led Danish and Norwegian weathermen to give weather information to the Allies. So now Germans turned to Admiral Karl Dönitz[17] and his submarines. Two German U-boats were assigned full-time duties as weather-reporting stations from August 1940 to January 1941. Subsequently, they are known to have occasionally gathered weather data while on other missions. As time went on, U-boats also ferried weather personnel and equipment, to and fro from weather station sites.

The German Luftwaffe also conducted weather reconnaissance patrols that ranged as far as Greenland. Weather Squadron 5 undertook this task. However, it was observed that weather gathering by air was too unreliable. Ironically, missions were often cancelled because aircraft were grounded due to bad weather. The Germans also had a Weather Trawler Programme which employed weather ships. The "fishing" trawlers were also found supplying vital meteorological data. Unfortunately, the British

---

17 A German admiral during the Nazi era, for three weeks after the death of Adolf Hitler he was named Hitler's successor as head of state, with the title of President of Germany and Supreme Commander of the Armed Forces.

were found effectively monitoring weather ship transmissions to such an extent the element of surprise was lost. One by one the weather trawlers were captured or sunk by the British Royal Navy. It is said that programme was not merely a failure, but an unmitigated disaster and could have also been one of the major contributors to Germany's defeat.

The Royal Navy captured the weather trawlers and before sinking they seized the Enigma[18] cypher machines, devices that transmitted and received messages in the secret German Enigma code. In addition, there were cryptographic items, rotors and few other equipment that helped the British crack the Enigma code. During 1940, the possible weather station sites were at locations under the control of Allies and anti-Nazi forces. The location of these sites were very remote and desolate areas infamous for their cold temperature extremes and natural hazards. In addition, there was a threat from polar bear attacks.

Jan Mayen Island[19], Spitsbergen[20], and Greenland[21] were amid the best locations for gathering and transmitting weather data. All were in the Arctic regions, where European weather fronts form. Over these sites weather stations were already in place and hence Germans had a keen interest to capture them. Jan Mayen Island was owned by Norway and inhabited by four Norwegian meteorologists, who faithfully transmitted weather data to the homeland. When it became clear that the Germans might attempt a physical occupation of the island these meteorologists immediately ceased transmitting to Norway and began sending reports to the British and also requested British for help. They were rescued and before they departed, they destroyed their radio equipment and anything else that might be of value to the Germans.

Since there was a radio silence, the Germans realised that this is an opportune time to take over the island for establishing their own weather station. They had launched an air reconnaissance mission to check if

---

18 The Enigma was a type of enciphering machine used by the German armed forces to send messages securely. Alan Turing was a brilliant mathematician helped Britishers to break this code

19 Jan Mayen is a Norwegian volcanic island in the Arctic Ocean, with no permanent population. It is 55 km long and 373 km² in area, partly covered by glaciers.

20 Spitsbergen is the largest and only permanently populated island of the Svalbard archipelago in northern Norway. Constituting the western most bulk of the archipelago, it borders the Arctic Ocean, the Norwegian Sea, and the Greenland Sea. Area: 37,673 km²

21 The world's largest island, located between the Arctic and Atlantic oceans, with an area 2.166 million km²

anyone was physically holding the island. A German weather troop was immediately formed and an interservice expedition was planned. It was decided that a fishing trawler Hinrich Freese would take these people to the island. Regrettably for the Germans, the British were taking no chances with Jan Mayen (codenamed as Island X by the Britishers). The Hinrich Freese arrived at Jan Mayen on November 16, 1940. But the light cruiser HMS Naiad caught the German trawler before it could land its weather team and equipment. Finally, the Allies returned to Jan Mayen on March 10, 1941 and established a weather station on the island with a group of 12 Norwegian meteorologists. Subsequently, Germans undertook bombing missions to inflict damage to this unit, but did not succeed much and in the bargain, lost one or two to aircrafts. These crafts are known to have crashed on one of the island's mountainsides, lost in heavy fog. In this case, it could be said that the nature's justice was such that, the aircrafts (sorties) launched to destroy the weather unit, finally met with an accident and got destroyed owing to bad weather!

Spitsbergen was another area of interest for the Germans in their never-ending quest to establish weather stations. It was a strategic location for weather gathering for them. During 1941, a 10-man Luftwaffe meteorological team was landed on the northeast corner of this island. Throughout October 1941, the Luftwaffe shuttled in nearly four tons of supplies. By November 11, several German weather stations were fully operational. This island witnessed, practically a cat and mouse game amongst the Germans and the Allied forces. Both the powers kept on winning and losing the control of this island and had mounted few important operations to take over the control of this island. In one of the campaigns, the Germans had to leave from Spitsbergen. But they had left an automated weather station behind that successfully transmitted meteorological data throughout the summer of 1942. Subsequently, the German fleet arrived at Spitsbergen on September 6, 1943, taking the Norwegians by surprise. A fierce battle took place and the Germans secured the island, they destroyed all Allied facilities, including the all-important weather station. After few days, the German fleet was forced to withdraw.

Greenland is another island where Germans were keen to have control for various reasons including the necessity to establish weather stations. During the World War II, Greenland was of considerable significance despite the island's remoteness and harsh climate. Greenland was a Danish colony, and after Denmark itself had been invaded in April 1940, this island was virtually abandoned. The United States, despite its neutrality in 1940, eventually controlled this island (1941). During the fall of 1940 the Norwegian supply ship Veslekari, carrying Danish and Norwegian hunters and 50 armed pro-German collaborationists, was caught by the free Norwegian warship Fridtjof Nansen. Their original mission was to seize the weather station. The Germans made their boldest and successful Greenland foray in 1943. In August, the German trawler Sachen sailed with a weather team to Sabine Island on Hansa Bay, near Greenland's coast. The German weather team, code-named Holzauge, effectively established a station and then hunkered down for the winter. The Germans did succeed in situating some covert weather stations along Greenland's east coast. They were able to provide Nazi U-boats with information about weather conditions in parts of Europe. There were some reports (1943-44) about the German forces planning to construct a base over there. But the US forces were on alert and they had also bombed a weather station on the northeast coast. Data from some captured German weather stations was used by the Allies in the build-up to D-Day in June, 1944. The last Germans to be stationed in Greenland were technicians manning the weather station Edelweiss II. This base was taken over during October 1944, with all the staff being taken prisoner.

By 1944, the tide of war had turned against Germany, and its resources were dwindling. But weather reporting was still so important that the Nazis continued to send secret expeditions to the Arctic. Clutching at straws in a wild effort to stave off defeat, the Germans planned three additional weather stations in the Arctic. The first expedition was codenamed Edelweiss. The second was labelled Goldschmid. A third effort, code-named Haudegen, was sent by submarine U-307 to Spitsbergen.

Weather expedition Edelweiss was aboard the trawler Kehdingen when it was caught by the ubiquitous cutter Northland. It finally got stuck in the ice and its officers and crew were taken into custody. The Americans could also capture the 12-man Goldschmid weather party. The weather station Haudegen was a cluster of huts with a seven-bunk dormitory and a library of 20 volumes. The German personnel heard of the German surrender by radio on May 7, 1945. But for next few months they continued to broadcast weather data in plain transmissions without code. They finally surrendered to a Norwegian ship in September 1945, the last German unit to capitulate in World War II.

The Normandy Landings[22]

It is said that perhaps one of the most important weather forecasts ever made during wars, was the one for D-Day, the Allied invasion of France.

June 06, 1944 (D-Day) is known to be the largest amphibious invasion in the history of warfare. This operation was codenamed as Operation Overlord. It involved the Allies using over 5,000 ships and landing craft to land more than 150,000 troops on five beaches in Normandy. It was a well-planned operation and a command team led by American General Dwight D. Eisenhower was formed in December 1943 to device the strategy for the naval, air and land operations. It required an extraordinary cooperation between international armed forces. The invasion was steered in two main phases: an airborne assault[23] and amphibious landings[24]. Just after midnight on June 6, over 18,000 Allied paratroopers were dropped into the invasion area. They were to provide tactical support for infantry divisions on the beaches. Allied air forces flew over 14,000 sorties in support of the landings. There was no resistance form Luftwaffe since the Allied air force had already secured air supremacy prior to the invasion.

The naval component of 'Operation Overlord' was called as 'Operation Neptune'. Nearly 7,000 naval vessels, including battleships, destroyers, minesweepers, escorts and assault craft took part in the naval operations. Naval forces managed escorting and landing over 132,000 ground troops on the beaches. Also, they had carried out bombardments on German coastal defences before and during the landings and provided artillery support for the invading troops.

For the success of Allied invasion, there was a need for good lighting conditions during the night, so the best option could have been a bright cloudless full moon night and calm sea conditions (light winds). During

---

22 Christopher Klein, "The Weather Forecast That Saved D-Day", Jun 05, 2014, https://www.history.com/news/the-weather-forecast-that-saved-d-day and https://www.iwm.org.uk/history/how-d-day-was-delayed-by-a-weather-forecast and https://www.iwm.org.uk/history/the-10-things-you-need-to-know-about-d-day and "How a weather forecast made history - the D-Day Landings", June 03, 2019, https://www.rmets.org/resource/how-weather-forecast-made-history-d-day-landings, accessed on Sept 18, 2021

23 Airborne assault occurs when paratroopers, and their weapons and supplies, are dropped by parachute from transport aircraft, often as part of a strategic offensive operation

24 Amphibious warfare is a type of military offensive that in present times uses naval ships to project ground and air power onto an enemy shore at a designated landing beach. During the Great War period such operations were conducted using ship's boats as the primary method of delivering troops to shore

June 1944 a full moon and low tide coincided on 5, 6 and 7 June. This means there was only a three-day window with the necessary astronomical conditions. The proposal for the invasion of France was to mount an attack on June 5, 1944.

Till the morning of June 4, the weather was quiet with a light breeze. However, the weather was turning unsettled with a series of low-pressure systems emerging out in the North Atlantic and heading towards the English Channel. Group Captain James Stagg was Eisenhower's chief meteorologists for the invasion. In those days, Stagg and his team had no key equipment and technologies like radar, satellites, computer models and communication systems. He was depending more on rudimentary systems like barometer and few other equipment for providing observations. Hence, weather forecasting for more than a day or two in advance was unrealistic.

Eisenhower had selected June 5 as a D-Day; however, Group Captain Stagg had urged for a last-minute delay owing weather conditions. There was a much of disappointment in Allied camp since they were planning for this operation for almost one year. But also, there was a realisation that the massive Normandy landings demand optimal weather conditions. High winds and rough seas could upturn landing crafts and disrupt the amphibious assaults. Also, wet weather could have bogged down the army movement and thick cloud cover could have obscured the necessary air support.

Predicting the English Channel's notoriously fickle weather was no easy job. A team of forecasters from the Royal Navy, British Meteorological Office and the US Strategic and Tactical Air Force were involved in this task. The Allies had a robust network of weather stations in Canada, Greenland and Iceland. They were routinely getting observations from weather ships and weather flights over the North Atlantic. In addition, there was a secret agreement with weather stations in the neutral Republic of Ireland. Particularly, a weather station in Ireland at a post office at Blacksod Point in the far west, proved crucial in detecting the arrival of a lull in the storms that Gp Capt Stagg and his colleagues believed would allow for an invasion on June 6. On the afternoon of June 4, when the weather began to deteriorate as the first storm approached, a rise in the barometric pressure was noticed by Stagg. It was a single observation received from a ship stationed six hundred miles west of Ireland. There were reports that the pressure is continuously rising. This led Stagg to conclude that there could be a break in the weather on June 6.

On the other side of the English Channel, German forecasters were also monitoring the weather conditions and their prediction was that the stormy conditions would continue without any break until mid-June. This led Nazi commanders to think that Allied invasion is unlikely at least for near future. This led them becoming bit casual towards manning their coastal defences. In terms of resources, both from observation and analysis (forecasting models) point of view, the Germans meteorological setup was inferior in comparison with the Allies.

It is important to note that amongst the meteorological services within the Allied forces, the US forecasters were of the opinion that the operation should be launched on June 5 only. However, Gp Capt Stagg kept faith in British forecaster and advised for 24h postponement of the operation.

This one forecast has been viewed as a pivotal moment in world history. If it would have gone wrong then the lives of thousands of men and massive amounts of equipment would have been lost. Also, if the weather would not had gone bad on June 5, then that would have allowed the Germans to realise the nature of build-up of forces done by the Allies, along the coast of southern England. It is important to note that weather on June 6 was also not a totally clear weather, but there was a period of reasonable sky clearance and dying of winds to undertake air and sea operations. On June 6, during early morning period, the Pathfinder planes for the paratroops ran into unexpected banks of clouds over the coast of France. So, some soldiers got dropped at incorrect dropping/landing zones. Broadly, the weather on the morning of June 6 was satisfactory for the invasion. This one correct forecast ensured that the yearlong efforts made by the Allied force did not go in vain.

Luck of Kokura[25]

Bockscar (Bock's Car), was the United States Army Air Forces B-29 bomber that dropped a Fat Man nuclear weapon over Nagasaki, the Japanese city during World War II. Till date, this is the last nuclear attack in history. Actually, the city of Kokura was the original target for the second nuclear bomb on August 9, 1945. However, owing to the target getting obscured (bad visibility) the bomber aircraft while in air decided to opt for 'plan B' and decided to bomb Nagasaki. Apparently, even today in Japan

25 Alex Wellerstein, "The luck of Kokura", August 22, 2014, http://blog.nuclearsecrecy. com/2014/08/22/luck-kokura/ accessed on Sept 30, 2021 and Kathleen Sears, *Weather 101*, Adams Media, London, 2017

there is an axiom called 'luck of Kokura' which refers to this incidence, where a bad weather saved the lives of tens of thousands of people there.

The Kokura mission was dubbed as CENTERBOARD II (Hiroshima was CENTERBOARD I) mission undertaken by a group of six aircrafts, all B-29 bombers. One of them was the strike plane with the Fat Man implosion bomb. Two other planes were instrument and observation planes. The fourth aircraft was a 'standby' plane, just in case the strike plain faces some problem. Fifth and sixth aircrafts were the weather planes, which had done an advance weather reconnaissance over Nagasaki and Kokura. These reconnaissance planes were for checking out bombing conditions for helping the bomber plane determine, whether the primary or secondary target would be used. The striker aircraft Bockscar took off from the island of Tinian and had arrived at a rendezvous point at Yakushima Island. It rendezvoused with one of the other B-29s (the instrument plane), but did not spot the other one (the photo plane). Subsequently, the pilot of Bockscar continued on to Kokura. However, the target was obscured by heavy ground haze and smoke. It was 7/10 clouds coverage. It was not possible to undertake bomb delivery on the target by visually identifying the target. Three bombing runs on Kokura were attempted, but no visual identification of the target was possible. Since Bockscar had limited fuel, the pilot decided to engage the secondary target, Nagasaki. In fact, Nagasaki weather was also not that good. It was obscured by smoke and clouds and the aircraft made the target approach by using radar. At the last possible moment, some cloud cover was broken and target identification was possible and the bomb was dropped on Nagasaki.

Five days after the attack, the Japanese announced their acceptance of the Allies' terms of unconditional surrender and the rest is history. It is actually the bad weather, which ended up saving Kokura, but some clearance in weather made it a doomsday for Nagasaki. Interestingly, if Kokura would have got bombed then in all likelihood it would have ended up killing a young Kokura college student named Tetsuya Fujita. After some years, this college student ended up becoming one the most renowned meteorologist. He became famous for developing a tornado damage scale that still bears his name and is known as Fujita scale.

The Cold War Period

The Cold War was the stressed relationship between the United States (and its allies) and the Soviet Union (and its allies) between the end of World War II (September 1945) and the fall of the Soviet Union (December

1991). Actually, this was a different type of war, which was technically not fought on the battle ground, but involved power positioning by the both the blocks in the realm of nuclear deterrence posture, geopolitics and geo-economics. The period of Cold War exceeds 45 years and more importantly since actually no war fought it would be difficult to develop a context of impact of weather on this war.

Still, two important issues at the backdrop of this war did emerge which have weather significance. One, during this war some efforts had happened involving intentional modification of weather for the purposes of the military gains. There was a realisation that the weather control could be as powerful a war weapon as the atom bomb. Two, issues concerning climate crisis.

If human activities could change climate, why not change it on purpose, to suit us better? From 1945 into the 1970s, much effort went into studies of weather modification. The US agencies tried cloud-seeding to enhance local rainfall. Also, the Russian scientists presented ideas of planetary engineering. All this led the military agencies to secretly explore the idea called the Climatological Warfare. There were different weather modification experimentations undertaken and good amount of the government funding was made available. However, it appears that post 1975, the major focus of the research was more towards contentious 'geoengineering' schemes for interventions that could restrain global warming, if it started to become unbearable[26]. Issues related to various aspects of Climatological or Weather warfare are discussed in detail in some of the following chapters of this book.

One very novel project which was undertaken during the Cold war period for military purposes actually is known to have helped in climate research too. However, there is also some very limited connection of this project with the issues related to climate change. Camp Century[27] was a classified US nuke installation in Greenland which was supposed to have a facility for 600 missiles aimed at the USSR.

---

26 Matt Novak, "Weather Control as a Cold War Weapon", Dec 5, 2011, https://www.smithsonianmag.com/history/weather-control-as-a-cold-war-weapon-1777409/ and "Climate Modification Schemes", Aug 2021, https://history.aip.org/climate/RainMake.htm, accessed on Sept 14, 2021

27 Jon Gertner, "The Top Secret Cold War Project That Pulled Climate Science From the Ice", Dec 06, 2019, https://www.wired.com/story/the-top-secret-cold-war-project-that-pulled-climate-science-from-the-ice/ and "Camp Century", July 19, 2018, https://www.atomicheritage.org/history/camp-century, accessed on Sept 14, 2021

Camp Century base was built within the Greenland Ice Sheet in 1959, where the average temperatures were around minus 60 degrees Celsius. Officially, it was a science station, but it essentially was a top-secret site for testing the feasibility of deploying nuclear missiles from the Arctic.

Construction of this site was completed by October 1960 by the Army engineers, who had used Swiss-made Peter Plows to dig deep trenches in the snow and ice. It was a very major engineering job and the trenches were covered with a roof of steel arches and topped with more snow. Inside the trenches, prefabricated wooden buildings were set up and care was taken to minimise melting. The largest trench, known as 'Main Street', was more than 1,000 feet long. For the purposes of fresh water requirements, the engineers had drilled a hole deep into the ice. The entire facility consisted of 26 tunnels, almost two miles in total and had all facilities required for human survival.

The last piece of Camp Century was the instalment of the PM-2, a portable, medium power nuclear reactor and the shipment for this alone consisted of 400 tons of equipment. The reactor was successfully installed in 1960 and operated for 33 months before being deactivated and removed. The entire facility was meant for the US Army's operation, codenamed "Iceworm". Here the purpose was to deploy ballistic missiles under the Greenland ice. The project continued till 1966 and eventually got cancelled and no missiles were ever deployed there.

Along with military men few geologists were also present in this facility. Their experimentation and analysis did realise some significant scientific discoveries, such as some the first studies of ice cores, revealing geological secrets going back 100,000 years. Of late, climate change scientists have warned of severe consequences should the Greenland ice sheet melt enough to reveal Camp Century. It is known that this facility's nuclear reactor had produced over 47,000 gallons of radioactive waste and this waste remains buried under the ice. There are scientific predictions that the Camp Century site will start losing ice by 2090. In general, this project could be viewed as a one of historical wrongs done, which could leave a major negative impact on the global climate in coming few decades.

There have been some important military campaigns fought during the period of Cold War. However, they were not involving both the powers, simultaneously. There were some conflicts involving one of the power blocks and some conflicts were amongst the states, which were not the part of both these power blocks. Some famous campaigns during that period include Vietnam War (1955-1975), Korean War (1950-1953), India-China war (1962), India-Pakistan War (1971), Yom Kippur War (1973), Falklands War (1982), Lebanon War (1982-1985), Civil War in Afghanistan (1989-1992) and the Gulf War (1991). In some of these wars, maritime power and air power was at display. There has been some impact of weather on all these campaigns, however there appears to be no impact of such a magnitude that could have aided to change the course of the battle itself. The type of season, type and nature of weather systems occurred during the phase of conflict and the nature of terrain in the zone of conflict must have dictated on the prevalence of weather over that region. Various states involved in all these conflicts have managed to continue with their campaigns in different (favourable/unfavourable) types of weather situations. Some of these wars have been short wars, while some have lasted for longer duration. Obviously, in some cases seasonal weather situations would have had some impact on the warfighting.

The 1991 Gulf War[28]

During 1989/90, the Berlin Wall came down. It ended the role of Communist regimes in Eastern Europe. Around the same period, it was seen that the US and Soviet leadership (Reagan and Gorbachev) was thinking differently. There was a push for reforms in the Soviet Union. The period 1985–87, witnessed negotiation of the Intermediate-Range Nuclear Forces Treaty (INF) and treaty became a reality by December 1987. By May 1991, after on-site investigations by both sides, 2,700 missiles were destroyed. The nine-year-old Soviet Afghan conflict came to an end by 1989 with the ending of the Soviet occupation in Afghanistan. Finally, on December 26, 1991 the Soviet Union itself dissolved into its component republics. With this the Cold War came to an end. During early part of 1991, the Gulf War took place. The Soviets did not oppose the US, when they had taken on their former ally Iraq.

Iraqi president Saddam Hussein invaded neighbouring Kuwait in early August 1990. Even after the United Nations Security Council had asked Saddam Hussein to withdraw from Kuwait, he did not listen. To liberate Kuwait from the clutches of Saddam Hussein, the US launched an

---

28 Casey Bukro, "Climate Surprises in a Land Of Sand", Feb 08, 1991, https://www.chica-gotribune.com/news/ct-xpm-1991-02-08-9101120423-story.html, accessed on sept 13, 2021 and Operation Desert Storm: Evaluation of the Air Campaign, Jun 1997, report no GAO/NSIAD-97-134 published by United States General Accounting Office Washington, DC

attack on Iraq. The major part of this operation was an air offensive called Operation Desert Storm.

Operation Desert Storm was mainly a sustained 43-day air campaign. It was the first large employment of US air power since the Vietnam War and gets recognised as the most successful war fought by the United States in the 20th century. The main ground campaign occupied only the final 100 hours of the war. The air campaign involved nearly every type of fixed-wing aircraft in the US inventory, flying about 40,000 air-to-ground and 50,000 support sorties.

Forty years have passed since the 1991 Gulf War. However, even today this war gets recognised as one of the classic wars of modern era. This is probably because this war demonstrated the relevance of various new technologies in warfighting. Over last four decades the focus of various militaries have remained towards using these technologies in their security architecture. Over a period of time much upgradation in the realm of these technologies have happened. Though, more or less the basic doctrinal idea about the employment of technologies in warfare have remained same. Also, much of research towards understanding how exactly this war was fought has happened. Obviously, as said in the context of history that the 'history is written by victors'[29] we have only the US side of the story about how this war was fought. Nonetheless, it is important to factor this available research towards understating this war from weather point of view.

A substantial air campaign was undertaken by the US during this war. In total around 1,600 US combat aircraft were deployed. The US bomb tonnage dropped per day was equal to 85% of the average daily bomb tonnage dropped by the US on Germany and Japan during the course of World War II. Operation Desert Storm provided a valuable opportunity to assess the performance of US combat aircraft and munitions systems under actual combat conditions. It was found that generally the weather conditions were favourable towards launching an air campaign. Also, the coalition forces were preparing and practicing for almost six months for this campaign.

The US weather services were monitoring daily weather of northern Saudi Arabia, the northern Persian Gulf, Iraq, eastern Jordan, south-eastern Turkey, and southwestern Iran between August 1990 and March 1991. During this period three operations were conducted, namely Desert Shield, Desert Storm and Provide Comfort.

---

29 This quote gets attributed to Winston Churchill, but its origins are unknown

There is a 245-page report[30] published by the USAF Environmental Technical Environmental Applications Center. This report provides the details of the type weather prevailed during the entire phase of these operations. The entire phase of operations has been divided into four distinct climate zones: the upper plain, which includes rolling grasslands between the Tigris and Euphrates rivers; the lower plain, which includes a fertile delta between the rivers and many swamps; the mountains in north-eastern Iraq, which includes ski resorts; and the desert, which covers southern and western Iraq and extends into Jordan, Kuwait, Saudi Arabia and Syria. The common misconception is that the Persian Gulf is hot and dry all the time. However, the US forces did encounter different types of weather from sand/dust storms to rain to slushy ground conditions.

Generally, there was no continuous hindrance from weather to undertake flying activities. Yet, it needs to be mentioned that the weather was worst in that region in 14 years and weather conditions even less conducive to an air campaign. Still the air campaign did took place and some sorties are known to gone waste owing bad weather. The weather did limit the effectiveness of the target sensors. IR, EO, and laser systems were all seriously degraded by weather conditions such as clouds, rain, fog, and even haze and humidity. They were also impeded by dust and smoke. At high altitudes and even at low altitudes owing to high humidity or other impediments, pilots were unable to discriminate targets effectively. They were reporting that they were unable to discern whether a presumed target was a tank or a truck and whether it had already been hit by a previous attack.

The assessment after the war indicates that, the air campaign planners were overoptimistic about various aspects and actually many of the early missions were cancelled because of adverse weather. It has been observed that the manufacturers' claims that their flying systems like aircrafts, weapons and sensors could perfectly operate in all weather conditions were actually half true. The flying platforms like F-16, F-117, and the Grumman A-6 Intruder did face difficulties in conduct of operations owing to clouds, haze, humidity, smoke, and dust. Low Altitude Navigation Targeting Infrared for Night (LANTIRN) pods were mounted under the fuselage of an F-16. The manufactures had claims that such navigation pods, enables pilots to fly at low altitudes, even in limited visibility, and thus avoid detection by unfriendly forces. However, it was observed that

---

30 "Gulf War Weather", March 1992, Report No: USAFETAC/TN--92/003

this system has very low capability (at times nil) to identify targets during poor weather conditions.

The Post-Cold War Phase

All the cases discussed in this chapter are actually based on the information available in the post-war analysis. Learning from these experiences indicates that the states must be factoring 'weather' as an important tenet during their war planning. Modern day warfighting (actually it could be said to have begun with the 1991 Gulf War) involves assistance from new technologies too. Like the air forces use precision guided munitions (PGMs) and navy uses submarine-launched ballistic missile (SLBM). Today, weather impacts not only the performance of the weapons delivery platforms like tanks, aircraft alone, but also that of weapon systems and other support systems too. In the post-Cold War period, few globally noticeable conflicts have taken place like the Iraq War (March 2003), Syrian War (continuing since March 2011), the Afghanistan War (2001-2021) and the Russian invasion Ukraine (Feb 2022). Weather did impact/impacting the warfighting abilities of the warring factions in these wars.

It is important to recognise the fact that weather does influence even the modern-day state-of-art military platforms. Drones or UCAVs (Unmanned Combat Air Vehicles) are known to brought a technology disruption in aerial warfare and the way we perceive airpower. The 44 days conflict over Nagorno Karabakh (September 27, 2020 to November 10, 2020) gets recognised as one of the turning points in the combat application of drone technology. The UCAVs at the disposal of the Azerbaijani side played a key role in this conflict. Their widespread use provided an opportunity for Azerbaijani forces to carry out surgically precise attacks on Armenian positions far from the front lines. They were able to correctly detect, monitor, and destroy various targets. However, it was observed that the drone operations are limited by the weather conditions like extreme temperatures, fog, rain and wind. The changes occurring in weather situation were known to have influenced the behaviour of the drone systems. During these military operations, the presence of UCAVs was noticeably lower during bad weather[31]. This explains that even in 21st century, weather continues to be an 'influencer' for warfighting.

---

31 Damir Ilić and Vladimir Tomasevic, "The impact of the Nagorno-Karabakh conflict in 2020 on the perception of combat drones", *Serbian Journal of Engineering Management*, Vol. 6, No. 1, January 2021, pp. 9-18.

Chapter four specifically undertakes few case studies in respect of some recent conflicts. Here the purpose is to identify the role played by the weather during these wars. It is expected that such case specific appreciation of the weather situation would help in a wider understanding of the environmental situation and help towards appreciating what weather-related factors, the states must take into consideration while planning for future wars. Similarly, wars are known to adversely impact the climate (the nature of damage is location and time specific) to some extent. The probable impact of war on climate is addressed separately in this book.

Chapter 3

21st Century Warfare and Meteorological Requirements

Weather conditions do have some impact on wars. During the 20th century, from the World Wars to Gulf Wars, the states involved in the wars did face various challenges owing to the weather. The next chapter deliberates how the longest war in the 21st century (Afghanistan conflict, which lasted for two decades) witnessed weather impacting some critical military operations. In this era of Industry 4.0, significant military technologies developments have occurred. Modern-day military technologies are recognised as state-of-art technologies, and the technology developers make efforts to ensure that their systems are all-weather proof as far as possible. Simultaneously, it has been observed that it is not possible to fully nullify the impact of weather on any fighting platform. Hence, even for 21st-century warfare, the weather situation continues to remain an essential concern in warfare. In the earlier chapter, we saw how unexpected weather twisted the fate of various military operations throughout history. This chapter looks at the present.

The impact of weather could be twofold. One, a general impact on everything associated with the warfare and secondly, specific impact of certain aspects of weather on specific systems. The exact nature of tools and tactics the armed forces apply would depend on the nature of the task they are undertaking. This nature of the task and the tools and tactics used and employed to achieve this task would play a role in deciding the specific nature of weather information required.

Globally, the armed forces are viewed as the institutions created by the state for the primary purpose of national defence against external threats and internal conflicts. The structure of the armed forces can differ significantly between countries. Usually, regular forces are the forces which remain ready for any eventualities like war. For this purpose, armies, navies and air forces are established. These forces also play an important role in international commitments like peacekeeping and peace support missions. Also, a few other services could be established mainly depending on the strategic requirements of the state. These could be para-military forces, auxiliary military forces and reserved military forces. Such forces usually play a vital role in supporting the operations and can undertake some specific operations independently, depending on their jurisdiction. Armed forces are well-trained professional forces established for specific roles. At times, based on the situation, armed forces are given new roles and responsibilities. Such situations offer opportunities for the armed forces to prove their relevance while extending their competencies. But, most of the time, they are neither equipped nor adequately prepared and trained for such tasks[1]. There is a possibility that owing to the nature of such tasks including time-criticalities such compromises in operating producers could be done. Under such circumstances the unit commanders need to be alert and should not overlook weather-related compulsions (if any).

For any commander, weather intelligence is of much importance. Weather conditions impact tactics, techniques, and procedures. Battlefield environmental conditions play a major role in the planning and progression of various military operations. It is not the weather condition alone which impacts the progression of any operations. The commander also needs to look at some other environmental factors while planning. They include terrain conditions, battlefield-induced contaminants (BIC), and illumination and background signatures[2].

Historically, it has been found that the physical landscape on which the actual battle happens also plays an important role in the outcome of that battle. The (physical) geography could either help one side advance their forces by offering a natural obstruction against an enemy attack or expose the forces to an incoming threat. Hence, armed forces always assess the terrain before launching any operation.

Terrain Appraisal

Military geography comprises the application of geographic information, tools, and technologies to military problems. Fundamentally,

---

1   The Armed Forces, SSR Backgrounder, https://www.files.ethz.ch/isn/195684/ DCAF_BG_10_The% 20Armed%20Forces.11.15-1.pdf, accessed on Dec 31, 2021

2   Battlefield Weather Effects, Field Manual FM 34-81-1, Washington DC, Dec23, 1993, http://www.bits.de/NRANEU/others/amd-us-archive/FM34-81-1%2892%29.pdf, accessed on Dec 31, 2021

from a geographical perspective, military operations comprise time, space, and the nature of what exists within the confines of that time and space. In a larger sense, military operations are geographic: they occur in places, and places comprise distinctive natural and human landscapes. Also, the type of operation dictates the nature of the geographical environment. Urban warfare would have a different geographical setting compared to jungle warfare. While during peacetime operations, like disaster relief operations (say, flood relief or earthquake) could have a different geographical milieu. So different operational environments and circumstances require different types of geographic information. Obviously, military strategies and operational requirements from training to equipment, are based on the necessary military geography-related information.

Historically, since the 19th century, the distinct academic subfield of military geography could be identified. The Second World War was a defining moment for military geography, as academic geographers embraced it. It got expanded in its scope and scale to support a global-scale war effort. The studies on this subject started becoming more analytical and integrative. Since the 1990s, military geography appears to have matured much as an academic subject. Particularly, the spread of operations other than war and the need to respond to asymmetrical threats has started military analysts to look at this subject in a more focused fashion[3].

This discipline has progressed based on the empirical evidence connecting war and geography. Research works are available that link the local topography, hydrographical settings, climate and coastal conditions with the military operations. These works also examine the influence of secondary factors like biological, health and environmental issues on military operations. Various wars have demonstrated the unique interaction between physical conditions and the geopolitical realities of different geographical settings. Particularly, in the 21st century, which is witnessing the ever-changing nature of warfare, there is a need for critical assessment of military geography. There are tangible and intangible features to armed conflicts. The tangible features can include geographical concerns, such as terrain and climate, but also includes those highly visible aspects of the quantity and quality of personnel and military equipment available[4].

---

3   https://www.oxfordbibliographies.com/view/document/obo-9780199874002/obo-9780199874002-0029.xml, accessed on Dec 03, 2021

4   Francis A. Galgano and Eugene J. Palka (Eds), *Modern Military Geography*, Routledge, New York: 2011 and a note written by Cdr (Dr) J. Bezuidenhout, University of Stellenbosch.

Terrain and weather impact combat more than any other physical factors. Weather affects battlefield operations, weapons, and electronics systems and more so also affects the soldiers that make it all work. Terrain features affect weather elements such as visibility, temperature, humidity, precipitation (rain/sleet/snow), winds and clouds (mainly low clouds and also help towards the vertical development of thunder clouds). The most common example of terrain affecting weather is that on the windward side of high terrain, say in the mountains, the rainfall rate will be more than on the leeward (opposite) side. On the other hand, weather conditions such as temperature, winds, and precipitation have a definite effect on the terrain and can boost or limit military operations, such as trafficability, water-crossing (fording), and the first-round precision of supporting field artillery fires[5]. For operations at the sea, sea conditions make a difference. Ocean surface topography or sea surface topography is also relevant mainly for undersea operations (say submarine activities). However, this effect is much lesser than ground terrain's impact on army operations.

At the tactical level, terrain, climate and its extremes affect soldier's performance. The armed forces are known to cater for the influence of weather and terrain in their doctrines. Based on the typical nature of climate and terrain of the region, the soldier clothing gets designed. Normally, their training involves conduct for exercises in desert warfare, jungle warfare, mountain warfare and high-altitude/cold climate warfare. Training soldiers to be ready to manoeuvre and fight in the face of changing weather is important for success. While the deployment of military units, in challenging climatic arenas, the soldiers are given sufficient time for acclimatisation. To operate both during peacetime and wartime, either for training or during the actual combat phase, continuous assessment of weather in the area of interest is essential. Data on the frequency of weather extremes for specific regions assist in advance planning. At the operational level, climate and extreme weather affect the strategy and organisation of effective campaigns, theatre operations, and battles. Military operations undertaken in environments of weather disturbances leading to heavy precipitation (rain/snow), tropical storms (hurricanes) or extreme desert heat are clearly affected by the expected climate. The climate will influence force projection and exit strategies after a series of military operations. Extreme weather events can cause delays and disruptions in plans for mobility, lines of communication, points of embarkation and logistical support. Restoring national utilities, food production, water resources,

---

5 http://www.bits.de/NRANEU/others/amd-us-archive/FM34-81-1%2892%29.pdf, accessed on Dec 02, 2021

etc. can be considerably hindered by the frequency of extreme weather. At the strategic level, climate and extreme weather conditions are considered before employment of resources for national and international needs[6]. The operating and maintenance cost projections are carried out by factoring the average climate conditions of the region of interest. The military industry also keeps the weather and terrain conditions in mind while designing their products.

Concept of Warfare

It is said that war has a continuing nature that exhibits four continuities: a political dimension, a human dimension, the existence of uncertainty and that it is a contest of wills. Carl von Clausewitz (1780-1831), a Prussian general and military theorist, a known authority on the subject of war, in his various writings, he has argued about the moral and political aspects of war. He has argued succinctly that, war is all about passion and a response about the hostile feelings of the people. He also highlights the uncertainty aspect of the war and mentions that war exists within social, political and historical contexts and hence has its unique character[7]. Generally speaking, the state's political objective is known to decide its military strategy. It has been observed that the broad conceptualisation of the nature of war since the Clausewitz era, continues to dominate even in the 21st century. Owing to the nature of technological developments and some irregular strategies adopted by the state and non-state actors, it has been observed that continuous changes are taking place in the nature of warfare over the years.

Various debates involving the understanding of military thought provide a 'viewpoint' about the nature of war, types of war, levels of war etc. There is no stranded (globally recognised) division about the nature of warfare. This is understandable since every war has its own context and circumstances. Wars happen owing to political requirements and based on the desired end result, the warfighting strategies and tactics are decided with lot of thought process. There are grand strategies, national strategies and military strategies. Broadly, the wars get categorised as either total wars or limited wars. Differentiation could also be done based on the geography, nature of tactics and the type of weaponry used. The war-related literature

---

6   Weatherly, J. & Hill, D. (2004). OS-02: The Impact of Climate and Extreme Weather Events on Military Operations.

7   https://www.benning.army.mil/mssp/Nature%20and%20Character/, accessed on Nov 30, 2021

provides various deliberations about the different methods of understating the nature of warfare.

For the purpose of this chapter, appreciation of the ever-changing nature and character of war has been taken as given. Here the focus is mainly on debating the relevance of weather in the context of such different categories of warfare. The identification of the 'categories of warfare for the 21ˢᵗ century mentioned below are not based on any specific scientific method. It could be viewed as an assessment based on various ongoing debates on the contemporary warfare.

Types of Warfare

Some important types of 21ˢᵗ-century warfare, could be identified as:

➤ Conventional Warfare

➤ Asymmetric Warfare

➤ Nuclear Warfare/WMD Warfare

➤ Cyber Warfare

➤ Space Warfare

It is important to note that various other types of warfare are also getting discussed presently, like Network Centric Warfare, Hybrid Warfare, Non-contact Warfare, Mosaic Warfare and a few other types. The weather could have a specific impact in context of various types of warfare. However, in broad terms, it could be said that weather-related discussion done below, particularly in the context of conventional warfare would cater directly or indirectly (to a great extent) for most of the other types of too. In the context of cyber warfare, there may not be any issues related with weather, expect to say that weather at times does impact commutation systems and it is important to keep track of this, during the phase of any defensive or offensive cyber operations. It is also important to quickly analyse if the problems experienced in the IT systems are owing to a cyber-attack or some space weather-related problems.

The discussion on the role and impact of weather on Space Warfare has been carried out in the subsequent chapters. From weather perspective, space warfare issues are bit different than the outline of discussion followed for other types of warfare in this chapter. The discussion on space aspects needs to be is more broad-based and also address certain aspects, which could be viewed beyond the stranded understanding of warfare. Hence, space aspects are discussed separately in this book.

Conventional Warfare

The wars, which happened during the period starting from say the first World War to the period before the 9/11 (terror attacks on the US soil, on September 11 2001) could be viewed as conventional wars. Normally, conventional warfare is about the military conflict taking place by the use of conventional weapons. Such wars could happen amongst two or more states (or alliances). Here mostly, the approach is to target the advisories' military forces and associated infrastructure. Normally, the civilian population never gets militarily attacked. Such wars are expected to be fought without the use of any weapons of mass destruction (WMDs). In case of the First World War, chemical weapons were used, while the Second World War ended with the use of nuclear weapons. Hence, it is obvious that some phases of these wars were not purely conventional in nature.

History demonstrates that geographically speaking, conventional wars (mostly) did take place in the region of 'the Heartlands'[8]. Sir Halford John Mackinder (1861-1947), an English geographer, academician and politician, regarded as one of the founding fathers of geopolitics and geo-strategy, has conceptualised the idea of Heartland. He argued that the huge crescent that starts in the Middle East, passes through the horn of Africa, proceeds through South Asia, and ends in northeast Asia (Korea) is the area where maximum wars have taken place and those were conventional wars[9]. However, Nicholas John Spykman (1893–1943), an American political scientist and a professor of international relations at Yale University, criticised Mackinder for overrating the Heartland as being of immense strategic importance due to its vast size and central geographical location. Obviously, geography dictated the importance of land power. However, Spykman conceptualised the idea of 'the Rimland'[10]. As per him the Rimland, a strip of coastal land that encircles Eurasia, was more important

---

8   Geoffrey Sloan (1999) Sir Halford J. Mackinder: The Heartland theory then and now, *Journal of Strategic Studies*, 22:2-3, 15-38

9   Martin van Creveld, "Modern Conventional Warfare: An Overview", https://indi-anstrategicknowledgeonline.com/web/MODERM%20CONVENTIONAL%20WAR-FARE%20AN%20OVERVIEW%20%20BY%20MARTIN%20VAN%20CREVELD%20HEBREW%20UNIVERSITY%20JERUSALEM.pdf, accessed on Dec 01, 2021

10 Antero Holmila (2020) Re-thinking Nicholas J. Spykman: from historical sociology to balance of power, The International History Review, 42:5, 951-966

than the idea of the Heartland. He argued for the importance of sea power. The possible relevance of air power started slowly sinking in the minds of military leadership after the Write brothers took their first flight in 1903. Subsequently, air power emerged as an important instrument of war policy during the Second World War.

From the Heartland to the Rimland and subsequently, with the presence of combat flying machines, there was a realisation that land, water and air are the mediums to flight wars. Various platforms and weapon systems essential to fight a war in these three mediums possibly got bracted as conventional warfighting systems over the years. Hence, to understand the impact of weather on conventional wars, it is important to understand how weather impacts the army, navy and air force operations.

Army Operations

The combat arms of the army normally include Infantry, Armor, Artillery, Air Defence Artillery and Special Forces. Some military establishments have their own aviation core exclusively established for the army. During the combat phase (or even otherwise, say during routine training), the unfavourable weather conditions would have an impact on the nature of operations. It is important not to use the weather inputs in isolation but along with other information like terrain conditions and light conditions and the nature of operations to be undertaken.

The common weather elements, which would impact the overall performance of the armed forces, include atmosphere pressure (pressure and density altitude), sky cover (types and amount of low, medium and high clouds including rain-bearing clouds), precipitation (rain, snow, sleet etc), humidity (relative and absolute), visibility, wind speed and direction, and temperature and dew point temperature. All these elements could have nuanced interpretations for every arm of combat arm.

There would be different requirements regarding the weather information for every arm of army. For example, say the information about the ambient temperature, pressure, wind speed and direction would have different meanings for Armor and Artillery operations. To appreciate how explicitly the weather elements would impact every arm the following paragraph provides some specific details.

The Infantry itself could have different subgroups like Light Infantry, Heavy Infantry and Mechanised Infantry. Light Infantry is expected to be more mobile. It could be said that Light Infantry is simply a walking force mainly carrying handheld equipment and weapons, while others carry heavy weaponry and vehicles. Obviously, the state of ground would be decided by the terrain features and type of current and past weather like rain or snow (if any). Under such a situation, the trafficability and movement rates would differ for Light and Mechanised Infantry. The surface wind (direction and speed) would impact firing; however, it would have different connotations for small arms firing and artillery firing. Similarly, units with big vehicles on their inventory would be required to be more concerned about the ambient temperatures. Apart from the human discomfort, the freezing or very hot temperatures would impact the lubricants used and engine warm-up periods and the ballistics of main guns.

Fundamentally, operating an armoured vehicle in cold weather is more or less similar to operating any other piece of machinery. Basically, to handle cold weather the operators need to ensure that the lubrication needs to be stepped up and adjusted for lower temperatures and engines need to be pre-heated where necessary. Also, the ammunition should be stored in warmth. These are all good measures when reasonably challenging weather conditions are there. There is a major impact on mobility, when the surface becomes very icy. With icy surfaces, steel tracks become slippery and it becomes difficult to control tanks since they start drifting. It is important to note that wheeled vehicles can typically have snow chains installed on their wheels, whereas tanks rely on their tracks only[11].

Air Operations

Since the beginning of the aviation era, the weather has been an important element in deciding on various aviation activities. On December 17, 1903, Wilbur and Orville Wright carried out four brief flights at Kitty Hawk, North Carolina with their first powered aircraft. Earlier, during 1900, they had journeyed to Kitty Hawk to begin their manned gliding experiments, as the mid-Atlantic coast was known for its regular breezes and soft sandy landing surfaces. The Weather Bureau is known to have played a vital role in these first flights. The first weather station in North Carolina was established by the US Army Signal Service on August 16, 1874 at the Cape Hatteras Lighthouse keeper's quarters as a weather reporting station. A second weather office was set up at the Kitty Hawk Life Saving Station in 1875. To find the best location to test their flying machine, the Wright Brothers wrote to the office in Kitty Hawk for advice. They got a prompt and friendly reply from Joseph J. Dosher, who worked at the office,

---

11 "Tanks in Cold Weather", Dec 15, 2021, https://aw.my.games/en/news/general/tanks-cold-weather, accessed on July 28, 2022

which assisted the Wrights to decide that Kitty Hawk was the best place to attempt their feat[12]. The importance of weather for aviation activities is so critical that, for many decades, a separate branch of meteorology called Aviation Meteorology is in place and it deals exclusively to the weather issues of the aviation sector. Various air forces in the world, also have their own special units for providing them timely inputs and mission-specific weather forecasts.

Broadly, air forces use four types of flying platforms: fighter aircrafts, transport aircrafts, helicopters and unmanned aerial vehicles (UAVs/drones). This flying mechanism offers the air forces various options for their unitisation. Fighter aircrafts have a major combat role; however, they are also used in electronic warfare and reconnaissance role. Major commitments for transport aircrafts are logistical in nature, but they could be used as airborne platforms for proving early warnings or for coordination of various flying units. On some occasions, transport aircrafts have also been used for aerial bombing purposes. Helicopters and UAVs are used, both for non-combat and combat purposes.

Apart from aerial combat and air defence missions, air forces undertake various other missions like providing close air support (CAS) to army developments, transportation operations for troops and equipment movements, para-dropping operations, transportation operations, reconnaissance gathering, search and rescue (SAR), weather observational missions, fire support, aerial refuelling, gathering of electronics intelligence and for undertaking aerial refuelling. For all these types of missions, it is important to know the weather conditions, both on ground and in air, for smooth operations. Particularly, aerial bombing operations are undertaken in different modes like say dive bombing and high-altitude bombing. Hence information about the weather elements is required at different altitudes. Also, the modern-day weapon (release) delivery on the target happens much away from the actual target. Hence, the weather requirements differ for missions carrying standoff weapons and laser-guided munitions.

Broadly, the aviation weather hazards are more or less similar for civil and military aviation. Particularly, for military aviation, the weather forecast accuracy is critical. For fighter aircrafts and helicopters, it is important to ensure that they are well prepared to handle any fast changes in weather. Universally, some specific weather elements, which are hazardous to conduct of aviation activities, get identified as 'Aviation Weather Hazards'.

---

12 "The Wright Brothers and the Weather Bureau", https://vlab.noaa.gov/web/nws-heri-tage/-/the-wright-brothers-and-the-weather-bureau, accessed on Jan 04, 2022

Such hazards include sharp variations in ground and upper air temperatures. Information about the dew point temperatures gives the aviators an idea about the likely formation of fog or icing conditions. Information about the Density Altitude (it depends on temperature) helps to determine if an aircraft has enough lift capability and performance to get off the ground. High-density altitude limits fuel, weapons, and passenger loads. Cloud cover in the sky and types of clouds present determine the easy/difficulty in operations. Overcast skies impact the accuracy of bombing operations (there is a problem in getting thermal signatures) and adverse weather conditions, particularly at night, significantly impact aviation activities. Surface and upper air winds (direction and speed), jet stream, wind shear turbulence, mechanical turbulence (terrain induced), convective turbulence, clear air turbulence (CAT), precipitation (rain/snow/sleet/icing), thunderstorms, sand, dust and snow storms, blowing snow, fog and misty conditions affecting visibility are known to impact aviation activities depending on their severity. It is important to note that the forecasting accuracy of high impact weather parameters are strongly dependent on availability of the integrated data sets (both observations and predictions)[13].

For army aviation and the naval aviation, the weather data and forecast related requirements would change as per the nature of missions. For helicopter flying, both in case of army and air force, not major variations in weather forecasts are expected. This is because on various occasions, their area of operations and nature of tasks could be similar to that of air force. However, on most occasions, air force helicopters are known to operate from the air force airfields, which are well-equipped for undertaking aviation activities. Naturally, the infrastructure available for the air force helicopters could be much better in terms of physical infrastructure and weather inputs than the army flying units, which could be operating from helipads and some makeshift arrangements. Some states do have army aviators also flying transport aircrafts. Under such situations, they need to have access to all required information. Presently, various army establishments are known to have started their own cells catering for meteorological requirements. In this era of 5G, it is expected that there would be no issues regarding the availability of almost real-time weather-related information.

---

13 Ismail Gultepe, "A Review of High Impact Weather for Aviation Meteorology", *Pure and Applied Geophysics*, May 2019, pp.1-53.

Naval aviation involves helicopters and ship-based fighter aircrafts operating in various roles. Obviously, the basic requirements about the weather inputs are more about sea state, costal winds and temperatures, weather conditions over the high seas etc. The specific requirements would be based on the area of operations.

The limitations and restrictions imposed by weather for naval aviation are more or less similar to the problems faced by air forces. The only major difference is that mostly they over oceanic regions. Generally, the temperature and humidity characteristics of the troposphere, over oceanic regions and land regions show some number of variations. Naval aircraft flying and engaging targets over the ocean need to cater for such differences. Also, low-flying fixed or rotary wing aircraft encounter ocean-related weather phenomena like sea fog. Ships operating close to coastal regions and firing over land usually encounter similar problems as faced by the army/air force in respect of weather and atmospheric conditions. Some air forces also fly what are normally known as deep penetration strike aircrafts. Such aircrafts get airborne (and also land) from the air force bases close to the cost for the targets in the ocean, which are within their range. They also require mission specific weather forecasts.

For modern-day warfare air operations also include drone/UAV operations. Drones have evolved as a potent platform in warfare. These unmanned systems are getting used in multiple role form reconnaissance to commutations to logistics. Also, drone systems (unmanned combat air vehicles or UCAVs) are getting used in combat operations too. Requirements of weather for drone operations are more or less similar to the actual manned aircraft operations. Alternatively, drone is also a useful platform to take inflight weather observations. There are weather drones which are specially designed drones and equipped with sensors to undertake weather observations. The data gathered from such systems helps to improve to accuracy factor of numerical weather forecast models.

Maritime Operations

The world's oceans play an important role in keeping planet earth warm. Mainly in the tropical region, most radiation from the sun gets absorbed by the oceans. The ocean doesn't just collect solar radiation; it also helps to distribute heat around the globe. The ocean water is constantly evaporating, which increases the temperature and humidity of the surrounding air to form rain and storms. Further, such weather systems are carried to the earth by trade winds. Almost all rain that falls on land starts off in the ocean. In areas which are mainly beyond the earth's equatorial areas (tropical regions), the weather patterns are driven largely by ocean currents, which are caused by wind, temperature and salinity variations and gravity. These currents mainly act like a conveyor belt, help transferring warm water and precipitation from the equator toward the poles and cold water from the poles back to the tropics. Therefore, ocean currents are known to regulate global climate, largely. Earth is fundamentally a water planet and water bodies cover more than 70 per cent of the earth's surface area. Navies operate in and from these oceans, which are actually the habitation for weather generation[14].

Realising that the sea has a direct influence on weather, climatic conditions and global warming; the humans have sought to unveil the secrets of this medium through oceanographic, meteorological and hydrographic studies. This knowledge is essential for exploiting the maritime environment fully and properly, whilst learning to minimise its adverse effects particularly concerning safety of life at sea[15].

Broadly, the weather forecasters combine ocean observations and knowledge of how ocean–atmosphere interactions shape weather in particular and seasonal and long-term climate, in general. Ocean observations like the sea condition, atmospheric and sea surface temperatures, the wind profile, atmospheric pressures, waves, sea swell, visibility and precipitation (if any) and other related variables are extremely important for undertaking any weather-related assessment. Together, these data sets become key input for various types of weather predictions including the Numerical Weather Prediction models[16]. Owing to all this, there are some international efforts (at the level of WMO too) to undertake and make available various sets of ocean observations all over the world. All this allows navies to have regular availability of the inputs for providing the knowledge about the weather situation in coastal areas and also in deep occasions.

Fundamentally, the oceans are a three-dimensional battle space. Hence, the naval forces are required to operate below and above the sea surface. They use the medium of air with the crafts based on the ships. In

---

14 https://oceanexplorer.noaa.gov/facts/climate.html, accessed on Jan 11, 2022

15 "Indian Maritime Doctrine", Indian Navy: Naval Strategic Publication 1.1, https://www.indiannavy.nic.in/sites/default/files/Indian-Maritime-Doctrine-2009-Updated-12Feb16.pdf, page 51, accessed on Jan 12, 2022

16 "How the ocean shapes weather and climate", https://public.wmo.int/en/our-mandate/focus-areas/oceans/weather-and-climate, accessed on Jan 11, 2021

addition, they are required to use outer space and the electronic medium too. Naval power is all about effectively using surface ships, submarines and aircraft. During maritime operations, various weapons get delivered from maritime platforms against other maritime platforms or targets ashore. Some weapons may even have to travel through the interface of two mediums, as in the case of submarine-launched missiles and air launched torpedoes and depth charges (it is an anti-submarine warfare weapon). In naval combat, the hunter and the hunted may operate in totally different mediums[17]. Obviously, the required weather information and forecast should cater for such requirement.

Geographical, meteorological, and oceanographic considerations constantly play a role in various ocean activities, including warfare at sea. As the nature of warfare at sea started evolving, the requirements for weather inputs started increasing. Obviously, there are different requirements for the surface and subsurface warfare. Scientists were required to design special equipment for undertaking observations at surface and subsurface levels. The distribution of salinity, temperature, and pressure within the sea govern its sound-transmitting properties and even the character of the bottom is an important factor. Therefore, oceanography[18] has become a vital factor in weapon systems studies, as well as in management of strategies and operations. The 'environment' of undersea warfare varies, both geographically and seasonally. Based on the actual happening in the earth's atmosphere, the actual weather strongly affects the temperature gradient in the hydrosphere, which sequentially, determines acoustic paths. Owing this, navies understood that they cannot depend on only one weapon system and need to have a judicious mix of weapon systems, which could be used effectively under different weather conditions. The advance knowledge of feasible detection ranges by various techniques can significantly increase the efficiency of barrier, hunter-killer, and large-scale ASW (anti-submarine warfare) operations. This idea applies to the performance of radar equipment in the atmosphere, along with the sonar equipment beneath the surface of the sea. Radar and sonar are very sensitive to their environment in their effectiveness of operation[19].

---

17 "Indian Maritime Doctrine", Indian Navy: Naval Strategic Publication 1.1, https://www.indiannavy.nic.in/sites/default/files/Indian-Maritime-Doctrine-2009-Updated-12Feb16.pdf, page 52, accessed on Jan 12, 2022

18 Is a branch science which deals with aspects like the marine life and ecosystems, ocean circulation, plate tectonics and the geology of the seafloor, and the chemical and physical properties of the ocean

19 William J. Kotsch, "Meteorology—Vital Element of Naval Planning and Operations: A

The numerous weather and oceanographic variables influence the different types of naval operations in many ways. Consequently, in the planning or conduct of these operations, it is necessary to thoroughly consider all weather and oceanographic requirements.

Amphibious operations are the military operations characterised by attacks launched from the sea by naval and landing forces against hostile shore[20]. The amphibious craft are sensitive to wind speed, wave height and period, the vertical assault technique is highly sensitive to wind speed, gustiness, and turbulence. Hence, prior knowledge of these, and other, conditions is mandatory for the efficient conduct of these types of operation. Carrier Task Force operations which include high-speed, high-altitude jet aircraft have different requirements of weather observations. There are different types of missions that require sustained operations at sea, including the refuelling and replenishment of units[21]. Target selection, correct delivery of payload on them and safe return of the flying platform on the ship is a much-complicated task. Correct and timely weather inputs allow to proper planning and execution of various tasks. Also, firing of missiles (they come in different shapes and sizes) from the ships, aircrafts and submarines demands stringent planning and depends on the weather services for task execution.

Additional characteristic of the military maritime environment is the inherent mobility of naval operations in a fluid medium. During land warfare, an area could be occupied and fortified. However, this is not possible during the maritime conflicts, since sea being a medium for movement. Hence, navies cannot dig in at sea, or seize and hold ocean areas. A sort of occupation on a permanent basis is not (strictly) possible. Therefore, there are no positional defences at sea and even identifying battle lines to indicate the progress of an operation is not possible. The only measure of combat effectiveness at sea is the effective use of ocean areas or the denial of the same to an adversary[22]. Broadly, the capability of a navy to

lecture delivered at the Naval War College 6 January 1961", *Naval War College Review*, Vol. 13, No. 9 (May, 1961), U.S. Naval War College Press, pp. 1-15

20 https://www.britannica.com/technology/amphibious-warfare, accessed on Jan 10, 2022

21 William J. Kotsch, "Meteorology—Vital Element of Naval Planning and Operations: A lecture delivered at the Naval War College 6 January 1961", *Naval War College Review*, Vol. 13, No. 9 (May, 1961), U.S. Naval War College Press, pp. 1-15

22 "Indian Maritime Doctrine", Indian Navy: Naval Strategic Publication 1.1, https://www.indiannavy.nic.in/sites/default/files/Indian-Maritime-Doctrine-2009-Updated-12Feb16.pdf, page 54, accessed on Jan 12, 2022

effect sea control or sea denial in the ocean areas of its interest becomes a major determinant in the outcome of war.

The maritime warfare is much beyond merely defending the country's coastline. Truly, the maritime realm actually gets used as a medium for power projection. Hence, beyond having a strong navy, various states are known to invest towards ensuring free and full use of the seas, for trade, transportation and to meet resource needs. All such activities have a major impact on the country's economic growth. The maritime environment offers power and dominance to those who are strong at sea; hence, there is always a competition between nation-states for dominating the oceans. This elbowing ranges from wielding political influence, fishing and mineral mining rights, offshore economic activities like prospecting for oil and gas on one hand to denying potential adversaries use of the seas by various 'hard' and 'soft' measures on the other. To achieve all this, a nation requires to develop adequate maritime power to effectively safeguard and progress its national interests[23]. Knowledge of ocean environment and that of associated climate and weather is a prerequisite for any ocean domination, both as a strategy and also for conducting tactical operations.

The meteorological requirements of the navy could vary significantly from mission to mission. The type of maritime hardware put in use and the tactics adopted to complete the mission may not be the same for all the missions. An amphibious mission is one of the most important missions undertaken for maritime power projection, in general. An amphibious operation is a military operation launched from the sea by naval and landing forces embarked in ships or craft involving a landing on a hostile or potentially hostile shore. An amphibious operation requires extensive air participation. These operations may involve high-risk, high-payoff efforts to accomplish critical missions. Modern-day Navy amphibious assault ships are the primary landing ships for assault operations. These ships use Landing Craft Air Cushion (LCAC), conventional landing craft and helicopters to move Marine assault forces ashore. Also, in a secondary role these ships are known to perform sea control and limited power projection missions[24].

---

23 "Indian Maritime Doctrine", Indian Navy: Naval Strategic Publication 1.1, https://www.indiannavy.nic.in/sites/default/files/Indian-Maritime-Doctrine-2009-Updated-12Feb16.pdf, page 50, accessed on Jan 12, 2022

24 https://www.globalsecurity.org/military/systems/ship/amphib-ops.htm, accessed on Feb 17, 2022

Along with the typical information about the weather conditions for the conduct of activities in the oceans, there is a requirement for the hydrological data too. Such data includes information in regards to range of tides, duration of tides, surf timings and impact of wind on surf for planning their movements. These inputs differ based on the weather conditions and the state of the sea. Also, the strength and direction of offshore currents need to be factored into planning various activities. For issuing the weather forecast there is a requirement of the availability of the tidal observations from ports and coastlines in the potential conflict areas, accurate bathymetric information, surf conditions, knowledge of sea surface temperature and few other parameters.

Submarines have emerged as an important platform for modern-day warfare. They can remain at sea for months and are capable of delivering a combination of devastating weapons, both conventional (mines, torpedoes and missiles) and nuclear (various types of missiles). The potency of submarines comes from its ability to remain largely undetected. Underwater ears and eyes for a submarine come in the form of SONAR (Sound Operated aid to Navigation and Ranging). This system (it has two types: Active and Passive)[25] can detect other ships and submarines, and undersea mountains, and inform the submarine about the happenings in its surrounds.

Although sound is the most successful means of searching and locating objects underwater, the sea environment poses various problems that impact acoustic propagation. The ocean is not a quiet medium. Fish movements, tidal waves breaking within the ocean and over shores, falling rain and shipping activities generate sound in the ocean commonly known as 'ambient noise' and is a permanent fixture present all the time. Timely knowledge of underwater currents does help sonar operators to cater for changes in ocean dynamics in their analysis of sonar data. Also, temperature variations within the ocean (which largely depends on ocean depths) affect the sensitivity of receiving systems to some extent. Velocity of sound in water largely depends on sea water temperature, salinity conditions and pressure. These factors divert a sound beam through refraction and reflection[26]. All in all, there are various complications involved in submarine operations. Also, submarines remain underwater for months and travel a good distance under the sea. Hence it is important

---

25   https://oceanservice.noaa.gov/facts/sonar.html, accessed on Feb 17, 2022

26   In discussion with Commander Vijay Sakhuja (Retd)

to provide them accurate and timely weather forecasts for ensuring ease in operations.

Overall, the requirement for weather inputs differs much from what is required for the land forces or air forces. Additional observational platforms are required for having a knowledge about what weather conditions are prevailing over and under the ocean surface.

For many years, two important observation platforms have been used to gain the sea conditions. They include weather ships and weather buoys. Under the North Atlantic Ocean Station Agreement, 13 stationary ocean stations were put in the oceans since 1947/48. This happened owing to the efforts by the International Civil Aviation Organization (ICAO). Here the purpose was to provide a permanent network of meteorological observations. The number of ships were reduced to nine during 1954[27]. Finally, the agreement of the use of weather ships by the international community is known to have mainly ended around 1985. Actually, by 1974 only four such floating platforms were left, and the penultimate station closed in the 1990s. The last remaining weather ship in the world, MS Polarfront was a Norwegian weather ship located in the North Atlantic Ocean and maintained by the Norwegian Meteorological Institute. Owing to high costs (also, there was a realisation that, satellite data also provides many of the required inputs) for maintaining such ships, on February 27, 2009, the cancellation of this station was announced and finally MS Polarfront was removed from service on January 01, 2010[28]. Presently, various merchant ships provide information about the weather. Also, military ships provide some limited information. Normally, military ships share information with their own weather forecasting agencies and also with the agencies of friendly navies. Presently, the in-use platform for collecting observations form the oceans are, the Weather Buoys. The buoy carries various instruments, which gather weather and ocean data from the oceans. One important category of buoys, is the moored buoys. They are connected with the ocean bottom using either cables, nylon, or floating polypropylene. Also, there are some drifting buoys too.

For the collection of undersea weather data, much work is also found happening in the area of submarine cable system. These communication cables are laid on the sea bed between cable landing stations (CLS) on the land to carry telecommunication signals across stretches of ocean. As of

27 C.E.N. Frankcom, "Ocean Weather Ships", *International Review* 40 (1963), 141-53

28 Quirin Schiermeier, "Last weather ship faces closure", *Nature*, Vol 459, p. 759, Jun 09, 2009, https://www.nature.com/articles/459759a#citeas, accessed on Feb 17, 2022

late 2021, there are approximately 436 submarine cables in service around the world. The total number of cables is constantly changing as new cables enter service and older cables are decommissioned. Presently, these cables are spanning a total distance of over 1.3 million km globally[29]. Currently, scientific community is working towards using the capabilities and features of fiber optic submarine cable systems equipped with sensors to measure temperature, absolute pressure, and three axis acceleration at regular intervals along the entire length of the cables. In this regard, a project has been undertaken by the three UN specialised agencies (International Telecommunication Union (ITU), World Meteorological Organization (WMO) and Intergovernmental Oceanographic Commission (IOC) of UNESCO). They are developing mini-observatories on trans-ocean submarine cables to measure key ocean seafloor observables[30]. Deploying oceanographic sensors on new undersea telecommunication cables is a promising solution for obtaining undersea data. These sensors can offer vital environmental data from sites in the deep ocean which are difficult (and expensive) to reach. Suitable sensors are already deployed on dedicated cabled ocean research observatories and can be integrated into future telecommunications cables to create SMART cable systems (a concept originated decades ago). Modern fiber-optic cables, capable of delivering power and high bandwidth, are getting used as part of dedicated sustained cabled observatories to obtain data on complex ocean systems beyond what is available from conventional methods, such as research vessels and fixed buoys[31]. Such efforts are expected to help maritime forces in a big way from the point of view of improving weather forecasting.

Broadly, any naval strategy or maritime strategy is all about the actions taken for achieving victory at sea. These actions have multiple dimensions from planning, preparing to actual conduct of operations. At the same time, the role of naval forces is also about power projection. A navel strategy also depends on the nature of threats it is expected to face both during short-term and long-term. One of the important elements, which the navies are required to take into account right from the process

29 https://www2.telegeography.com/submarine-cable-faqs-frequently-asked-questions#:~:text=How%20many%20cables%20are%20there,and%20older%20cables%20are%20decommissioned accessed on July 29, 2022

30 "ITU-WMO-UNESCO IOC Joint Task Force", https://www.itu.int/en/ITU-T/climatechange/task-force-sc/Documents/Functional-requirements-2015-05.pdf, accessed on Feb 12, 2022

31 Bruce M. Howel et al, "SMART Cables for Observing the Global Ocean: Science and Implementation", https://www.frontiersin.org/articles/10.3389/fmars.2019.00424/full, accessed on Feb 17, 2022

of planning is the nature of weather conditions likely to prevail over the area of interest. The performance of maritime platforms, largely depends on the prevailing meteorological and hydrological conditions and precise information on these fronts improve the effectiveness of maritime forces.

Nuclear Warfare

Post Hiroshima and Nagasaki incidences, the closest the world have got to a likelihood of nuclear, war was during 1962 Cuban missile crisis. It is a reality that the idea of Nuclear Deterrence has worked so far with no nuclear weapon state ever using these weapons. For all these years, there have been serious efforts towards ensuring that global stockpile of nuclear weapons gets reduced. Towards this end, various arms control and disarmament measures were put in place. But, during the US's Donald Trump presidency (2017-2021), nuclear issues again got at the Center Stage after many decades. President Trump is said to have undermined decades of arms-control efforts by expanding the US arsenal. He doubled the number of low-yield nuclear weapons, possibly raising the risk of nuclear war by making nukes apparently more 'useable' in a fight between major powers. Simultaneously, Trump's nuclear doctrine expanded the list of external threats that officially justify nuclear retaliation. Perhaps most notably, the list of threats now includes a major hacking event. The US Navy subsequently, deployed the low-yield W76-2 variant of its Trident II submarine-launched ballistic missile. Also, at the opposite end of the yield spectrum[32], the US is known to have accelerated development of high-yield SLBMs and cancelled a Pentagon plan to decommission the megaton-class B83-1 gravity bomb[33].

The US President Trump started to engage nuclear North Korea (Kim Jong Un and Donald Trump summit in Singapore in June 2018), but could not move much in that direction, while with Iran, during 2018 he withdrew from the formally known Joint Comprehensive Plan of Action

---

32 The explosive yield of a nuclear weapon is the amount of energy released when a particular nuclear weapon is detonated. It is usually expressed as a TNT equivalent, the standardized equivalent mass of trinitrotoluene that if detonated, would produce the same energy discharge, either in kilotons or megatons. Normally, average grade (small category) nuclear weapon yield could be between 600 to 2200 kilotons of TNT per metric ton. By comparison, in case of very small tactical devices could be 0.5 to 50 kilotons of TNT per metric ton.

33 David Axe, "Donald Trump Is A Nuclear President—His Legacy Is More Nukes, Fewer Controls", Dec 24, 2020, https://www.forbes.com/sites/davidaxe/2020/12/24/donald-trump-is-a-nuclear-president-his-legacy-is-more-nukes-fewer-controls/?sh=78865538bd47, accessed on July 10, 2022

(JCPOA, 2015) accord, which was restricting on Iran's nuclear programme in exchange for sanctions relief. Such actions actually lead to 'dilution' of deterrence. The Russian invasion of Ukraine (2022) has also led to some hard talking and nuclear threatening. All this indicates that nuclear weapon states do not have the luxury to enter into any form of dormant mode at any point in time. They would be always required to remain prepared to fight a nuclear war.

It is important to factor in meteorological aspects in the matrix of nuclear triad, a three-cornered military structure comprising of land-launched nuclear missiles, using air power to deliver nuclear warhead on the target and a nuclear weapons carrying submarines. All these three platforms could carry variety of missiles. A theater-range cruise missile armed with a nuclear warhead can be launched from surface ships or submarines and is known has sea launched cruise missile (SLCM-N), for example, the missile deployed by the US during mid-1980s: the nuclear-armed version of the Tomahawk land-attack cruise missile (TLAM-N) which can be delivered both from surface ships and nuclear submarines. Similarly, there are different types of air launched and land-based missiles. Mostly, the missiles with a range of more than 5000 km are known as intercontinental ballistic missiles (ICBM), which are known to be primarily designed for nuclear weapons delivery. Technically, such missiles can also deliver chemical or biological warheads. Then there are systems like the multiple independently targetable re-entry vehicles (MIRVs), which allow a single missile to carry several warheads, meant to hit different targets. At present, much work is happening towards development of hypersonic missiles, which fly minimum five times the speed of sound. Russia has already tested these missiles during the 2022 Ukraine conflict. It has been reported that the future hypersonic missiles could also be nuclear tipped and particularly states like Russia and China are working towards it.

As mentioned earlier, a nuclear weapon could be dropped over a target either by using a land-based missile or by an aircraft or by a submarine launched missile. This indicates that essentially army, air force or navy could be used for launching such an attack. Broadly, the meteorological requirements would be the same as discussed in the conventional warfare section above. Weather situation should be favourable for launching a missile or aerial attack, both at the target and also at a location from where the attack is getting launched. For launching an attack from submarine, the required weather parameters should be factored in while launching the mission. It may be noted that the nuclear weapon being an area weapon, there would not be very stringent requirements for very accurate targeting.

Hence, even in somewhat unfavourable weather conditions over the target area, such attacks could be launched.

It is important to factor in weather much extensively when an attack has been launched on a target, which is close to the attacker. Particularly, in a proximity warfare situation (say North and South Korea or India and Pakistan), when both the states are sharing land or sea borders, any attack without a critical assessment of prevailing weather situation could be very harmful even to the aggressor country. This is because, if the exact wind pattern has not been taken into account, then there is a possibility that nuclear radiation could cross the political borders and ends up impacting the aggressor country itself. There is also a theoretical possibility that the adversary (a nuclear weapon state) could denote a small nuclear weapon (tactical weapon) in their own area (a vast barren and deserted area), when the weather (temperature and wind profile) is suitable for transferring the nuclear radiations in the enemy land.

For any state having strategic forces, it is important for their leadership to engage meteorologists, both for strategic and tactical planning. Strategic nuclear targeting is a serious business and nuclear weapon states undertake a detailed assessment for identifying nuclear targets. It is important that meteorologists are part of this process and as peacetime exercise they should develop weather summaries for such targets. Also, there is a need to clearly identify the type of weapons delivery platform and the possible geographical location from where such attack would be originated. All such inputs would help meteorologists to prepare themselves much in advance.

NBC (Nuclear, Biological and Chemical) operations are very sensitive to environmental conditions, which affect the transport and diffusion of CB agents. Humidity, air temperature, ground temperature, wind direction and speed, low-level temperature gradient, precipitation, cloud cover, and sunlight are some of the critical elements to study and take into account while planning for NBC operations. The degree of impact rest on upon the synoptic situation and the local impact of topography, vegetation, and state of the ground. The low-altitude stability of the atmosphere is an important factor in deciding, whether there will be a good horizontal transport of radioactive or CB clouds[34].

---

34 Battle Field Weather Effects, Field Manual FM 34-81-1, US Army < Dec 23, 1992, http://www.bits.de/NRANEU/others/amd-us-archive/FM34-81-1%2892%29.pdf, accessed on July 23, 2022

Chapter 4

War and Weather: Case Studies

A Case Study is one of the important methods in the realm of qualitative analysis, which encompasses a careful and complete observation of a system. It provides valuable insights into phenomena or situations under investigation. Case studies are used to explore and investigate the issue. It would be of interest to use this method to undertake the assessment of impact of weather during the conduct of military operations. This method allows as to describe, evaluative and compare the impact a weather system on the outcome of the wars amongst other things. This chapter undertakes three specific case studies to appreciate the impact of weather on the warfare, particularly on some important wars fought in the 21st century. No specific format has been used for undertaking these case studies. This is mainly because the duration of each case has been different and also the relevance of weather could change from case to case. The nature of data availability helps to decide on the approach to undertake the analysis. Here descriptive assessment has been undertaken and in addition some contributory investigations have been embarked on.

Three cases identified for this chapter are the wars fought post 9/11 in Iraq and Afghanistan, while the last study is on the ongoing war in Ukraine. First two wars are the wars fought in the desert and high mountain areas, while the war in Ukraine is an urban war with lot of challenges owing to snow. Typical weather conditions generally prevail in desert and mountain terrain, but since the wars continued for many years even some changes in climate of the region were observed. The wars in Iraq and Afghanistan were not the limited period wars, they were fought for many years. Ukraine was expected to be a short war, but has prolonged with so signs of abating. In all these wars, after the initial thrust of the war, which was fought more in classical manner, for rest of the period these wars were (are) in a mostly urban war mode. The basic difference is that the wars in Iraq and

Afghanistan were the wars against terrorism while, the Ukraine-Russia war is the typical state vs state conflict. Snowfall was a major weather issue for the wars in Afghanistan and Ukraine.

Case: Iraq War 2003

In 2002, the then US president, George W. Bush, argued that the US is vulnerable to the threat from Iraq, particularly after the September 11 (9/11) attacks. He had intelligence inputs about the Iraq's alleged continued possession and manufacture of Weapons of Mass Destruction (WMDs) and its support for terrorist groups. This had mainly promoted him to attack Iraq.

Iraq War, which is also known as Second Persian Gulf War had two phases. The first phase was a very brief phase (March-April 2003) when conventional war was fought amongst the allied forces (US, UK and few other states) and Iraq. In this Iraqi, defence establishment got thoroughly overpowered and the Allied forces claimed victory. The second phase was much longer and lasted from 2003 till 2011. This phase ended with the formal withdrawal of the US (and allied) forces in December 2011[1]. This case study[2] factors the nature of weather during the war and its impact on warfighting capabilities.

President Bush's ultimatum to Saddam Hussein was delivered on March 17, 2003 at 2000h, Eastern Standard Time. It demanded that President Saddam Hussein and his two sons should leave Iraq within 48 hours. Non-compliance would result in war-at a time chosen by the US. Iraq rejected the ultimatum.

Just 90 minutes after the deadline, a 'decapitation' missile strike with 36 cruise missiles occurred on an underground bunker in a building near the Al Rashid Hotel, south Baghdad. This was followed by the dropping of 4 Bunker Buster Joint Direct Attack Munitions (JDAMs) delivered by two F-117 Stealth bombers into the smashed superstructure.[3] The first Gulf War of the 21st century had begun.

Broadly, the pulling down of a huge statue of Saddam Hussein on April 9, 2003 at Firdos Square in central Baghdad by the US troops and

---

1   https://www.britannica.com/event/Iraq-War, accessed on Sept 21, 2021

2   This study is an updated version of author's earlier publication Ajey Lele, *Weather and Warfare*, Ch 6, Lancer, New Delhi, 2006, pp.117-141

3   K.Santhanam et al, *"Iraq War 2003: Rise of the New Unilateralism"*, (Ane Books: New Delhi, 2003), p.158.

local Iraqi population, which was also captured on television cameras and seen around the world by billions in real time, could be termed as the end of the first phase of war.[4] However, that had not got peace to Iraq (unfortunately, it is not there even today).

In Iraq, the classical (conventional) war was mainly fought during March 17, 2003 to April 9, 2003. The subsequent phase (which lasted for almost seven years) has essentially been an urban war. In meteorological parlance, this means that the US (allied) forces have seen six-seven full cycles of every season. Per se, weather is the least reported/debated dimension of any war. Many a time weather restricts the conduct of operations either fully or partially. Obviously, no military normally likes to discuss its own failures and at times they also have been seen to take a convenient view that the bad weather was responsible for their failures. Likewise, various military hardware manufacturers claim that their systems are 'weather proof'. However, it has been found that this happens mainly in ideal and controlled situations. During actual conflict situations, the missions were found getting impacted from weather. Under this backdrop a critical and balanced analysis of the claims of the arms dealers, wartime reportage and briefings given by the state authorities becomes essential.

This assessment draws on no privileged sources. The outline of the campaign on which this analysis is based is constructed from events as they were reported by the news, print and web media. A care has been taken as far as possible to analyse these reports under the backdrop of climatological and topographical realities of the region and neighbourhood.

Allied war machinery particularly the US machinery, had started moving towards the Iraqi theatre for deployment much before the actual commencement of the war. The distance (air travel) between the US and Iraq is more than 11,000 km. The port distance amongst the US and Iraqi port is more than 10,000 nm. To reach Iraq, the US naval forces had to cross different oceans, they also had encountered difficult weather conditions in their respective countries. Hence, from the point of view of the deployment of the forces, the weather was one of the critical aspects. However, this chapter restricts itself in assessing the weather situation over Iraq Theater alone during the period conflict phase.

The War

The 2003 invasion of Iraq was a war that began March 20 2003 fought between a coalition of willing consisting primarily of the US and British forces, and Iraq. It began without the explicit backing of the United Nations

---

4   The New York Times, Apr 10, 2005.

Security Council. Approximately 250,000 United States troops, with support from 45,000 British, and smaller forces from other nations, entered Iraq primarily through their staging area in Kuwait. Plans for an invasion force from the north were abandoned when Turkey officially refused the use of its territory for such purposes. Coalition forces also supported Iraqi Kurdish militia troops, estimated to number upwards of 50,000.

Facing them was a large, but under equipped, military force. The regular Iraqi army was estimated at 280,000–350,000 troops, with four Republican Guard divisions with 50,000–80,000 troops, and the Fedayeen Saddam, a 20,000–40,000 strong militia, which used guerrilla tactics during the war. There were an estimated thirteen infantry divisions, ten mechanised and armoured divisions, as well as some special forces units. The Iraqi Air Force and Navy played a negligible role in the conflict.[5]

The classical phase of war when intensive fighting took place lasted only for 21 days in Iraq (March 20: The war against Iraq begins - April 9: Baghdad falls, statue of Saddam Hussein symbolically toppled).[6] However, transition from war fighting to reconstruction which continued for more than seven years has also seen many bloody battles may be with slightly lesser usage of firepower. The most drastic difference between the 1991 Gulf War and 2003 Gulf War is that of involvement all of arms of security forces, since beginning in the year 2003. Almost from the start coalition air, ground, sea and Special Forces provided mutual support for each other, whereas in 1991, the air campaign lasted for 38 days, before ground forces were introduced. In the year 2003 speed of warfighting had also increased. Armoured and light-armoured vehicles backed up with a good and fast logistic chain had moved from desert terrain with great speed.[7]

The '23 day' war in Iraq took place during the months of March and April. Weather-wise these months belong to a changeover period meaning a phase between end of winter and beginning of summer. These months are the wettest months of the year in most parts of Iraq. The Urban Warfare phase of this conflict continued for more than seven years, so naturally, the coalition forces had experienced the vagaries of weather of all seasons. Before deliberating the details about the weather impacting war-waging

---

5   https://www.encyclopedia.com/places/asia/iraq-political-geography/iraq and http://edition.cnn.com/2003/WORLD/meast/02/18/sprj.irq.deployment/index.html accessed on Sept 22, 2021

6   Iraq War timeline is available at http://www.infoplease.com/ipa/A0908792.html, accessed on Sept 22, 2021

7   Jonathan Eyal (Ed.), War in Iraq Combat and Consequences, Whitehall Paper 59, London, 2003, pp.1-6.

capabilities of the coalition forces it could be worthwhile to have a brief look at the general climate of Iraq.

Terrain, Climate and Weather Realities[8]

Iraq is the land of the oldest civilisation, where urban life and the written word originated some 5,500 years ago. Numerous wars fought during the last five thousand years have changed Iraq's demographical, geographical and topological landscape immensely. There is a saying that, "there are no natural hills in southern Iraq, and if you see a hill, in most cases it's the mound of a buried ancient settlement."

The 1991 Gulf War has also contributed in some way towards damaging Iraq's topographical and climatic conditions. However by the first decade of 21st century, the climatic conditions have limped back to normalcy indicating that the changes caused by incessant aerial bombing were of temporary nature.

Geographical Details:

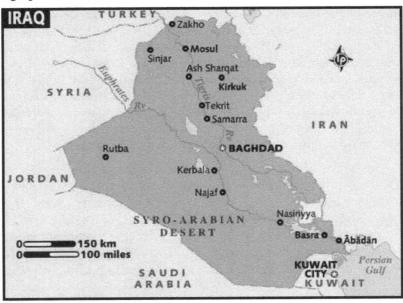

https://www.lonelyplanet.com/maps/middle-east/iraq/, accessed on September 22, 2021

---

8   The following discussion is based on K.Santhanam et al, "Iraq War 2003: Rise of the New Unilateralism", (Ane Books: New Delhi, 2003), p.111-118 and http://www.southtravels. com/middleeast/iraq/weather.html and www.globalsecurity.org, accessed on Jun 07, 2007

Location: Middle East, bordering the Persian Gulf, between Iran and Kuwait

Area: 437,072 sq km (Land: 432,162 sq km and Water: 4,910 sq km)

Coastline: 58 km; *territorial sea:* 12 nm (Approximately 22km)

Boundaries: (6)

Iran: 1,458 km, Saudi Arabia: 814km, Syria: 605km, Turkey: 331km, Kuwait: 242km and Jordan: 181km

Elevation extremes:

Lowest Point: Persian Gulf 0 m, Highest Point: Haji Ibrahim 3,600 m

Topography: Mountains, plateaus, hills and valleys, planes and inland water-covered areas are the major geomorphic forms available in varying combinations

Iraq has four broad topographic regions; they are:

(a) Mountain Region: About 21 per cent of the total area.

Elevation: 1700m-3500m.

Temperatures (in winter) may drop sharply to -15^0 C.

(b) Undulating Lands: Hilly landscape located south and west of the mountain region. 9.6 per cent of total area. Average altitude range 200-1,000 meters.

(c) The Depositional Plain: Plain of the Tigris and the Euphrates rivers in central and southern Iraq; area of 30.2 per cent of the total area. These twin rivers control water resources in Iraq. Both rivers have their headwaters in the humid mountains of Turkey where much of the precipitation falls as snow; subject to wide seasonal fluctuation.

(d) The Western Plateau (Deserts): Largest physiographic region covering the country. 39.2 per cent of total area; has number of plains with distinct relief and rock formations.

Climate

The climate of Iraq, in terms of temperature and rainfall, may be classified into three main types.

(a) Mediterranean Climate: This type is characterised by cool, wet winters. It is more restricted to the mountainous areas. Snowfall is not uncommon; rainfall varies from 400 mm in the low area to 1000 mm in high.

(b) Steppes Climate: Is transitional between the Mediterranean type in the north and the desert in the south; high temperature and less rainfall are the main limiting factors; rainfall range between 200-400 mm, during the cool season when the evaporation rate is the lowest.

(c) Hot Desert Climate: Lowlands in Iraq are a hot desert. In winter times, warm and sunny weather prevails, and the temperature rarely drops under freezing point.

Dry and hot summers, cool wet winters and a pleasant spring and fall are the main climatic characteristic of Iraq. Roughly 90 per cent of the annual rainfall occurs between November and April, most of it in the winter months from December through March. The remaining six months, particularly the hottest ones of June, July, and August. The influence of the Persian Gulf on the climate of Iraq is very limited. Near the gulf the relative humidity is higher than in other parts of the country.

In the western and southern desert region, the climate is characterised by hot summers and cool winters. This region also receives brief violent rainstorms in the winter that usually total about 10 cm. Most nights are clear in the summer, and about one-third of the nights are cloudy in the winter.

In the rolling upland (foothill) region there is basically no precipitation in the summer and some showers in the winter. The winter rainfall normally averages about 38 cm. The nights are generally clear in the summer and in the winter dense clouds are common about half of the nights.

The alluvial plain of the Tigris and Euphrates Delta in the southeast receives most of its precipitation accompanied by thunderstorms in the winter and early spring. The average annual rainfall for this area is only about 10 to 17 cm and about 50 per cent days in winter are cloudy, and in the summer the weather is clear most of the time.

In the mountains of the north and northeast, the climate is characterised by warm summers and cold winters. Precipitation occurs mainly in winter and spring, with minimal rainfall in summer. Above 1,500 m, heavy snowfalls occur in the winter, and there is some thunderstorm activity in the summer. Annual precipitation for the whole region ranges from 40 to 100 cm. Few nights are cloudy in summer and about half of the days are cloudy in winter.

A large daily and annual temperature range is a pronounced continental climatic characteristic. The annual average temperature in Baghdad is 22.5°C while the mean daily minimum temperature in January is 4° C. The average temperature in Iraq ranges from higher than 48°C in July and August to below freezing in January. The cool season begins in November and runs through March, the months during high temperatures in Baghdad average 23°C. The southern and southeasterly *sharqi*, a dry and dusty wind with occasional gusts to 80 kmph, occurs from April to early June and again from late September to November. Air operations may be reduced during the windy season.

Winter months often experience cyclonic activities. Climate mainly affected by *western disturbances*; which originate in the Caspian and Mediterranean Seas. The yearly average number of these east-moving cyclones is 120. Most precipitation is associated with these weak cyclones.

Occasionally, a well-developed cyclone may remain stagnant over the country for several days. This draws in large amount of maritime air associated with considerable amount of rain lowlands, and heavy snowfalls in the mountains.

Climatological Data

Baghdad (representative of Central parts of Iraq)

	Jan	Feb	Mar	Apr	May
Rainfall (mm)	27.1	27.5	26.9	18.8	7.3
Avg.Temp.°C	9.4	11.8	16.2	21.6	27.7

Basrah (representative of SE parts, close to Persian Gulf)

	Jan	Feb	Mar	Apr	May
Rainfall (mm)	34.2	18.9	17.3	16.7	6.5
Avg.Temp.⁰C	12.2	14.2	18.8	24.2	30

Mosul (representative of Northern parts of Iraq, close to Turkey)

	Jan	Feb	Mar	Apr	May
Rainfall (mm)	63.2	67.5	70.0	52.9	20.6
Avg.Temp.⁰C	7.0	8.9	12.4	17.4	24.1

Rutbah (representative of Western parts of Iraq)

	Jan	Feb	Mar	Apr	May
Rainfall (mm)	16.7	17.0	21.7	18.2	9.5
Avg.Temp.⁰C	7.1	9.2	12.6	18.2	23.8

Annual Temperatures (°C)

Region	Winter	Months	Summer	Months	Ex-tremes	
	Min	Max	Min	Max	Min	Max
Western/ Southern Desert	9^0	16^0	20^0	40^0	-14^0	49^0
Rolling Upland	3^0	13^0	25^0	40^0	-12^0	49^0
Tigris/ Euphrates Delta	4^0	18^0	25^0	40^0	-7^0	51^0
Mountains	-4^0	5^0	15^0	25^0	-30^0	42^0

Based on topographical and climatological realities and taking into consideration their own and Iraqi military capabilities the coalition forces could have factored the limitations posed by the weather and terrain possibly on following lines, during their military planning.

Over Iraq almost 90 per cent of the annual rainfall occurs between November and April, most of it in winter months from December through March. Hence, end March could be the best period to start any campaign and extend till May/June.

An average of 50 per cent cloud cover over Baghdad in December and January, declining to almost 40 per cent in February. Fog, low ceilings, clouds and rain characterise winter season (Dec-Mar). None of these conditions were totally conducive for bombing and photo reconnaissance operations. Hence particularly from Air Force angle, these months were not suitable.

Aerial reconnaissance, both by UAVs and satellites usually do not yield high-quality results during winter months due to presence of snow and cirrus clouds (high clouds above 25000 feet). Cirrus clouds are associated with western disturbances and are observed even during summer months. Hence form point of view of intelligence gathering winter months are dreadful.

Weather may not pose a problem for USAF attack aircrafts like B2, F-15, and F-117, which are equipped with targeting radars, but other crafts like A-10 and AV-8B require clear weather for operations. Also, aircrafts using IR weaponry will face difficulties during bad weather.

Oil wells on fire are capable of hindering close air support missions. This is mainly because the smoke from burning oil wells will affect air operations due to reduced visibility and smoky atmosphere.

Laser-guided bombs (LGBs) face difficulties in rain and fog during winter and sandstorms and excessive heat during summer. Also, relative humidity more than 60 per cent during winter months (till end of March) may affect the performance of LGBs.

Rain severely affects helicopter operations. Mainly landings would be carried out over marshy fields and it could be difficult to use various helipads due to wet soil. Landings are tricky over the region of Central Iraq (areas nearby Baghdad), which is partially an area of marshland and lakes.

Bad weather affects air operations and hence in turns the ground operations. This could compel the coalition forces to plan ground operations even based on weather conditions and forecasts.

Understanding the Weather

21 Day War and Weather

On March 20, 2003 Bush announced the beginning of combat operations and weather created first hindrance on 6th day of the war that is on March 25. By March 22 the US and UK forces were in the vicinity of Basra. By March 24 the bridge crossings of the Euphrates near Nasiriya were sized. Simultaneously lead elements had reached within sixty miles of Baghdad. However, further progress was delayed by a large sandstorm on 25th.[9] The US F/A-18 warplanes based on carriers in the Gulf attacked other guard positions near Baghdad. But within hours, military action slowed considerably because a whirling sandstorm whipping across the region. The storm, carrying sand from as far away as Egypt and Libya, stalled any significant US and British advance.[10] Still the US forces attempted long-distance pounding with B-52 aircraft by dropping huge payloads of bombs south of the capital, however, these efforts met with very limited success.

Press reporters travelling with coalition troops had noted that on occasion the fighting units were halted with visibility reduced to just a few meters. Though, the weather had not prevented the air strikes and they were found targeting the Medina division of the elite Republican Guards, digging in for a decisive encounter.

The chairman of the US Joint Chiefs of Staff, General Richard Myers had acknowledged that bad weather had slowed down the advance. As per Major-General Victor Renuart of US Central Command 1,400 air sorties against the Iraqi Republican Guard were scheduled for March 25. Many of them were cancelled due to bad weather. Rivulets of sand were flowing across the desert floor and all operations were ceased as a result of the storm. The forces attempted to continue with military activity with all-weather precision weapons, but the coalition was forced to call back some combat missions from aircraft carriers in the region. A dozen aircraft were launched from the USS Harry Truman in the Mediterranean on 25th on two strikes, but returned to the carrier a few hours later without reaching northern Iraq.[11]

---

9   Jonathan Eyal (Ed.), War in Iraq Combat and Consequences, Whitehall Paper 59, London, 2003, p.15 and Carl Drews, "Sandstorm Over Baghdad", Oct 2004, https://acomstaff.acom.ucar.edu/drews/sandstorm/, accessed on Sept 22, 2021

10   http://www.pbs.org/newshour/bb/middle_east/jan-june03/roundup_3-25.html#

11   "Sandstorms slow Baghdad advance", March 25, 2003, http://news.bbc.co.uk/2/hi/middle_east/2885359.stm, accessed on Sept 16, 2021

During the start phase of the war (the third week of March), heavy dense cloud conditions created difficulties for aviation units. The reports from aircraft carrier USS Harry Truman had indicated that weather posed greatest threat for carrier fighter jets crossing into Northern Iraq. Finding the tanker in the clouds was toughest and scariest task for F/A-18 Hornet pilots. An F-14 pilot stationed aboard the carrier Truman described the dense skies around him as "goo" as he searched for the KC-135 Stratotankar, a mid-air refueler.[12]

Australian Army Chief, Lieutenant-General Peter Leahy, during media briefings on March 25 had accepted that weather had played a spoilsport in the coalition forces campaign at Iraq. Replying to a question from media he had mentioned that high winds, sand storms and poor visibility was instrumental in degrading the performance of weapons system on both sides. However, he had further added that the Coalition forces have very robust systems and very robust equipment that's designed to cope with a wide range of climatic and weather conditions. And that they can operate day or night under any weather conditions.[13]

The occurrence of sandstorms is bit routine for the region. There were indications that the last week of March may experience some sandstorms. The weather conditions generally remained poor during 25-27 March 2003. A strong weather system in the Middle East had triggered a series of dust/sandstorms that became nearly continuous activity and slowed operations throughout the theater. On the first day, several moderate to strong thunderstorms swept west to east through Iraq and Kuwait. Both ahead of the storms and after the storms, strong winds caused blowing sand, reducing visibility to near zero at times. Sand, dust and raindrops mingled to form what troops described as a mud storm. On the second day, the storm center passed across northern Iraq and moved into Iran by midnight.

Strong westerly and southwesterly winds from this low-pressure system, blew across central and southern areas of Iraq, keeping the sandstorms going throughout the theater. On March 27, most of Iraq's skies cleared as the dust settled under an approaching high-pressure area. But Kuwait and the Persian Gulf were still experiencing blowing dust,

---

12 http://vh10634.moc.gbahn.net/news/iraq/ships0325.html, accessed on Jan 23, 2006

13 http://www.globalsecurity.org/wmd/library/news/iraq/2003/iraq-030325-australia01. htm, accessed on Aug 24, 2021

hindering ground and air operations around Kuwait and naval operations in the gulf.[14]

These storms, which had made worst weather situation for war fighters, had derived its initial power from a collision of cold air driving out of northern Europe and warm air over the Mediterranean Sea, and its winds were focused over the flat terrain of Iraq by the funnel-like curve of the mountain ranges of Turkey to the north and Iran to the east. The intensity of the storms has shown that protective clothing and protective shelter has many limitations. As per one American solider "if sand were measured like humidity, it would have been 100 per cent on Tuesday (25th)".[15]

At the same time, some amount of air effort did happen even during the phase of sand storms. Coalition aircraft continued to attack air defence, command and control, and intelligence facilities in the Baghdad area. It was reported that the coalition aircraft continued to achieve high sortie rates despite the weather. In the days just prior to the sandstorms, the air component flew an average of 800 strike sorties daily, however during the sandstorm phase this rate had reduced drastically. Even during the sandstorms, surveillance aircraft continued to provide data that enabled the coalition to target Iraqi units over an area of several hundred square miles, when the Iraqis thought that weather would shield them from air attack.[16]

Other than this three to four days period with widespread dust storms and poor visibility conditions, the coalition forces did not encounter much of problem form weather. However, the season being a changeover period form winter to summer, the coalition forces had to undergo certain hardships like sudden rising of dust in the atmosphere and reducing visibility. Loose sand created problems for ground troops from the point of view reducing their mobility. Troops found difficulties in working in NBC suits, because of the heat and dust.

The desert environment of Iraq, in general, did present the coalition with significant challenges. The sandstorms early in the conflict phase and, later, the extreme summer temperatures demonstrated the debilitating

---

14 Gregory Fontenot, On Point: The United States Army in Operation Iraqi Freedom, (Naval Inst Press: Maryland), 2005, Chapter 4, et pasium.

15 http://www.jsonline.com/news/gen/mar03/128526.asp, accessed on Jan10, 2006

16 Anthony H. Cordesman, The Iraq War: Strategy, Tactics, and Military Lessons (Washington, DC: The Center for Strategic and International Studies, 2003), pp.69-84. see also (n.13)

effects the environment can have on people and equipment. In general, following was observed:

(a) There were a number of heat casualties.

(b) High temperatures reduced the load carrying capacity of all helicopters had created difficulties for ground crew servicing the aircraft and aircrew attempting to rest. Helicopters parked on aircraft pans unsheltered from the heat suffered adverse effects on their systems.

(c). Ammunition to the value of approximately £14M was written-off because of its reduced 'life expectancy' when stored unprotected in high temperatures.

(d) Several equipment types, including radars, UAVs, airfield navigation aids and CIS, were less reliable in the high temperatures and dusty environment. In some cases, the air conditioning did not cool equipment sufficiently and in others, it caused condensation on sensitive electronic equipment.

(e) Personal comfort Clothing, food and accommodation all had contributed in some way to combat effectiveness in the desert environment. [17]

The coalition forces were well equipped with a full backup of combat meteorological services. Particularly, the US and UK forces had well trained manpower to provide forecast information for any location up to five days ahead. The met services essentially depended on their global forecasting system models. Furthermore, to this global picture, more detailed information was made available for a limited area from a higher resolution forecast model.

The Met Office contribution to provide timely forecasts to commanders, both deployed and at home, was an important element in the overall allied forces philosophy of obtaining information superiority. Most models were designed to produce a joint operational area forecast to meet the coalition aim of 'one theatre, one forecast'. The forces and planners had sufficient advance warning about the likelihood of severe sand storms over the region on 25-27 March 2003. These sandstorms, which were caused by an active low-pressure area, were predicted four to five days in advance

---

17 http://www.mod.uk/linked_files/publications/iraq/opsiniraq.pdf, accessed on Dec 23, 2005

and factored into operational planning. As the event approached, the higher resolution models were able to add more precision and accuracy in them, to address tactical and operational needs as well as planning. Overall the quality of advice from the coalition forecasts was excellent, and no significant weather event went unannounced to commanders.[18]

Military meteorologists were monitoring the movement of the weather system susceptible to the development of sandstorms, since the beginning of third week of March. Initially, this storm front developed over the Mediterranean Sea and moved through parts of Egypt, Jordon and Syria towards Iraq region. Over Iraq a major short wave trough and a frontal system had converged. During this phase, thunderstorms formed along the storm line. Behind thunderstorms, strong winds churned dust from Saudi Arabian desert into major sandstorms covering southern and central Iraq and Kuwait. The USAF had used latest software tool, called Dust Transport Application (DTA) to track the storms impact. The model combined wind speed, precipitation, and other factors with a dust source database to evaluate the type of dust particles the storm front would lift into the atmosphere. The visibility conditions and the duration of bad visibility periods were forecasted accurately.

Based on the advance weather forecasts, the plans were changed. The Air Forces shifted from the Laser-guided bomb (LGBs) to the Joint Direct Attack Munition (JDAMs), because the dust particles had started blocking the infrared sensors of LGBs. The JDAMs were found largely resistant to the dust. However, it was observed that the arrival of JDAM did not eliminate the need for accurate weather forecast.

The terrain characteristics of the region played a vital role in modifying the pattern of weather over the region. The Air Force weather forecasters provided weather briefings for continual assessments of operating conditions. They also had a daunting task in finding the right time for the Army's airdrop at Basur in northern Iraq. While the sandstorms were sweeping across southern and central Iraq, it was raining hard in northern Iraq. The mountainous sections of northern Iraq had more vegetation and did not experience the same fierce dust storms, but bad weather over the drop zone was hazardous for dropping operations. This situation was the real challenge for the forecasters who were expected to identify a two-hour *weather window* in which weather would be clear for air droppings.[19]

---

18 Ibid

19 Rebecca Grant, "Storms of War", Air Force Magazine, July 2004, vol. 87, no.7, pp.

Bad weather conditions did impact both the fighting units and the logistical units. The sand storms not only restricted the combat capabilities of the allied forces, but also created re-supply nightmares. They took a toll on Allied supply lines and created hurdles towards the planned fast advance to Baghdad. There were cases like a rudimentary ad-hoc Army base 100 miles south of Baghdad running out of rations. The timeless enemy in this region turned out to be wind and sand. This 'enemy' plagued the re-supply lines for the coalition forces in the battle zones for some time (few days). Few units were at zero balance on food. The local commanders understood that without adequate water, food, fuel and ammunition, regime change in Baghdad could become more problematic.

When the storms had hit the region — around the same time a couple of dozen re-supply trucks carrying food and water were to have arrived. But with winds nearing hurricane-force strength, reducing visibility to zero-zero conditions, the land movement had come to a grinding halt. The units had sent people out in (sand) blizzard conditions, and they couldn't find the trucks, which were then more than a day overdue.[20]

Luckily the storms did not last for prolonged durations and hence the logistic supply chain had resumed quickly. It appears that the Allied forces had not anticipated of having this level of trouble in regards logistics. Also, the forces had encountered difficulties in ground combat during this phase particularly because they were not accustomed to fighting under such weather conductions, but the enemy was.

Weather and Urban Warfare

Urban warfare does not have its Clausewitz, nor is it ever likely to have one. Neither centuries of experience nor libraries groaning under the weight of case studies have been sufficient to create a reliable and practical theory of war as it is conducted in the urban environment. Professionals and amateurs alike have been forced to try it out on the ground.[21] The tremendous growth of urban areas worldwide has reduced the amount of open, manoeuvrable terrain available to attacking or defending forces. Many urban areas have grown together to form giant urban obstacles extending for many kilometres. These areas are generally located on or

---

20 Charlie Brennan, "Conflict with Iraq: Weather, combat create resupply nightmare", Scripps Howard News Service, March 27, 2003, http://cfapps.naplesnews.com/sendlink/printthis.cfm, accessed on Dec 24, 2005

21 http://www-cgsc.army.mil/carl/download/csipubs/spiller3/part3.pdf, accessed on Nov 12, 2005

near traditional movement corridors in regions rich in natural or industrial resources. They play an important role in the economic and political life of many countries.[22] Any attacking nation has to cater for such 'ground realities' because its aim is not that of destruction, but to take the control of the region and allow it to function normally.

The US was forced to learn the nuances of urban warfare in occupied Iraq. They tried to 'wall in' a hostile population for more than seven years. The US forces had tremendous advantages in resources and troops, but they were fighting an asymmetric enemy who was striking at will, unannounced and with the help of unconventional tools and tactics. For this reason, the coalition forces were forced to remain constantly in the state of readiness.

Fighting an urban warfare in various cities of Iraq, which have got different terrain and weather features, was a difficult task. Cities like Baghdad, Fallujah, Mosul etc. were having multilayered densely packed areas that made the warfare more difficult and more dangerous. In all these years, the coalition forces had got experienced in operating in all types of weather seasons in the region. The performance of human, equipment and vehicles was found to fluctuate depending on the general atmospheric conditions in the region. The forces had to switch over to different set of clothing depending on the season and their deployment locations. Also, during the initial phase of the urban conflict, the forces were much concerned about the likely prospects of biological or chemical attack and hence used to remain equipped with NBC suits.

On various occasions in these seven to eight years, the weather had hampered the military operations. It is not possible to narrate all incidences, but few significant ones are discussed below.

Thirty Marines and a Navy corpsman were killed in a helicopter crash near Iraq's border with Jordan, January 26, 2005 was the deadliest day for US forces since the start of the war in Iraq. The cause of the chopper crash was weather-related.[23] It was reported that due to bad weather, the CH-53 Sea Stallion chopper crashed near Ar Rutbah in western Iraq.[24] CH-53E Super Stallion was the largest helicopter in the US military and it was flying

---

22 http://www.globalsecurity.org/military/library/policy/army/fm/71-100-2/Ch8.htm, accessed Sept 22, 2021

23 "Deadliest day for U.S. in Iraq war", Jan 27, 2005, http://edition.cnn.com/2005/WORLD/meast/01/26/iraq.main/, accessed Sept 22, 2021

24 http://www.airborneranger.com/forums/index.php?showtopic=260, accessed on Jan 14, 2005

over the desert.[25] A top US General had confirmed that there was severe weather at the site of the US Marine helicopter crash in western Iraq. He had also confirmed that there were no reports of enemy fire in the area and it was obvious that the weather was responsible for the crash.[26]

In Iraq Theater, sand is thought to be one of the worst enemies of the helicopters, wearing down rotors and seeping into engines and electronics. On few occasions it had blinded pilots, especially on landing, when the helicopters kick up huge clouds of dust. Also, it was found that, the sand mixes with lubricants and turns them into sticky masses of gum.[27]

Coalition forces were mentally prepared to fight the adverse weather conditions before entering Iraq. Nevertheless, many of them in the past had never encountered such type of vagaries of weather. Some troops, who stayed bit long in Iraq, and faced all phases of weather, became bit comfortable with the weather conditions. But since the conflict had spread for a longer duration, the troops were rotated and new troops were inducted at periodic intervals. Obviously, new set of troops faced the problems of acclimatisation with the weather and terrain conditions. This also had some impact towards the progression of the urban war.

In the year 2004, the summer spell prolonged for much of a time. In month of November, the daily temperatures touched 40°C or more, and rain clouds and dust storms popped on many times without warning. In spite of the US military being all weather fighting force, unexpected weather conditions endangered few missions, caused delays and sometimes missions were cancelled altogether. Particularly at places like Mosul (located near the mountainous Turkish border about 225 miles northwest of Baghdad) the weather was mostly unpredictable. While the climate in much of Iraq alternates between hot and dry or cold and dry, the northernmost regions experience a full range of seasons. It did hail over Mosul during December, when the allied forces were fighting a grim battle with insurgents. During the month of November, the region experienced twice the expected rainfall.[28]

---

25 http://www.military.com/NewsContent/0,13319,FL_helo_012705,00.html, accessed on Jan 23, 2005

26 http://www.military.com/NewsContent/0,13319,FL_helo_012705,00.html, accessed on Jan 23, 2005

27 http://www.defensetech.org/archives/001360.html, accessed on Jan 12, 2005

28 C. Mark Brinkely, "Weather wages own war", Army Times, www.keepmedia.com/ShowItemDetails.do?item_id=680990&oilID=255&bemID=P, accessed on Dec 12, 2007

How the bad weather leaves a mark on the moral of the troops and other personal operating in this environment could be easily judged from the following statement: "The weather is warm now. We often turn on the ceiling fan (or panka) in an attempt to move around the muggy air. April is a month of fresh beginnings all over the world but in Iraq, April is not the best of months. April is a month of muggy warmth and air thick with dust and sand- and now of occupation. We opened the month with a dust storm. We breathed dust, ate dust and drank dust for a few days. The air is clearer now but everything is looking a little bit diminished and dirty. It suits the mood".[29]

Some more incidences about the impact of weather on the security operations conducted by the US force have been documented. Since these operations continued from 2003-2011, many incidences had occurred, where there was a visible impact of weather on military operations. Owing to long period operations, the soldiers had also developed the experience about the type of weather, which occurs over Iraq during various seasons. Experienced solders used to brief the new batch of solders about the weather related challenges. Moreover, military meteorologists were able to develop region specific weather forecasting models. The larger focus about the US operations which lasted from 2003-2011, has been more on understating how these military operations have impacted the weather and the climate change. Some deliberations about this subject are undertaken in the part on climate change in this book.

Inferences

The coalition forces were aware that climatologically March and April were the best months available for military operations in Iraq and even in these months, weather could play a critical role. The forces were prepared to work around the weather for the success of their campaign.

During the classical phase of war, the forces had encountered only one bad patch of weather, which lasted for three to four days with maximum intensity of worst weather conditions only for a day. This period constitutes 15 to 20 per cent time of the 21-day war. Apart from this the weather had relatively little impact on the progress of classical phase of war.

However, this period itself constituted almost one fifth/one sixth period of actual war fighting and this clearly demonstrates the relevance

---

29 Baghdad Burning, April 09, 2005, views expressed on this issue are available at http://riverbendblog.blogspot.com/2005_04_01_riverbendblog_archive.html#11130 7454974312560, accessed on Dec 12, 2007

of weather in war fighting and that too during a 'fair weather' time. The sand storms had some effect on air operations and caused damage to equipment, but military preparations to make the invasion an "all weather" operation appear to have paid off to an extent.[30] Simultaneously, the war also demonstrated the limitations of LGBs. This war proved that lasers don't operate well in mist, fog, smoke or sand storms.

JDAM was found to be the most effective weapon during adverse weather conditions. However, the nature of warfare itself put restrictions on the usage of JDAMs. The smaller JDAMs (500 pounds) were used to take down parts of buildings containing enemy troops, and the larger JDAMs (2000 pounds) were used to flatten buildings that are away from other structures during adverse weather conditions. But accuracy is most important, particularly in an urban warfare scenario. Few cases of missing a target and destructing adjoining buildings were also reported. This explains that bad weather puts some limitations on the usage of JDAMs while fighting urban warfare. [31]

The desert environment of Iraq presented the coalition with significant challenges, against which a number of equipment improvements and other preparatory steps were taken. The forces were found suitably prepared and equipped to operate in demanding environmental conditions. But it was observed that micro-terrain and micro-climate of the region demands greater education for the troops particularly when they have to fight a prolonged duration war in urban settings. A case in point could be Baghdad and Basra. Around Baghdad, there's enough shade and vegetation in the river valley that the dust isn't as pervasive as out in the desert or even down in Basra, where there's not much of a windbreak for hundreds of miles. However, the scenario changes altogether when huge sand storms envelop the region.

Even after the US withdrawal from Iraq, the situation continues to remain unsettled. Iraqi forces had to undertake some security campaigns to ensure that anti-state forces are kept under control. One such campaign is famously known as Mosul Campaign. During June 2014, an estimated 1500 fighters of the Islamic State of Iraq and Syria (ISIS) seized control of Mosul, Iraq's second city. Although many residents fled, others stayed

---

30 Lee Bowman, "Conflict with Iraq: Mideast weather playing nice — for now", Scripps Howard News Service, April 4, 2003, http://cfapps.naplesnews.com/sendlink/printthis.cfm, accessed on Dec 12, 2004

31 James Dunnigan, "Is JDAM Smart Enough for Street Fighting?", http://www.strategypage.com/dls/articles/20030324.asp, accessed on Jan 25, 2005

behind, enduring the restrictive civil and social policies of ISIS. In December 2016, the military activity, known as the liberation campaign, began in east Mosul, concluding in west Mosul in June 2017[32]. During this campaign on occasions the Iraqi forces did face the challenges owing to bad weather conditions. During Nov 2016, the Iraqi forces were not able to move from their holding positions along Mosul's eastern outskirt. High humidity and clouds were found obscuring the view for aircraft and drones[33] (a support provided by the US lead air campaign). Generally, at places poor visibility did create problems for conduct of operations.

One of the important lessons of this war is that impact of weather on the performance of logistics units was not correctly envisaged. The weather did affect the movement of supply convoy though it was for very short duration and in particular region only. But this proves that not only combat operations, but support operations also suffer from adverse weather conditions and any disturbance in them could have an impact on overall military objective.

Case: War in Afghanistan

The War in Afghanistan was a conflict that took place from 2001 to 2021. It began when the United States and its allies invaded Afghanistan and toppled the Taliban-ruled government. Unfortunately, Taliban government has come back to power after the US forces left the Afghanistan soil after 20 years.

On September 11, 2001 (9/11) Al-Qaeda operatives had hijacked four commercial airliners, crashing them into the World Trade Center in New York and the Pentagon in Washington, DC. A fourth plane crashed in a field in Shanksville, Pennsylvania. Close to three thousand people died in this attacks. Although Afghanistan is the base for al-Qaeda, none of the nineteen hijackers were Afghan nationals. The then US President George W. Bush vowed to 'win the war against terrorism,' and later zeros in on al-Qaeda and Osama bin Laden in Afghanistan. Bush eventually called on the Taliban regime to deliver to the US authorities all the leaders of al-Qaeda[34]

---

32 Lafta, R., Cetorelli, V. & Burnham, G. Living in Mosul during the time of ISIS and the military liberation: results from a 40-cluster household survey. Confl Health 12, 31 (2018)

33 "Iraqi Special Forces Pause at Edge of Mosul, Weather Cuts Visibility", Nov 2, 2016, https://www.news18.com/news/world/iraqi-special-forces-pause-at-edge-of-mosul-weather-cuts-visibility-1307557.html, accessed on Sept 23, 2021

34 https://www.cfr.org/timeline/us-war-afghanistan, accessed on Sept 23, 2021

who were hiding there, but with the negative response from the Taliban leadership finally the US and their friends invaded Afghanistan.

The War

The US military, with a support from the United Kingdom (UK), begins a bombing campaign against Taliban forces. With this began the Operation Enduring Freedom. Initially, what could be called as support in principle, was received from Canada, Australia, Germany, and France[35].

The major combat phase in Afghanistan conflict was during 2001-2003. It all started with bombing phase on October 7, 2001. The US efforts for this phase, consisted primarily of the air-strikes on Taliban and Al Qaeda forces. The purpose of these operations was to help the Northern Alliance and Pashtun anti-Taliban forces to advance by directing US air strikes on Taliban positions. In October 2001, about 1,300 Marines were deployed to pressure the Taliban at Qandahar.

The Taliban regime got unravelled after it lost Mazar-e-Sharif on November 9, 2001, to forces led by Dostam. Northern Alliance forces—despite promises to the United States that they would not enter Kabul—did so on November 12, 2001, to popular jubilation. The Taliban subsequently lost the south and east to US supported Pashtun leaders. The Taliban regime ended completely on December 9, 2001, when the Taliban and Mullah Umar fled Kandahar, leaving it under tribal law. Subsequently, the US and Afghan forces conducted 'Operation Anaconda' in Paktia Province in March 2002. On May 1, 2003, US officials declared an end to 'major combat'[36]. Subsequently, the period until the withdrawal of the US (2021) could be viewed as the period of urban warfare. During the period 2003 to 2021, there have been many occasions of breach in peace. The tactics used by Taliban were asymmetric in nature and they were using different tactics for different locations. Like in cities they were conducting suicide attacks, while at other places they were using guerrilla tactics. Basically, what Afghanistan was witnessing post 2003, was an insurgency situation involving Taliban. Around 2007, the presence of Taliban had increased sharply in many parts of Afghanistan. As per some reports possibly, the Taliban had a permanent presence in 54 per cent of Afghanistan[37] and there was a possibility of the country falling into Taliban hands.

---

35 https://www.cfr.org/timeline/us-war-afghanistan, accessed on Sept 23, 2021

36 Kenneth Katzman and Clayton Thomas, "Afghanistan: Post-Taliban Governance, Security, and U.S. Policy", December 13, 2017, https://sgp.fas.org/crs/row/RL30588.pdf, accessed on Sept 23, 2021

37 Richard Norton-Taylor, "Afghanistan 'falling into hands of Taliban'", Nov 22, 2007,

Geography and Climate

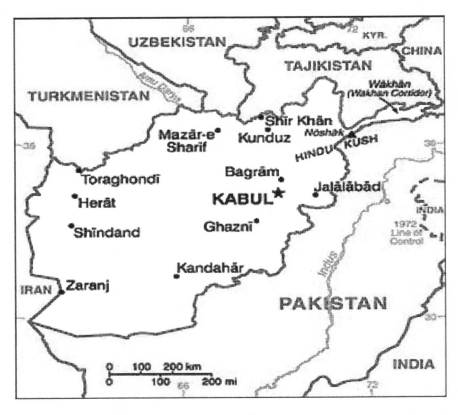

In Afghanistan, the climate is usually arid continental, with cold and relatively rainy winters/spring and hot and sunny summers. However, there are substantial differences depending on area and altitude: the South is desert, many areas are rather cold because of altitude, and the Far East is relatively rainy even in summers, since it is partly affected by the Indian monsoon. Precipitation is generally scarce, at semi-desert or desert levels. Afghanistan has four seasons; spring, summer, autumn and winter. Widespread snowfall is experienced in parts of the mountain region in the winter. The snow season is between October and April, but varies depending on altitude. Some details based on geographical zones are given below.

https://www.theguardian.com/world/2007/nov/22/afghanistan.richardnortontaylor, accessed on July 06, 2022

Northern plains: Here the climate is continental, with cold winters and very hot summers. In winter, cold waves are possible (ground temperature could reach -20/-25 °C) and in summer the peaks could be 45 °C or more.

North-central: Afghanistan is a mountainous country, and it's crossed by the range of Hindu Kush in its various chains, but also by the Pamir in the far north-east, in the frigid Wakhan Corridor, near the border with China. Many cities, starting from the capital Kabul, are located in narrow valleys, shaped by rivers between the mountains, at higher or lower elevations. There are many very high peaks like Noshaq (7,492m), Shar Dhar (7,038m) and Lunkho e Dosare (6,901m) and few others. At high altitudes, above 4,000 meters, there are vast glaciers.

South: Here the climate is warmer, and snowfalls in winter are rare.

Following three places have been taken as representative locations (please refer the map above) which could provide a broad idea about the pattern of weather prevailing over different parts of the country.

Kabul

Month (Kabul)	Min (°C)	Max (°C)	Mean (°C)	Avg precipitation (mm)
January	-7	5	-1	35
February	-5	7	1	60
March	1	13	7	65
April	5	18	11.5	70
May	9	24	16.5	25
June	12	30	21	1
July	15	32	23.5	6
August	14	32	23	2
September	9	29	19	2
October	4	23	13.5	4
November	-1	15	7	20
December	-5	8	1.5	20
Year	4.3	19.7	12	310

Kandahar

Month (K'har)	Min (°C)	Max (°C)	Mean (°C)	Avg precipitation (mm)
January	0	13	6.5	50
February	3	16	9.5	40
March	7	23	15	45
April	12	28	20	15
May	15	34	24.5	3
June	19	39	29	0
July	23	40	31.5	2
August	20	39	29.5	1
September	14	34	24	0
October	9	29	19	2
November	3	22	12.5	6
December	0	16	8	20
Year	10.5	27.8	19.1	185

Mazar-i-Sharif

Month (MIS)	Min (°C)	Max (°C)	Mean (°C)	Avg precipitation (mm)
January	-2	9	3.5	30
February	0	12	6	35
March	5	17	11	45
April	11	24	17.5	30
May	16	31	23.5	10
June	22	37	29.5	0
July	26	39	32.5	0
August	24	37	30.5	0
September	17	32	24.5	0
October	9	25	17	5
November	3	16	9.5	15
December	-1	10	4.5	20
Year	10.9	24.1	17.5	185

General Discussion

The western forces did encounter day-to-day difficulties in Afghanistan owing to typical terrain and weather conditions. Afghanistan's environment was very challenging for Army aviation, since it possesses both desert and high mountains, which limit aircraft and aircrew capabilities. There were major issues with the rapidly changing weather conditions. Like, aircraft icing was a major issue for the aviation units. Owing to the typical topography of mountain ranges like high altitude and compartmented and complex terrain structures, there used to be increase in the ferocity of the weather conditions. Also, such terrain conditions were also found leading to frequent disruptions in communications and shorting of radio ranges. The Afghanistan desert has its own unique challenges. Extreme heat and dust have been the key features of this environment. As per some statistics, around 75 per cent of aircraft accidents in such theatres are related to brownout flight conditions[38].

Some detailed research has been carried out to understand the impact of weather and terrain on the warfare in general and human loss of life in particular[39]. Empirical studies indicate that there is some (not overwhelming) evidence that winter itself did limit insurgent military action and this led to decreased coalition fatalities in Afghanistan theatre. Also, there were some indications that soldiers' bodies did have negative impact of both harsh winter and summer weather. Troop movement and conduct of operation were impacted by visibility and wind speed. Broadly, it has been found that taken together, temperature, wind speed and visibility all played sizable roles in explaining coalition fatalities.

Research[40] comparing with the previous conflict in somewhat similar terrain and weather conditions brings about very interesting resets. The war in Afghanistan (2001-2003) represents the first large-scale conflict involving military troops in a cold, mountainous climate since the Korean War (1950-1953). An analysis was steered to identify the degree of cold weather injuries, especially frostbite, in the deployed military people. The results indicate that there were only 19 cold-weather injuries in

---

38   https://apps.dtic.mil/sti/pdfs/ADA623049.pdf, accessed on Sept 27, 2021

39   Timothy Allen Carter and Daniel Jay Veale, "Weather, terrain and warfare: Coalition fatalities in Afghanistan", Conflict Management and Peace Science 30(3), 2013, pp 220–239. It may be noted that, in aviation, a brownout (or brown-out) is an in-flight visibility restriction due to dust or sand in the air

40   Hall A, Evans K, Pribyl S., "Cold injury in the United States military population: current trends and comparison with past conflicts", J Surg Educ. 2010 Mar-Apr; 67(2):61-5

comparison with the 6300 cases of cold-weather injury reported during the last major cold-weather conflict, the Korean War. This decline results from the shorter and weather-dependent engagements, cold-weather training, and cold weather protective gears with the US and allied personnel. Possibly, technology has played an important role to overcome the difficult of the past.

The military meteorologist gained much experience after they were deployed in the Afghanistan theatre. Even before the first mission was launched in Afghanistan, three young met personal during October 2001, are known to have begun their weather reconnaissance from a secret vantage point in the remote mountains of South Asia. They collected the data and dispatched a transmission via secure text to the task force commander. After this, the commanding general launched the first operation of the war based on the first weather forecast issued for this war. Over two decades, many weather forecasts got issued to support the operations to topple the Taliban and rout al-Qaeda. Many forecasts have been mission-specific and there were different types of missions including missions like kill Osama bin Laden. Finally, during July/August 2021, the weather forecasts were issued for the withdrawal phase too, when the US forces and other units left Afghanistan.

It was found that specific weather inputs when properly integrated from the beginning, has helped to execute the missions with tremendous precision. The real challenge was to undertake missions during not so perfect weather conditions. Many missions were actually launched based on real-time intelligence with only very brief windows of opportunity. It was skill of the forecasters to identify the brief window of favourable weather for launching the mission. During the initial phase of the campaign, there were major limitations for forecasting owing the absence of real-time weather observations and credible computer models for making predictions. As days processed, the allied forces were able to establish a system by making bests use of resources available. Met units dispatched remote weather sensors from low-flying helicopters, which used to transmit their observations via satellite communication.

Forecast uncertainty was primarily tied to complicated terrain. Also, sustaining the stream of observations was hard. The typical topography was a major challenge. It was difficult to get a perfect picture of weather changes from valley to valley by using different sensors for every valley. The Hindu Kush Mountain range fans out from the northeast of the country with ridges and valleys running in multiple directions. The fault lines running east-west has created a ridgeline that mostly ends up in developing stratus clouds (these are low clouds mostly at a height 800 feet or below) and fog sweeping down from Central Asia. South of the ridgeline, the city of Herat would be sunny and hot. North of the ridge, the city of Bala Murghab would be grey and chilly with little visibility for aircraft take-offs and landings.

The real challenge posed by the weather was its constantly changing nature, owing to orography and typical pattern of mountain ranges in Afghanistan. The mountains capture cloud moisture from passing storm systems and with the heating taking place owing to sunshine, by late afternoon or evening the convection used to start building up. Hence, the mornings would be crystal clear, and by noon clouding would start building up. Particularly, such situations made helicopter flying difficult and risky. On the other hand, the rising elevation and tapering channels on the highway from Kandahar to Qalat were responsible for creating tens of meandering dust devils and sand-sky brownouts in the summer and induced whiteout blizzards in winter. It was observed that Ghazni and Wardak provinces get totally covered with snow overnight[41].

As early as the year 2002, the US forces decided to start training Afghanistan military and police forces. A task force, TF Phoenix was established to raise the Afghan army. It was expended to train, equip, and advise about the missions[42].

Afghanistan's Special Mission Wing 777 was established during 2005 mainly to handle combats in respect of counter-narcotics, counter-insurgency and counter-terrorism operations. This wing had its own meteorological section, which was responsible for scrutinising and forecasting the weather. Such forecasts were of great assistance mainly to aviation units. It was found that the terrorist organisations mostly felt that bad weather conditions offer them safe cover. However, the improved accuracy in forecasting did help the Special Mission Wing to conduct timely and successful operations even during marginal weather conditions, since forecasters were able to correctly predict the gaps for weather getting cleared for a short duration of time.

---

41 The information after FN 40 is based on Jonathan D. Sawtelle, "After 9/11, weather fore-casting played a pivotal role in Afghanistan military operations", Sept 10, 2021, https://www.washingtonpost.com/weather/2021/09/10/weather-operations-afghanistan-post-911/, accessed on Sept 28, 2021

42 T.X. Hamme, "Raising and Mentoring Security Forces in Afghanistan and Iraq (Ch 4)", in Richard D. Hooker, Jr., and Joseph J. Collins (Eds), Lessons encountered: learning from the long war, National Defense University Press: Washington, DC, 2015, pp. 277-344

The US has long experience in military met aspects. Their weather services began in 1917 originating as the US Army Weather Service. It was transferred in 1947 to the Air Force, with the provision that the Air Force would still provide meteorological services to the Army. In Afghanistan Theater, the US forces took time to handover the weather services to the Afghanistan forces. Possibly, knowing the importance of such services, particularly for the military aviation, the US took time to establish independent Afghanistan structures. Since 2001, the forecasting was provided by the US military personnel only. Finally, the Bureau of Meteorology[43] was recognised in 2017 to aid the special mission wing in predicting the best times for flying.

In order to strengthen the Afghanistan's military met services, the US agencies provided accurate meteorological materials/instruments and shared their skills with their Afghan colleagues. Also, they were trained in the use of advanced meteorological radar and websites. Healthy data sharing practices were put in place. Particularly, many special air operations are most often nocturnal, and during daylight operations, there was a need for accurate meteorological calculations. All such techniques and knowledge was shared with the Afghan counterparts.

The major challenge for the foresters was in regards to the issue of the short-term forecast. This is because special operations (air) missions used to last from 20 minutes to two hours. Hence, it was necessary to issue accurate forecasts and also specify a possible clear weather window during the adverse weather period.

One interesting case demonstrating the need for correct and timely forecast was the situation of 2018, when Kunduz was besieged by the enemy. During this period, a group of senior Ministry of Defence commanders were determined to fly to the province to assess the situation. The weather was very bad for two continuative days. It was impossible for any type of aircraft to fly. Still based on some timely and accurate forecast, a helicopter-borne rescue mission took off and reached Salang Pass north of Kabul and contacted the meteorological office to request a detailed weather report to complete the trip toward Kunduz. It was told by the forecasting office that if they didn't depart from the mountain range during a two-hour window of milder weather, they might be stuck two more days. The helicopter pilots

---

43 It may be noted that Afghanistan Meteorological Department was established during 1955 and a member of WMO since 1956. This depart works under the Afghanistan civil aviation authority.

took advantage of this information to race the senior commanders and supplies of ammunition to the endangered troops in Kunduz[44].

Broadly, it could be said that in the two decades of war, the principal ingredients of that war included various military and non-military efforts. The air power was used both during traditional military operations and also in anti-terror operations, logistical operations etc. Air operations also included use of UAVs. Ground operations had different facets and from limited area ground offensives to major offensives like Operation Anaconda (2002) were conducted. On most occasions the ground and air forces were working together. Operation Anaconda, was conducted in the Shahikot Valley of Afghanistan. It was a complex battle fought in rugged mountainous terrain under difficult conditions. There were issues related to terrain and weather, while conduct of this operation. During various small and major military actions, on occasions weather had impacted air force and/or military activities. Similar types of issues continued to happen at times during the entire course of two decades of war waging.

Case Study: Ukraine-Russia War

Background

During 1918, Ukraine had declared independence from Russia during a conflict fought by multiple countries and armies over several years. However, later Soviet forces had overthrown independent Ukraine and it came under the Soviet Union during 1922. Subsequently, during the period 1939-1944, parts of Poland and Romania were annexed by the Soviet Union and presently this region is known as the western Ukraine. Finally, with Cold war ending during 1991, followed by the disintegration of the Soviet Union, Ukraine declared independence. During 1994, under the Budapest Memorandum Ukraine gave up its nuclear arsenal in exchange for a commitment from Moscow 'to respect the independence and sovereignty and the existing borders of Ukraine.'

However, during 2014, Ukraine overthrew its own government (there was a pro-Western revolution) which was of pro-Russian. All this led to Russia's annexation (March 2014) of the Crimean Peninsula. Secessionists in

---

44 The information after FN 40 is based on Hossein Rahimi, "Afghan special operations forces rely on meteorologists to ensure mission success", Jun 25, 2020, https://unipath-magazine.com/weathers-role-in-warfare/ and Elliott Sprehe, "Weathermen enable special operations forces in Afghanistan", May 04, 2010, https://www.af.mil/News/Features/Display/Article/142971/weathermen-enable-special-operations-forces-in-afghanistan/, accessed on Sept 28, 2021

eastern Ukraine, supported by Russia, declared themselves independent, as the Donetsk People's Republic and Luhansk People's Republic. Technically, the 2022 Ukraine war is actually a continuing of the war which started during 2014 in the eastern region known as Donbas.

Russia never liked the Ukraine's friendship with west and was always skeptical about the possibility of the western military presence in its backyard. Ukraine was keen to forge its own path as a sovereign state and was keen on aligning more closely with Western institutions, mainly the EU and NATO. A more nationalist, Ukrainian-speaking population in western parts of the country generally supported the idea of greater integration with Europe, while a mostly Russian-speaking community wanted closer ties with Russia.

President Putin of Russia got infuriated when during January 2021, the Ukraine President hinted to the US President about Ukraine's keenness to join the NATO forces. This actually led Russia to start making a major military presence in the region close to Ukraine. Putin started conducting various training exercises in the region and also began building up a massive military presence. Russia kept on indirectly indicating to the rest of the world, that their military build-up was somewhat on the lines of coercive diplomacy tactics. Putin kept on assuring the world, that he has no plans of invading Ukraine. However, on February 24, 2022, Putin announced a 'special military operation' to assault Ukraine. This war was expected to be very short war, however Ukrainian political and military leadership, wholeheartedly supported by their citizens are continuing to resist Russia in spite of receiving some major losses[45]. Ukraine has lost some of the major cities in the southern and eastern region, they include Sievierodonetsk, Donetsk, Luhansk, Mariupol and Kherson. The war continues as of Aug 2022 and Russian forces are also known have received some major losses, particularly among its middle and junior ranking officers. Belarus being a friend of Russia, they are able to launch attacks by using Belarusian airspace.

---

45 This entire discussion is based on: Matthew Mpoke Bigg, "A history of the tensions between Ukraine and Russia", March 26, 2022, https://www.nytimes.com/2022/03/26/world/europe/ukraine-russia-tensions-timeline.html and Jonathan Masters, "Ukraine: Conflict at the Crossroads of Europe and Russia", Apr 01, 2022, https://www.cfr.org/backgrounder/ukraine-conflict-crossroads-europe-and-russia and Dan Bilefsky, Richard Pérez-Peña and Eric Nagourney, "The Roots of the Ukraine War: How the Crisis Developed", April 21, 2022, https://www.nytimes.com/article/russia-ukraine-nato-europe.html, accessed on Jun 27, 2022

Before invasion of Ukraine, Russian forces were there in the region for many months. Hence, broadly from the weather perspective, it could said that, both the forces had to operate under fluctuating weather conditions, since they had to withstand to the weather prevalent during various seasons.

Terrain and Climate

https://geology.com/world/ukraine-satellite-image.shtml, accessed on May 28, 2022

Ukrainian state is generally flat. The mountainous region is in the west (the Carpathians) and in the south of the Crimean Peninsula (the Crimeans). Russian federation is to the north and east of Ukraine and Belarus to the north. Poland, Slovak Republic, Hungary, Romania and Moldova are at the western and southwestern borders. Crimean Peninsula and Black Sea are to the south of the country. The northern part of the country is dominated by the forests and river Dnieper divides Ukraine approximately in half. This river is one of the major rivers of Europe, which flows from Russia into Belarus rising in the Valdai Hills near Smolensk, Russia, before flowing through Belarus and Ukraine to the Black Sea[46]. It

---

[46] https://www.worldtravelguide.net/guides/europe/ukraine/weather-climate-geography/

needs to be noted that from a military perspective, Belarus being a friendly country, Russia had an option to launch attacks on Ukraine from northern side and Russia has effectively used that option.

Coal is a main fossil fuel of Ukraine. The country is extremely mineral rich with, both metallic and non-metallic minerals. There are various mineral resources in high concentrations and are found in close proximity to each other. Apart from coal and natural gas, the state has rich reserves of iron ore, manganese, graphite, sulphur, kaolin, titanium, nickel, magnesium, timber, and mercury[47].

The climate in Ukraine is mostly with continental climate characteristics (so is the case with Ukraine's neighbours Romania, Poland and Belarus) except the Crimea peninsula, which has partially characteristic Mediterranean climate (this portion was annexed by Russia during 2014) and gets recognised as the warmest part of Ukraine. On occasions, the temperature in summer reaches above 30°C, owing to the slight impact of the warmer climate that is coming on the land from the Black Sea. While even during winters, the temperatures could be as low as -30°C, when the strong northeast winds blow from the direction of Russia, which are known as very cold wind Bora[48] winds.

Standard weather seasons for Ukraine are spring, summer, autumn and winter. With melting of snow and ice, the spring season begins. Another feature of this season is strong and gusty winds. Normally March, April and May are considered as spring moths with the temperatures found in the range of around +15 to +20°C. The summer of Ukraine is characterised primarily by hot weather and lasts still September with the temperatures up to +25°C. There is a very little summer precipitation and the southern regions of the country with subtropical climate, have many sunny days. While much increase in precipitation happens during the autumn period with good number of rainy days during the months of October and November. Harsh winter begins from December with the

---

and https://www.countryreports.org/country/Ukraine/geography.htm, accessed on Jun 29, 2022

47 https://ukraineinvest.gov.ua/industries/mining/#:~:text=Ukraine%20has%20 extremely%20rich%20and,magnesium%2C%20timber%2C%20and%20mercury, accessed on July 05, 2022

48 The bora is a northerly to north-easterly katabatic wind in areas near the Adriatic Sea (body of water separating the Italian Peninsula from the Balkans). Analogous terminology is used for north-eastern winds in other littoral areas of eastern Mediterranean and Black Sea basins.

onset of winter and the period of winter extends till February. The winter period witnesses major drops in temperatures up to, say to -20°C. This season witnesses average rain/snowfall in plains, while in the mountainous areas the precipitation volume increases substantially[49].

Interesting feature of the climate at Ukraine is that, even there could be 300 sunny days in a year except in the region around the city of Odessa (a major seaport located in the south-west of the country, on the north-western shore of the Black Sea). In the lowland part of the country, the annual rainfall is between 300 mm to 700 mm. The Crimean Mountains[50] during a year receives around 1000 to 1200 mm of precipitation, while in the Carpathians, precipitation is slightly higher, 1200 to 1600 mm. The most rainfall happens is in summer and autumn period[51].

Following tables[52] present information about the temperature details of few important places in Ukraine. These places broadly represent various geographical zones of Ukraine and also the fighting is found taking place around these places. These temperatures provide some indication that under what conductions the soldiers might be fighting during the war.

Kiev

This capital city, located in the north of the country has always been under the Russian radar.

Kiev - Average temperatures (1991-2020)

Month	Min (°C)	Max (°C)	Mean (°C)
January	-5.3	-0.9	-3.1
February	-4.9	0.6	-2.2
March	-0.8	6.3	2.8
April	5.6	14.9	10.2

---

49 https://seasonsyear.com/Ukraine, accessed on July 06, 2022

50 The Carpathian Mountains form a 1,500km-long range in Central and Eastern Europe. It is arching across 7 countries, from the Czech Republic, across Poland, Slovakia, Ukraine and Hungary, and down to Romania and the tip of Serbia,

51 http://hikersbay.com/climate/ukraine?lang=en, accessed on July 06, 2022

52 https://www.climatestotravel.com/climate/ukraine and https://www.worldweatheron-line.com/football/donbass-arena-donetsk-weather-averages/ua.aspx and https://www.worldweatheronline.com/football/donbass-arena-donetsk-weather/ua.aspx, accessed on July 06, 2022

May	11	21	16
June	14.8	24.5	19.6
July	16.7	26.5	21.6
August	15.7	25.8	20.8
September	10.7	19.9	15.3
October	5.3	12.8	9
November	0.5	5.1	2.8
December	-3.7	0.3	-1.7

In the north-west parts of the country _Lviv_ is situated and close to the Poland border. For this city, the climate is a bit less warm in the summer, since it is located at 300 meters above sea level.

Lviv - Average temperatures (1991-2018)			
Month	Min (°C)	Max (°C)	Mean (°C)
January	-5.5	0	-2.8
February	-4.9	1.6	-1.6
March	-1.4	6.7	2.7
April	3.9	14.2	9.1
May	8.6	19.6	14.1
June	11.8	22.7	17.2
July	13.8	24.6	19.2
August	13.2	24.3	18.7
September	8.8	18.8	13.8
October	4.4	12.9	8.7
November	0.4	6.6	3.5
December	-4	1.2	-1.4

In the center-south, in _Dnipro_ (formerly Dnipropetrovsk). Here the summer is little warmer than in Kiev.

Dnipro - Average temperatures (1991-2020)			
Month	Min (°C)	Max (°C)	Mean (°C)
January	-6.1	-0.9	-3.5
February	-5.8	0.6	-2.6
March	-1.2	7.1	2.9
April	5.1	16	10.6
May	10.9	22.7	16.8
June	15.1	26.6	20.8
July	17.1	29.1	23.1
August	16.3	28.7	22.5
September	11	22.4	16.7
October	5.2	14.4	9.8
November	-0.1	5.8	2.8
December	-4.2	0.6	-1.8

Parts of the _Donbas_ are controlled by Russia backed separatist groups

Donbass Arena (this is an inferred information)			
Month	Min (°C)	Max (°C)	Mean (°C)
January	-6	-2	-4
February	-5	0	-2.5
March	0	6	3
April	6	15	10.5
May	12	22	17
June	17	26	21.5
July	19	29	24
August	19	29	24
September	13	22	17.5
October	7	14	10.5
November	2	6	4
December	-3	1	-1

General Discussion

This case study has been undertaken during the period when this war is still unfinished. The exact details about the weather impacting this war are yet to emerge. Specific actual weather observations from the areas in Ukraine, which were under Russian attack are not available for obvious reasons. However, based on the various reports about general weather conditions in the region and the normal weather patterns of the area under the military operations some extrapolation of possible weather impact on the ongoing conflict could be carried out.

Almost one year before the start of actual war, during March/April 2021, Russian forces had begun building military setup in the region on the pretext of conducting military exercises. These exercises helped Russia to prepare for the war and also to position their soldiers and military equipment close to the Russia-Ukraine border. At times, the troops were rotated/partially withdrawn and the second build-up had begun during Oct 2021. Broadly, Russian forces were on ground almost for one years and this must have given them a reasonable idea about how weather can impact their warfighting capabilities in different seasons.

During the pre-war phase in 2021, Ukraine experienced few unusual weather events, which were mostly related to record-breaking temperatures (for both, highest and lowest records). There was a sudden snowfall during mid-May, when the average temperature had dropped around 3 °C below normal. This delayed the arrival of the summer. However, when it arrived, it end up beating the records in another direction and during the month of July, Ukraine became 3.3 °C hotter than the climate normal. Various high temperature records were broken between June 1 and July 15, 2021[53]. Also, the rainfall was more than the normal expectations and some flooding took place. All this is bound to have impacted the progress in military activities which were being undertaken by the Russian forces. At various locations, almost post 2014, Ukrainian forces have been on high alert. By now, there had acquired enough experience to operate under varying weather conditions. At times, for them good weather situation with clear skies actually becomes a limitation, because for Russia targeting becomes much easier.

---

53 Anastasiia Bushovska, "Ukraine Breaks Records for Highest and Lowest Temperatures in 2021", October 12, 2021, https://www.climatescorecard.org/2021/10/ukraine-breaks-records-for-highest-and-lowest-temperatures-in-2021/, accessed on July 02, 2022

Vladimir Putin had travelled to Beijing during February, 2022 and it was reported that Xi Jinping had asked him to wait until after the Olympics to invade Ukraine. The XXIV Olympic Winter Games, commonly known as Beijing 2022 were held between, February 4 2022 to February 20, 2022. It appears that, Putin did not realise that delaying the invasion could mitigate the advantage the weather was offering to him during early February. During the end of January and early February period, the frigid winter weather had frozen the Ukrainian landscape, making it strong enough to support Russian tanks. There were expectations that the Russian military could exploit this hardened terrain to invade. But, Putin had agreed to wait, possibly thinking that the weather would remain cold even during March. In fact, mid-twentieth century averages were indicative that major cities in Ukraine like Kyiv and Kharkiv, the hotbeds of fighting in the present war used to remain much colder even during March. However, for some decades now, they have warmed by more than two degrees. During February, 2022 it was observed that the temperatures across Ukraine had soared over 5°C above their mid-twentieth century averages[54].

Finally, when Russia invaded Ukraine on February 24, 2022 the ground had become very muddy. Satellite images showed the Russian tanks and rocket launchers abandoned in the mud. In northern Ukraine, Russian vehicles kept to roads and had formed long columns, making them vulnerable to any form of aerial attack. Far from the blitzkrieg (saturation bombing) Putin appears to have expected, the invasion from the north progressed at a snail's pace. The weather on the tactical battlefield was disadvantageous to the Russian forces.

During the beginning of the invasion, the Russian forces realised that the roads leading to the capital Kiev had slowed down the movement of their tanks due to mud. Such situation is called "Rasputitsa", which is a combination of muddy conditions caused due thawing snow and rainy weather. It looked that the history had repeated itself this time. In the past, similar conditions had caused havoc among Napoleon's Army in the nineteenth century when the French invaded Russia. Also, Hitler had met with the same faith when he was pushing towards Moscow during World War II. It was a bitter winter during early 1940s, which had slowed the German advance during Operation Barbarossa. Even during Feb 2022,

---

54 Dagomar Degroot, "Is Climate Change Influencing the Invasion of Ukraine? Possible Connections Echo Little Ice Age Histories", March 13, 2022, https://www.historicalclimatology.com/features/is-climate-change-influencing-the-invasion-of-ukraine-possible-connections-echo-little-ice-age-histories, accessed on July 07, 2022

Putin's decision to attack during Rasputitsa ended up putting their wheeled armoured fighting vehicle (AFV) and trucks in the mud[55].

Russia's military struggles in Ukraine could also be compared with their performance during the 1939 war with Finland, which they eventually won after incurring major damages, both in terms of men and machine. This war had begun with a Soviet invasion of Finland on November 30 1939 and ended on March 13 1940, when both the parties had signed the Moscow Peace Treaty. Eventually, Finland lost 10 per cent of its land and also got deprived of access to sea.

On paper, this war actually was no contest. Finland's entire military numbered around 280,000 men and 400 artillery pieces, 32 tanks, and 75 combat-capable aircraft. While the Soviets' Leningrad Military District alone had 500,000 men, 5,700 field guns, 6,500 tanks, and 3,800 aircraft. Soviet leader Josef Stalin was confident that they would just walk over the 800 mile Soviet-Finland border by using tanks and heavy artillery. His idea was somewhat similar to the famous Germany's strategy of blitzkrieg into Poland. However, the Red Army suffered owing to Finnish soldiers using guerrilla tactics. The Ski-mounted Finnish troops inflicted heavy losses on the Soviets and the war, which was expected to get over in 15 days as per the Soviet estimates, prolonged for 105 days. Here weather became a major disadvantage for the Soviet army's ground movements. Somewhat similar military struggles the Russian forces are undergoing in Ukraine during 2022[56].

Somehow, Russia was found not having a total dominance in the air despite its superior firepower, at least during the initial stages of the war. This was because the weather was not conducive for full-scale air operations. The low cloud-base had hindered the air operations and also possibly, the satellite reconnaissance. During the third/fourth week of February 2022, light and moderate snowfall was falling continuously for some duration, impacting visibility significantly. Indubitably, Russia forces are having PGMs and other state of art weaponry, which is supposed to be an all-weather weaponry. Here the targeting is done not visually, but by using GPS (Glonass) supported weapons. Still possibly, Russia was not

---

55 "Russian tanks advance in Ukraine: What is 'Rasputitsa'?", Mar 14, 2022, https://www. wionews.com/world/russian-tank-advance-in-ukraine-what-is-rasputitsa-462047, accessed on July 6, 2022

56 Benjamin Brimelow, "Russia's military struggles in Ukraine are starting to look like a bloody Soviet attack on a smaller neighbor during World War II", Mar 21, 2022, https:// www.businessinsider.in/stock-market, accessed on Jun 26, 2022

ready to take any changes owing to the possibility of collateral damage and possibly not much sure about the accuracy of the weapons in bad weather conditions.

A benefit for the Ukrainians was that the Russians were attacking them in their backyard. The Ukrainian forces had some comfort zone of operating in their own terrain. The continuous snowfall had made the terrain look somewhat uniform and made it difficult for the Russian aviators to identify the targets correctly. Russians were aware that the weather is a double-edged sword. Many of Ukraine's surface-to-air missiles (SAMs) are radar-guided and not much impacted by the weather. Obviously, Russians were aware that their aircraft becomes susceptible to Ukrainian SAMs, which are mainly guided by infrared[57].

Broadly, the weather is found to have played an important role in Ukraine's north at the beginning of the invasion. Here the ground was not sufficiently frozen and that forced Russian tanks to circulate in long convoys on paved roads, making them vulnerable to the Ukrainian forces' Javelin anti-tank systems. There was a situation, when it was eminent that the massive Russian force approaching towards Kiev would launch a major offensive for the capture of the capital. However, it was found that the big Russian convoy[58] was not able to make the progress as expected and inclement weather and unfavourable ground conditions was one of the reason behind this. The ground temperatures were around -10°C. Also, it must have been extremely difficult for the troops to stay inside the military vehicles in cold conditions for days. Experienced soldiers claim that siting in the vehicles, which are not moving gives a feeling of sitting in refrigerators[59]. Weather has also played an important role in warfighting over the Donbas region. During early phases of the conflict, for several days, rain had battered Donbas and subsequently rise in temperatures had happened. All this had made ground softer and made it difficult for the Russian forces to do anything off paved highways[60].

---

57 "Russian tanks advance in Ukraine: What is 'Rasputitsa'?", Mar 14, 2022, https://www.wionews.com/world/russian-tank-advance-in-ukraine-what-is-rasputitsa-462047, accessed on July 6, 2022

58 Said to be around 65 km long, near Kyiv and it had shown hardly any movement for three days and subsequently it just fizzled!

59 Brendan Cole, "In Putin's Ukraine Debacle, Even the Weather Has Turned Against Him", March 09, 2022, https://www.newsweek.com/russia-ukraine-weather-winter-cold-snap-putin-zelensky-1686364, accessed on July 06, 2022

60 Bad weather in Donbas could favor Ukrainians: US official, April 14, 2022, https://english.alarabiya.net/News/world/2022/04/15/Bad-weather-in-Donbas-could-favor-

By early July 2022, the Russian forces had captured a major area of Donbass region. The Russian army had claimed victory in Luhansk province and had intensified its shelling of the key Ukrainian strongholds of Sloviansk and Kramatorsk. The spring thaw had restricted Russian armour on roads in the first phase of the invasion owing the weather leading to bad road conditions. However, improving weather situation had led to making the ground dry for sweeping manoeuvres[61]. This indicates that with the improving weather situation, the Russia forces are likely to make quick advances towards achieving their military aim.

Between February to June 2022, both in the north and east, the Russians had faced various problems in respect of military commutations and coordination, troops moral, serviceability of fighting platforms and other equipment and providing other logistical supports like food and water. All in all, the war had not gone according to the Russian plan. Owing various reasons Russia was required to follow a slow and halting pace. A critical look at the climatic conditions over the warzone till the first half 2022, indicates that weather was one of the important elements towards stalling the progress of Russian military.

Ukrainians-US-official, accessed on Jun 26, 2022

61   Andrew Salmon, "Better weather may shift Russia's fortunes in Ukraine", May 4, 2022, https://asiatimes.com/2022/05/better-weather-may-shift-russias-fortunes-in-ukraine/, accessed on Jun 26, 2022 and https://www.euronews.com/2022/07/05/ukraine-war-russia-sets-sights-on-donetsk-region-after-claiming-victory-in-luhansk, accessed on July 08, 2022

Chapter 5

Weaponising the Weather

Background

Military historians and strategists have much debated the impact of weather on warfare. However, in a relative sense there is a finished debate on the aspects of use of weather as an instrument to wage a war. The most obvious reason for this is, the major absence of real-life (war) situations, where there are evidences of weather being used as a weapon. However, particularly in the 21st century, where the notion of warfare is constantly found getting evolved owing to the technology influence (e.g. Cyber warfare, Space warfare) it is important to understand the nuances of weather warfare, a technology driven warfare. To appreciate the possible future of weather warfare, it is essential to take a look at the genesis of this idea and actual use of weather weapons in warfare. It is also important to understand the possible rationale behind the states opting for this form of warfare, the legal aspects and the nature of ongoing research.

The science of weather modification poses a two-fold problem to the international community. Atmospheric activity and weather phenomena are transnational in character. There exists a possibility of the happening of inadvertent weather modification. Like sustained forest fires could impact the weather cycle of a particular region. On some occasions, there also could be health hazards for the population staying in the adjoining region. Advertent modification would increase or decrease the rainfall over the area under experimentation (or attack). This amounts to using weather as a weapon over enemy territory.[1]

---

1   S. Bhatt, "Some Reflections on International Law and Relations Involving Weather Modification Activities, Including some Special Feathers Relating to India", *Journal of Indian Law Institute*, Vol 13:2, 1973, pp. 253-254.

Particularly, inadvertent weather modifications happen regularly (majority of it have already happened globally, resulting into climate change). Over the years, major changes in the weather patterns have been observed owing to human actions (mostly, done inadvertently till the issue of global warning/climate change getting scientifically established) done for purposes other than changing the weather. Human activities have accidentally been able to change all facets of the weather at and near the Earth's surface. Various acts like rampant industrialisation leading to air and water pollution, human activities leading to decrease in groundwater table, cutting of jungles and excessive load put on the use of natural resources is severely impacting the weather. All this has been partially responsible for increase or decrease in patterns of precipitation and other weather changes, which could be global or local (effects typically create weather changes occurring on scales ranging from 1 sq km up to 10,000 sq km) in nature. The list of accidental weather changes is almost endless. Largely, the knowledge that humans were altering the weather became commonplace about 200 years ago[2].

In the 21st century, a good amount of weather modification experiments are known to be happening in various parts of the world, with 52 countries (some reports say 56[3]) having active cloud seeding programmes.[4] These experiments are mainly happening at a lower scale (in reference to geography) and basically with an aim to assist the people of the region. On the other hand, there is a long (and limited) history of weather warfare. Particularly, in the post-World War II period, few cases have come to the notice, where it is evident that for military purposes, atmospheric tampering has been carried out. Progress made in the field of satellites, information technology and commutation sciences and with the easy availability of supercomputing power, there have been vast improvements in weather prediction capabilities. The 'flipside' of these developments is that it could allow the humans (states) to tamper with the weather intentionally as a part of their war-fighting strategy.

Theoretically, the weather gets identified as a state of the atmosphere. It is about the heat and cold conditions and also about the precipitation. Changing these conditions intentionally for control rainfall, hail, lightning,

---

2   https://www.sciencedirect.com/topics/earth-and-planetary-sciences/weather-modification, accessed on Jun 18, 2022

3   Sahana Ghosh, "What is cloud seeding? Aug 01, 2019, https://www.cnbctv18.com/economy/what-is-cloud-seeding-4098671.htm, accessed on July 30, 2022

4   WMO Expert Committee on Weather Modification Research Report, November 2014.

cyclones, and any other tropospheric weather phenomenon gets recognised as weather modification. Weather phenomena occur in the tropospheric region. However, there is some influence on the process of formation of weather from the activities in the upper atmosphere, which happen beyond the troposphere. Also, topography and terrain play an important role in weather formation. Hence, it is also important to study and focus on other aspects, which may assist (at times) the weather modification processes. These categories are[5]:

> Geoengineering/Climate Engineering: This is the inadvertent (unintentional or "accidental") or intentional attempt by humans to control the temperature of the world and/or modify nature on massive scales to achieve the desired result (such as melting the arctic).

> Space Weather Modification: The inadvertent or intentional attempt by humans to alter the upper atmosphere (ionosphere, mesosphere) through rockets and satellites, chemical releases and injection of high-powered electromagnetic radiation (by using specially developed instruments like ionospheric heaters, lasers, and charged particle beams).

In general, Weather modification techniques are at the core of design for any weather weapon. Hence, it would be prudent to deliberate first on some aspects associated with weather modification before deliberating the history and other features associated with weather warfare.

Weather Modification

Weather modification is the act of intentionally manipulating or altering the weather. Magical (enchanted) and religious practices to control (read manipulate) the weather is mentioned in various cultures thousands of years before the modern era. Since long the most common form of weather modification is the process of cloud seeding employed to increase rain or snow.[6] The idea and practice of modifying the weather is essentially for the purposes of reducing human suffering. The creation of artificial rain particularly, assists the farming community and ensures the smooth supply of drinking water over the drought-affected or rain-deficient regions. There

---

5 https://weathermodificationhistory.com/interactive-timeline/, accessed on Jun 18, 2022

6 http://weatherwarfare.worldatwar.info/2012/12/what-is-weather-modification/, accessed on Aug 20, 2018.

are some modification techniques known to offer good results towards fog dispersal, suppression of hail etc.

Weather modification comprises of three major categories: suppression of weather patterns, intensification of weather patterns, and in some cases the introduction of totally new weather patterns. The two basic approaches to accomplish weather modification include cloud seeding and directed-energy.[7]

Apart from assisting the community, weather modification also directs destructive weather against a competitor or enemy, as a tactic of military or economic warfare, both in tactical spheres and strategic spheres.

There could be number of weather modification techniques which could be used for purposes of damaging the morale of the enemy. Some of the techniques could involve cloud seeding, fog clearance, or fog generation. For cloud seeding to succeed, specific atmospheric conditions are required, like the availability of water vapour in the atmosphere. It is clear, however, that humans have now attained the technical sophistication to attempt the modification of certain weather phenomena, especially related to clouds and precipitation. The accuracy factor with regard to the overall concept of weather and environmental modification still has some limitations. There are some techniques/ideas which are at present, more in the theoretical domain and much more research is required to make them workable; for example, creation of artificial earthquakes.

From a warfare point of view, weather is intentionally tampered to ensure that, the 'outburst' would assist the overall process of causing harm to the enemy by leading to a significant amount of destruction. Such destruction could be caused by creating flash floods, causing landslides or ensuring a drought-like situation over the enemy's territory. However, much of the damage could also be inflicted by planning and executing damage to the environment, bursting dams or destroying huge bridges on the river. Such acts are doable by sabotage. Here, no weather modification techniques would be required to be used; hence, in the classical sense, such acts may not fall into the category of weather warfare. For the purpose of this chapter, the scope is restricted to acts involving intentional tampering with weather for security purposes.

The science of weather modification has a long history. Various historical evidence demonstrates some association between the weather

---

7   "Weather Warfare", http://www.newworldwar.org/weatherwar.htm, accessed on Mar 12, 2018.

and wars. However, in some cases there is a lack of scientific evidence to reach to any definitive conclusion. No specific scientific correlation has been found yet, with regard to the empirical evidence, which indicates that rainfall had occurred after every large battle in the past from the time of the Napoleonic wars (1803–1815, a series of major conflicts pitting the French Empire and its allies, led by Napoleon) to the American Civil War (1861-65, the Civil War in the United States began after decades of simmering tensions between northern and southern states over slavery, states' rights and westward expansion) and few other conflicts, like the Seven Years' War (1756-1763, involving every great European power of the time and spanning five continents, affecting Europe, the Americas, West Africa, India, and the Philippines). Various such occurrences were collated together during 1869 by an American engineer who published a book called *War and Weather* (1871).[8] Interestingly, this is known to have led the US administration to task a retired military general with undertaking experiments to appreciate the possibility of the impact of gunpowder and explosives on rain-making. A grant of US$ 9000 was made available for undertaking the query; however, the results of the experiments were inconclusive.[9]

The 19th century, saw important experiments carried out by a Serbian immigrant named Nikola Tesla, who came to the US in the 1890s. Tesla experimented with electromagnetic flux and studied the earth's gravitational field. During his research, he discovered that the ionisation of the atmosphere would alter when it was charged by radio wave transmissions in the low-frequency range of 10 to 80 Hz[10]. During the early 1900s, various experiments were conceptualised for scientific rain-making, like giving electric shocks to the clouds, producing rain with the help of X-rays, spraying liquid air in clouds, blasting clouds with sand, ice drops on clouds, and more such ideas. Agencies like the US Army Signal Corps were tasked to work on programmes related to weather control. The investments towards developing techniques for weather control was not restricted to only rain-making; some efforts were also made towards storm control, stopping of forest fires and controlling a few other natural events.[11]

---

8 Edward Powers, *War and the Weather or the Artificial Production of Rain*, S.C. Griggs and Company, Chicago: 1781

9 Willy Ley, "The us do Something about the Weather: For your Information", *Galaxy Science Fiction*, Feb 1961, pp.72-73, https://archive.org/stream/Galaxy_v19n03_1961-02#page/n37/mode/1up, accessed on Feb 23, 2018

10 http://www.amigospais-guaracabuya.org/oagmc088.html, Jan 1, 2005

11 A detailed database on all these aspects is available at https://weathermodificationhis-

All this clearly indicates that the idea of manipulating the weather for the benefits of the civil population and also for the armed forces was there, even one and a half centuries ago. In addition, around the same time the idea of weather warfare was being discussed and debated.

Scientists from General Electric Irving Langmuir and Vincent Schaefer, altered clouds by "seeding" them with dry ice pellets. Bernard Vonnegut, a co-worker, also had verified that a smoke of silver iodide crystals would accomplish the same result. These US scientists on November 13, 1946, had verified the theory experimentally, which was advanced in 1933 by the Swedish meteorologist, Tor Bergeron, and the German physicist, Walter Findeisen, that clouds are likely to precipitate, if they contained the right mixture of ice crystals and supercooled water drops[12].

The actual experiment to check the possibility of manipulating weather was carried out on November 13, 1946 by a team of Curtis Talbot, a pilot working in the General Electric Research Laboratory, and Vincent Schaefer, a scientist. They flew to a height of 14,000 feet, approximately 30 miles east of Schenectady, which is the city in New York, near the confluence of the Mohawk and Hudson rivers. As a part of an experiment, they threw three pounds of dry ice (frozen carbon dioxide) into the clouds. They observed long streamers of snow falling from the base of the cloud around which they had undertaken cloud seeding. This probably was the first artificially manufactured snowfall or snowstorm[13].

Artificial rainfall has its origins in the research carried out during the 1940s related to aircraft icing and the growth of cloud particles. Various experiments were being conducted during this research. During this period, scientists discovered that dry ice and silver iodide induce precipitation in miniature supercooled clouds. A major project called Project Cirrus was undertaken, which involved a study of cloud physics and the mechanics of artificially induced precipitation. This project, contracted to General Electric, was sponsored by the US Army Chemical Corps, Navy and Air Force. In 1953 the Department of Defense initiated a broad-based experimental programme. This was the Artificial Nucleation Project, with a purpose to study the physics of precipitation control in

---

tory.com/newspapers/, accessed on Sept 02, 2018

12 "Weather and Climate Modification", *Report of the Special Commission on Weather Modification*, National Science Foundation, Washington DC 1965, p.1

13 "Weather Warfare: Weather Modification Technology in Warfare", 23 July, 2021, https://www.unrevealedfiles.com/weather-warfare-weather-modification-technology-in-warfare/, accessed on Jun 19, 2022

a variety of meteorological situations[14]. All this indicates the direct or indirect involvement of military meteorologists in various projects of weather modifications almost since the Second World War.

There have been a few important projects undertaken during the 1970s, which were not only dealing with the study and practice of weather modification but also to appreciate how certain human activities and practices could impact the weather. In a sense, it becomes evident that, the notion of human activities impacting environment was even prevalent then. Obviously, from the warfare perspective, it could be safe to argue that the converse of this idea, meaning, intentionally doing some activities to manipulate the weather over the geography of one's adversary, could have been at least visualised then. One interesting project worth mentioning is a civilian project and appears to have no connection with warfare. However, the knowledge, data and experience gathered through such projects could have helped military meteorologists to better understand how weather patterns get disturbed by human activities.

Scientists from the Argonne National Laboratory, the University of Chicago, Illinois State Water Survey, and the University of Wyoming participated in a cooperative scientific programme to study the inadvertent modification of weather by an urban-industrial complex. It was viewed that normally, under the urban settings the knowledge about winds, temperature, and visibility exists but, precipitation changes are not critically monitored. Hence, the focus of the project was to study urban-related alterations in precipitation processes and quantitative changes in surface precipitation. Also, the study of cloud and precipitation processes was undertaken. St. Louis area was the site of this field project called METROMEX (Metropolitan Meteorological Experiment). The scientists were also working on various laboratory and atmospheric modelling aspects along with field observations. The first field operations and data collection for METROMEX occurred in the summer (June-August) of 1971. It is important to note that such projects were provided with adequate infrastructure. Apart from standard meteorological equipment for observation and as measurement tools, mobile meteorological observatories, radars and meteorological aircrafts were made available[15].

---

14 James N. Corbridge, Jr. and Raphael J. Mosesi, "Weather Modification: Law And Administration", *Natural Resources Journal*, Vol 8, No 2, Apr 1968, pp.207-235

15 Stanley A. Changnon, Jr., Floyd A. Huff and Richard G. Semonin, "METROMEX: an investigation of inadvertent weather modification", *Bulletin American Meteorological Society*, Vol. 52, No. 10, October 1971, pp. 958-966

Over centuries, the human ability to observe and predict various types of weather systems has increased vastly. Yet, during the same period, weather modification investigations have progressively waned. Extravagant claims, unrealistic hopes, and failure to provide scientifically demonstrable achievement are some of the factors responsible for such a decline[16].

The presence of the Internet could be viewed both as a boom and bane for the science of weather modification. The Internet is allowing more visibility to the subject and more amount of research is now freely available and exchange of ideas are taking place among the experts. At the same time, significant speculation is taking place on the Internet on the subject of weather control. Hence, it is difficult to judge the actual status of ongoing scientific research[17]. A good amount of scientific research has undergone (and is underway) over the years on various aspects of weather modification. Most of the research is happening in isolation and no scientific collaboration is visible among different nation-states. In addition, no major political patronise is visible, except some small projects getting funding form research agencies. Only, on some occasion's states, are found experimenting with artificial rainfall particularly when they are facing drought situations. It could be said that the earlier expectations have not matched with the actual success on the field.

At present, researchers are found depending on various tools like sounding rockets, satellites, balloons, drones, lasers, radars, sonars, automatic weather stations and supercomputers to enhance their research. The experimentations are at various stages of development in areas like Ionospheric Heater, Cloud Seeding, Cloud Ionisers, Stratospheric Aerosol Injection, Contrail Induced Cirrus and Water Vapour Pollution[18].

The basic difference between the act of weather modification and the act of weather warfare could be visualised from the perspective of 'capability' versus 'intent' matrix. Developing competence in the field of weather modification is more of an act of technology development and

---

16 *Critical Issues in Weather Modification Research*, A report by Committee on The Status of And Future Directions in U.S. Weather Modification Research and Operations, The National Academies Press, Washington, DC, 2000, p.1

17 It needs to be mentioned that secrecy and ambiguity have been part of much of the scientific research in the arenas of nuclear, missile, space and various defence technologies too (even in non-internet era)

18 Jim Lee, "Ten Technologies to Own the Weather Today!", May 7, 2018, https://climateviewer.com/2017/11/07/ten-technologies-to-own-the-weather-today/, assessed on June 24, 2018

experimentation, while using this expertise for the purposes of gaining strategic advantage for the state, clearly demonstrates the resolve to use such expertise in warfare. Another aspect which is beyond weather modification, but still can play some role in modifying the weather is intentional tampering of the topographical and terrain features.

Wendy Watson-Wright, Assistant Director General and Executive Secretary of the Intergovernmental Oceanographic Commission (IOC) of the United Nations Educational, Scientific and Cultural Organization (UNESCO) defines geo-engineering as "the deliberate large-scale intervention in the Earth's climate system, in order to moderate global warming." She further argues that despite the attention it is gaining, [it] is an option that "involves considerable uncertainty and risk." A major correlation can be established between geo-engineering and weather warfare. However, this chapter refrains from specifically debating on this issue, mainly because at present there is less clarity about the technological capabilities with regard to geo-engineering. Issues like the artificial creation of earthquakes etc. are still not in the realm of reality. Reference is made to only those projects which are ongoing. In a separate chapter, some discussion on geo-engineering has been undertaken.

Weather and Warfare

Weather and climate influence human life in many ways. Variations in weather modify agriculture production and transportation and influence human behaviour. Variations in long-term climate can even determine the fate of a given civilisation. For various reasons, humans have always attempted to understand, predict and even modify atmospheric phenomena. Despite these efforts, lack of infrastructure and the sheer complexity of the problem has permitted scientific meteorology to develop only during the past century. Even now, our knowledge of the atmosphere is far from sufficient.

Weather could be defined as a natural phenomenon that occurs in the atmosphere. It is a known fact that the weather impacts the war-fighting process. Almost a century ago, it was argued that war does not affect the weather but, weather does affect war.[19] However, that is not the case anymore, we are experiencing both the things happening. It is essential to be familiar with the climate of a war zone in advance and to have accurate

---

19 Robert DE Courcy Ward, "Weather Has Effect on War: Study of Climatic Conditions Has Been of Importance in Europe", April 23, 1917, https://www.thecrimson.com/article/1917/4/23/weather-has-effect-on-war-pwar/, accessed on July 24, 2018

knowledge about possible weather phenomena like the probability of the occurrence of severe cold and hot weather; patterns of rainfall, including heavy rainfall; understanding about patterns of winds and information about possible visibility conditions over own and enemy territory. Militaries require a complete knowledge of essential weather elements for planning a campaign or for organising a solitary mission. This knowledge is essential for a decision on various activities of war-fighting – from selecting proper clothing to planning various operational missions.

History is replete with examples[20] where weather has impacted the wars. One of the most comprehensive historical surveys of weather and war was published in 1907 by Lord Bentley. On various occasions the weather has played such a crucial role in war-fighting that it has actually led to a change in the path of history. Some examples of this include the English defeat of the Spanish Armada (1588), Operation Barbarossa, Adolf Hitler's attempt to invade the Soviet Union (1941) and the famous D-Day invasion/Operation Neptune (1944), the largest seaborne invasion in history, when some 156,000 American, British and Canadian forces landed on five beaches along the heavily fortified coast of France's Normandy area. Another classic case from history, which indicates that even during harsh weather conditions with good knowledge of weather patterns and topographical and terrain conditions, movement of troops is possible, is that of Hannibal taking his troops, cavalry and African war elephants, across a high pass in the snowclad Alps to strike at Rome (218 BC). Some of these examples have already been discussed in detail in the earlier chapter.

The influence of weather-related events has weighed so much on the minds of war fighters, that some major military lexicons have had their origins in such events. For example, the Japanese pilots in World War II who deliberately crashed their aeroplanes onto enemy ships were known as Kamikaze (divine wind) fighters. In 1281, two Mongolian fleets led by Kublai Khan were threatening to invade Japan. The defeat of the weaker Japanese forces was evident, but a vicious typhoon wreaked havoc and the Mongolian ships had to retreat. Thus, a divine (kami) wind (kaze) saved Japan from a Mongol invasion.[21]

---

20 Weather and War: Three ways that weather changed the course of history, https://www.metoffice.gov.uk/learning/weather-and-history/weather-and-war, accessed on April 15, 2018

21 Lt Col Gary D. Atkinson, "Impact of Weather on Military Operations: Past, Present and future", Jun 01, 1973, a thesis by an USAF officer, US Army War College, p.2

Largely, the science of weather has always been relevant in war-fighting for centuries. However, it took many centuries for the states to keep meteorologists within the ranks of fighting forces. Gradually, the military leadership realised the importance of meteorology on the relevance of tactical and strategic operations. Modern military meteorology is said to have its origin in the late wars. Probably, every war could be said to have its own story of meteorology. In the summer of 1917, it became evident that meteorological personnel and equipment were required by the American Expeditionary Forces in France. By 1918, meteorological personnel were involved in the actual day-to-day work in the French, British, and American armies. There was clarity about what to expect from military meteorology and meteorologists. There were three clear focus areas: (a) Statistical information, or past weather (b) Current information, or present weather and (c) Forecasts, or future weather. A very strong argument was put then, for the requirement of men in uniform to serve as military meteorologists.[22] The process of having separate military units for meteorology is said to have begun around 1918-20. Subsequently, no direct references are found (from 1920 till date) in connection with tasking military meteorologists for weather warfare operations. But it is evident (circumstantial indications), particularly for states like the US, Russia and China, that their military meteorological units were/are involved in experimenting with various weather modification techniques. The military units dealing with meteorology are either found experimenting with a few weather modification techniques or outsourcing their projects to other agencies.

The use of various categories of military platforms from tanks, ships, aircrafts, submarines, remote vehicles to even space planes, offer major challenges to military meteorologists who have to forecast the weather for fighting in the air, on land and over and under the oceans. The lethality factor of modern-day weapons has demonstrated that they impact not only the enemy forces, but also the surrounding environment. The tendency of attacking military camps, ammunition centres and other critical infrastructure like energy production and storage sites, nuclear and electric power plants, is making the earlier belief that 'war does not affect weather' redundant. In fact, "the environment has long been a silent casualty of war and armed conflict. From the contamination of land and the destruction of forests to the plunder of natural resources and the collapse of management systems, the environmental consequences of war are often widespread and

---

22 William Gardner Reed, "Military Meteorology", *Geographical Review*, Vol. 12, No. 3 (Jul, 1922), pp. 403-411

devastating".[23] The wars like the 1991 Gulf War, had resulted in damaging and burning various oil-wells in the region. This did impact the weather patterns in the region temporarily.

Hence, broadly, it could be said that weather is both a boon and bane for war-fighting and also war-fighting leaves an adverse impact on the atmospheric conductions. There is a third aspect associated with the weather in warfare and that is, intentional tampering of weather as a strategy of war.

Weather Warfare

The artificial creation of imbalances in environmental fields (due to which the weather disturbances occur) to suit the military requirements of a nation could be termed as the conception of weather weapon technology. Weather weapon means usage of scientific means to create or modify atmospheric disturbances. It could constitute creation/clearing of fog on airstrips operated by the air force, creating flash floods in enemy territory to frustrate the enemy's logistics, creating drought conditions to cripple the enemy's economy, guiding a course of hurricanes and tornadoes to naval ports of opponent countries, generating massive forest fires by induced lightening or even creating panic by directing virus laden clouds to precipitate on the enemy populace.

There is no precise definition of weather warfare. Any use of weather modification techniques for military purposes could be considered as an act of weather warfare. Alternatively, the usage of various types of weather weapons to gain a political or military advantage against the enemy also gets labelled as weather warfare.

Types of Weather Weapons

Various atmospheric modifications could be carried out with an aim to gain political or military advantages. Broadly, acts categorised as war-fighting efforts and specific environmental alterations made, could be identified with the results (divesting) achieved. These could be categorised as weather weapons. Such weapons could mainly include flood weapons, drought weapons, cyclone weapons, hail weapons and fog weapons. At the same time, the usage of these weapons requires the availability of typical favourable environmental conditions, in the vicinity of the 'target region' at that point in time. This means if the region is without any clouds, then flood weapons cannot be used. In short, suitable weather conditions need

---

23 UN Secretary General Ban-ki Moon, *The Guardian*, Nov 6, 2014.

to prevail to undertake weather modification experiments. Also, there are a few other categories of weapons which, at present, are theoretical possibilities, like the Earthquake Weapons. Actually, such a weapon category is known as Tectonic Weapons. The use of such weapons means the intentional creation of earthquakes, volcanoes, or other seismic activities (over an identified target location area) by interfering with the Earth's natural geological processes. In addition, certain intentional acts which can damage the environment and create mayhem, could be stage-managed. Such acts could involve bursting of dams, sabotaging the nuclear or chemical facilities or creating forest fires. All these acts cannot be categorised as classical acts of weather warfare, but have the potential to cause similar damage as that by the usage of weather weapons.

Weather Warfare: The Prelude

Immediately after the end of the second world war, the US and UK armed forces began experimenting with the weather. During 1947, the US Navy, Army, and Air Force, working with General Electric Corporation, made the first effort to modify a hurricane under Project Cirrus, by dropping about 180 pounds of dry ice into clouds. The crew members did confirm that there were pronounced modifications of the cloud deck seeded and they were in no position to allude to the reasons behind this. Subsequently, the hurricane did change its direction and made a landfall close to Savannah, Georgia. However, the local population was in the know about the experimentation undertaken and the administration had to face public outrage and threat of lawsuits. At the same time the scientific community also did not consider Project Cirrus as a success and the project eventually got cancelled[24]. For many years from the side of the US government there was no official acceptance of this project. Much later the details of this project were made public after the declassification of the documents[25].

Actually, before the modification of cyclone, during 1946-47, three scientists working at the research laboratory of General Electric Company namely Irving Langmuir, Bernard Vonnegut and Vincent Schaefer had modified clouds by 'seeding' them with dry ice pellets. This snowmaking

---

24 Timothy Alexander Guzman, "Is Weather Warfare a Conspiracy Theory?", October 21, 2017, https://www.globalresearch.ca/is-weather-warfare-a-conspiracy-theory/5614348, accessed on Aug 09, 2018. Some other information for this section has also been taken from the same source.

25 http://documents.theblackvault.com/documents/weather/CirrusFinal.pdf, accessed on Sep 12, 2018

in the laboratory led to the birth of the cloud seeding project called the Project Cirrus[26].

The main focus post-second World War, was on cloud seeding. This was known as the most important method for weather modification, meant for enhancing precipitation from clouds. The idea of cloud seeding is known to have got first conceived after World War II. Here the aim was to increase the precipitation efficiency artificially. Over the years, this idea has become a much-practised activity at many arid regions of the world.

As mentioned earlier, these three scientists had verified experimentally the theory proposed in 1933 by the Swedish meteorologist Tor Bergeron, and the German physicist, Walter Findeisen. The Bergeron Findeisen theory was predated by the work of the Dutch scientist, August Veraart in his 1930 experiments conducted in Holland with dry ice and supercooled water-ice. Actually, the idea of rain-making is not an idea of present era. There are evidences available indicating that many traditional societies, have practiced some type of religious or ritualistic rain-making experiments[27].

In the present era, two US Government patents on methods of rain-making were issued before the turn of the 20th century. Also, during 1971, the US government (on name of Robert G. Knollenberg Mattoon, Ill) has patented a weather modification (production of rain or snow) technique of 'introducing into natural atmospheric clouds seeding agents having a high solubility in water and a large endothermic heat of solution in water. Precipitation in the form of rain or snow begins'[28]. Along with the US weather bureau, the US Air Force and Navy are known to be actively involved in various weather modification experiments during mid-1950s. Actually, the 1946 validation that clouds could be modified for creating rain by scientific methods arose out of the World War II investigations of fog particles by Langmuir and Schaefer. The military possibilities of this discovery led the armed services to support a broad theoretical, laboratory and field programme in cloud modification like the Project Cirrus[29].

26 https://nyheritage.contentdm.oclc.org/digital/collection/p16694coll20/id/5747/rec/33, accessed on Jun 18, 2022

27 Report (1963) of the US appointed special commission on weather modification, https://www.nsf.gov/nsb/publications/1965/nsb1265.pdf, accessed on Jun 18, 2022

28 https://patentimages.storage.googleapis.com/cc/e6/38/df0017485b1932/US3613992.pdf, accessed on Jun 19, 2022

29 https://www.sciencedirect.com/topics/earth-and-planetary-sciences/cloud-seeding, accessed on Jun 19, 2022

Under Project Cumulus, undertaken by the British Royal Air Force (during 1949 and 1952), is known to have carried out the cloud seeding experiments over southern England. These experiments were allegedly responsible for the 1952 flood in the Devon village of Lynmouth, resulting in 34 deaths and the devastation of various structures. In the 1950s, the US Forest Service carried out a project called Skyfire. Since, lightning is the major cause of fires in Rocky Mountain forests, the lightning fire problem project was conceptualised as Project Skyfire. The aims of Project Skyfire were broad in character. First, to gain a better understanding of the occurrence, behaviour, and control of lightning fires. The aim was to test the possibility of preventing or reducing the severity of lightning fires through cloud-modification operations. A second major activity of this project was the study of the jet stream[30]. The most significant result of this project was that, there is a possibility 38 per cent reduction in cloud to earth lighting strikes from the clouds seeded by silver iodide generators[31]. However, it appears that not much further progress has happened in this arena.

Interestingly, after the disaster of Project Cirrus the US agencies still continued with idea of controlling the hurricanes. An attempt was made on September 16, 1961 with Hurricane Esther by the National Hurricane Research Project (NHRP) along with the United States Navy aircraft, when eight cylinders of silver iodide were strategically dropped into Esther's eyewall, which led to the weakening of the winds by at least 10 percent. On the very next day, more flights were made without silver iodide falling into the eyewall resulting in no reduction in wind speed. This was considered a success leading to Project Stormfury led by the US Navy and the US Department of Commerce.

Under Project Stormfury from 1962 to 1983, the US Government tried to disturb the inner structure of hurricanes in the Atlantic by flying aircraft into them, and seeding them with silver iodide[32]. The literature available on this subject clearly does not indicate the exact 'intent' behind these experimentations however, in most of the cases there was a direct

30 J. S. Barrows," Lightning Fire Research in the Rocky Mountains", Journal of Forestry, pp 845-846, https://www.fs.fed.us/rm/pubs_exp_for/priest_river/exp_for_priest_river_1954_barrows.pdf, accessed on July 30, 2022

31 Department of the Interior and Related Agencies Appropriations Part 1 & 2, By United States. Congress. Senate. Committee on Appropriations, https://books.google.co.in/books?id=2sagKAYLK9UC, accessed on July 31, 2022

32 "Weather Warfare", http://www.newworldwar.org/weatherwar.htm, accessed on Mar 12, 2018

involvement of the armed forces. Hence, it could be safe to argue that, at least the relevance of this technology to assist the armed forces in their military operations must have been debated. Possibly, weather modification could have been then viewed as a 'force multiplier'.

The US was found experimenting with the weather in post-World War II period with their, both civilian and military agencies. Interestingly, during the year 1952 itself, a department on 'weather modifications' existed in the White House. The mere existence of such an office strongly implies that the technology to modify and control the weather was being experimented on even then. The US Department of Defence started studying the ways to manipulate the weather during the year 1958. By 1960, artificial rainfall became a reality. Obviously, this technology generated interest among the scientific and policy community of major powers. Post-1960, the erstwhile USSR and the US started experimenting in various areas related to environmental engineering like creation of electromagnetic pulses (EMPs) in the atmosphere, studying techniques required for the intentional depletion of the ozone layer, stimulating plasma resonances, carrying out ionospheric heating experiments to manipulate the conductivity of the auroral ionosphere, where weather systems operate and originate[33].

All such experimentation carried out by the defence agencies indicates that they were testing technologies for this new form of warfare. Obviously, in every test, be it a success for failure, there was a learning for the defence agencies.

Weather Warfare: The Past

During early 1950s, a Nobel prize-winning physicist, Irving Langmuir and a pioneer in rain-making (who had worked with Vincent Schaefer of the General Electric Research Laboratory) argued that weather control can be as effective as the nuclear bomb in warfare. He was of the opinion that the effect of 30 milligrams of silver iodide under ideal conditions could equal to that of one nuclear bomb in terms of energy liberated[34]. During

---

33 Ajey Lele, *Weather and Warfare*, Chapter 8, Lancer: New Delhi, 2006, pp. 157-168 and http://www.cuttingedge.org/news/n1206.cfm, accessed on Sep 10, 2018. Also, various details on this operation and other issues discussed in this paper are available in N. Seshagiri, *The Weather Weapon*, National Book Trust India, New Delhi, 1977

34 The December 11, 1950 Charleston Daily Mail (Charleston, WV) ran a short article quoting Dr. Irving Langmuir, https://newspaperarchive.com/charleston-daily-mail-dec-11-1950-p-5/ and Matt Novak, "Weather Control as a Cold War Weapon", Dec 05, 2011, https://www.smithsonianmag.com/history/weather-control-as-a-cold-war-weapon-1777409/, accessed on Jun 19, 2022

the early phase of the Cold War, the US was possibly looking for options of weapons, which possibly could give them the destructive power somewhat similar to the nuclear weapon but without having any 'liabilities' of nuclear weapon.

The US President's Advisory Committee on Weather Control was formed during August 1953. Its specified purpose was to determine the efficacy of weather modification measures and the extent to which the government should involve in such activities. During mid-1950s, there were open discussions in media about methods and options for weather modifications. Both the US and Soviet scientists were found openly discussing idea like using coloured pigments on the polar ice caps to melt them and unleash distressing floods, releasing large quantities of dust into the stratosphere for creating precipitation on demand. These ideas also included concepts like building a dam fitted with thousands of nuclear-powered pumps across the Bering Straits. This dam, proposed by a Russian engineer called Arkady Borisovich Markin was expected to redirect the waters of the Pacific Ocean, which would theoretically raise temperatures in cities like New York and London. Markin's stated purpose was to relieve the severe cold of the northern hemisphere, but the US scientists' apprehensions about such weather control was that it could eventually cause flooding[35].

The first known major use of modifications techniques in warfare in recent times was done by the US in the Vietnam conflict (1955-75). Operation Intermediary Compatriot/Operation Popeye, was the first successful weather warfare operation. During the late sixties/early seventies, the US agencies had launched it during the Vietnam conflict. It was a secret operation which came to light only after two to three years of its launch. The US Senate report of July 26, 1972 on Oceans and International Environment indicated that in 1967 the Joint Chiefs of Staff had asked President Lyndon B. Johnson for authorisation to implement operational phase of weather modification to carry out cloud seeding over Laos, Cambodia area for causing flash floods to reduce trafficability along infiltration routes.

Operation Popeye was long running and large scale operation. It operated from March 20 1967 until July 5 1972. The objective was to extend the monsoon season over North Vietnamese and Viet Cong re-

---

35 Matt Novak, "Weather Control as a Cold War Weapon", Dec 05, 2011, https://www.smithsonianmag.com/history/weather-control-as-a-cold-war-weapon-1777409/, accessed on Jun 19, 2022

supply routes, denying the use of trails and roads. The objective was to increase rainfall sufficiently in carefully selected areas to deny the enemy the use of roads by:

(1) Softening road surfaces

(2) Causing landslides along roadways

(3) Washing out river crossings.

(4) Maintain saturated soil conditions beyond the normal time span.

The initial operation area was over parts of Laos and North Vietnam. It was then extended and redrawn to include parts of South Vietnam and Cambodia. In total, the Pentagon admitted that US C-130 aircraft operating from Udorn Royal Thai Air Force Base flew 2,602 missions and expended 47,409 cloud seeding units. As per Pentagon the project cost was $21.6 million for seven years of programme. Operation Popeye was a possible contributor to the catastrophic 1971 floods in North Vietnam, which covered over 10% of the country. Thailand, from where the flights were operated, was unaware that it was hosting the operation. Only Laos had been informed of the operations, according to the Pentagon. As per the experts, Vietnam region was an ideal target for flash flood weapon and these artificially generated flash floods caused more damage to the area than even three years of sustained US bombing.

The programme was to increase rainfall sufficiently in carefully selected target areas to further soften the road surfaces, cause landslides along roadways, and to wash out river crossings. Such events are normally expected to occur anyway during the height of the rainy season over this particular region. By seeding clouds, it was intended to extend the period of occurrence beyond the normal rainy season and to supplement the natural rainfall as vital to maintain the resultant poor traffic conditions[36].

The Americans had also used the drought weapon over Cuba in 1970 as a backup for Pentagon's secretly prestigious project Nile-Blue. In 1970, the US stepped up the project because Cuban Premier Fidel Castro had staked the honour of his government of success of that year's sugar crop. During this period, Castro set a harvest goal of 10 million tons of sugar. The CIA thought that Castro's failed promise would demoralise his people and make Cuban Communism a failure. The cloud seeding brought erratic

---

36 Deborah Shapley, "Weather Warfare: Pentagon Concedes 7-Year Vietnam", *Science*, New Series, Vol. 184, No. 4141 (Jun. 7, 1974), pp. 1059-1061

weather in Cuba and lead to squeeze rain out of clouds before they reached the island and the sugar harvest fell short. In fact, Castro had also offered to resign, but finally decide to continue in office[37]. Basically, this drought weapon caused premature perception of rain-bearing clouds near Cuba, ruined its sugar crop but, failed to create a major storm in the Cuban political setup then.

The Soviets were also very keen in developing weather weapons. The Soviet weather modification project was referred to as the Woodpecker system.[38] It involved the transmission of extreme low frequency (ELF) waves at about 10 Hertz using Tesla transmitters in Angarsk and Khabarovsk in Siberia, Gomel, Sakhalin Island, Nikolayev in the Ukraine, Riga in Latvia and also a site 60 miles south of Havana in Cuba. Thousands of personnel were involved in this project. They had plans of devising a technology to create disruption in the atmosphere over the US. It was also thought that such technologies could be used to alter the course of the jet stream (a zone of very high wind speeds in upper troposphere) and set up long-term weather blocks. On the other hand, surprisingly there were some indications of a joint collaboration between the Americans and the Soviets in this area. There was an article in the December 16, 1980; edition of the *New York Times* discussing a joint U.S.-Soviet project involving the transmission of ELF waves from Antarctica designed "to interfere with the earth's magnetic field." Noting much is known in this regard.

Weather Warfare: The Present

Two distinct features of the 21st-century world could be identified as a leapfrog in technology development leading to Industry 4.0 and the issues of climate change. Droughts, floods, hurricanes, forest fires, earthquakes etc have almost become a new norm for 21st-century world. In some parts of the world there have been enormous sufferings owing to the vagaries of the weather. This has essentially made the humans (more) aware about the impact and implications of environmental disasters. Now, the question is that, with increased technological capabilities on the one hand and the knowledge of possible damage the environmental disasters could cause, are states getting attracted towards venturing in manipulating the weather artificially to suit their military requirements? Are they keen (and

---

37 http://jfk.hood.edu/Collection/Weisberg%20Subject%20Index%20Files/C%20Disk/
    CIA%20Cuba% 20Policy/Item%2014.pdf, accessed on Aug 15, 2018

38 During the last phase of the Cold War, Soviets built an early warning detection system
    to listen out for NATO and U.S. ballistic missiles. It was a very powerful device that
    would interfere with radio receivers .

confident) to intentionally create mayhem over the enemy land as a form of weather warfare'?

Actually, it is difficult to answer the above question correctly simply because no one really knows. Modifying the weather for the goodness of the individual states has been happening for many decades, but in a very limited form. Acts of hail suppression, artificial rainfall, fog clearance etc., have been happening for many years. However, in spite of the 21st century witnessing many major disasters like tornadoes, typhoons, tsunamis, hurricanes etc., there has been no experimentation undertaken like say changing the direction of the tropical cyclone/hurricane to save coastal cities and also, there is no debate happening to think of modifying the weather in order to save from any possible natural disaster. One main reason for this is, possibly the humans understand their inability to undertake such tasks. Interestingly, at the same time few states have significantly increased their investments in undertaking weather modification experiments. But, there have been few allegations in regards to manipulating the weather intentionally for the state's gain. However, some call such allegations as part of conspiracy theories.

During a conference at Tehran (July 2018), an Iranian general accused Israel of manipulating the weather over the Islamic Republic, claiming that the Jewish state was stealing clouds and snow and contributing to climate change. According to him, the Iranian scientific centres have confirmed a foreign role in the drought conditions across the country. He quoted a study based on a dataset of four years (approximately during 2013/14 to 2017/18 period) analysing the climate of high altitudes from Afghanistan to the Mediterranean Sea. As per this study, all heights above 7,200 feet have snow - except in Iran. He claimed the reason behind it, was the weather modification capabilities of Israel[39]. The political leadership of Iran in yesteryears like Ahmadinejad and Mousavi had made some claims few years back indicating that the European countries were using "special equipment" to ensure the rainwater falling in their region leads to leaving nothing for Iran. Also, for the last few years, the Iranian political leadership is found blaming intentional tampering with weather systems by their opponents for continuous drought like condition in the last few years. However, in general no scientific organisation including the meteorological services from Iran, have been found in agreement with these theories.

39 Travis Fedschun, "Iran general blames Israel for 'cloud theft', then is rebuked by Islamic Republic scientist", July 3, 2018, http://www.foxnews.com/world/2018/07/03/iran-general-blames-israel-for-cloud-theft-is-behind-climate-change.html, accessed on Aug 23, 2018

After the end of Vietnam War and Operation Popeye, there has been no evidence to suggest that the US has indulged in any activity, which has led to the modification of the weather over the regions of their advisories during any of the wars/military campaigns they have fought post 1970. However, there has been much debate on various experiments undertaken by some of the agencies of the US, since these attempts have a direct correlation with developing technologies for modifying the weather. Literature is full of debates and discussions, particularly with regard to one project called The HAARP Programme. Also, many in the world have taken note of the August 1996 report *Weather as a Force Multiplier: Owning the Weather in 2025.*

The US military has developed advanced abilities that allow it selectively alter the weather patterns. The technology, which is being perfected under the High-frequency Active Auroral Research Program (HAARP), is an appendage of the Strategic Défense Initiative – 'Star Wars'. This idea was initiated by then President Ronald Reagan (SDI, 1983); however, initially focus was more on nuclear aspects and developing technologies essentially involving missile defence. The idea of HAARP came into being around 1992. From a military perspective, HAARP is a weapon of mass destruction, operating from the outer atmosphere and capable of disrupting (manipulating) agricultural and ecological systems around the world.

HAARP, located in Gokona, Alaska, is an array of high-powered antennas that transmit, through high-frequency radio waves, massive amounts of energy into the ionosphere (the upper layer of the atmosphere). This construction was funded by the US Air Force, the US Navy and the Défense Advanced Research Projects Agency (DARPA). Operated jointly by the Air Force Research Laboratory and the Office of Naval Research, HAARP constitutes a system of powerful antennas capable of creating 'controlled local modifications of the ionosphere. According to its official website, www.haarp.alaska.edu, HAARP will be used 'to induce a small, localised change in ionospheric temperature so physical reactions can be studied by other instruments located either at or close to the HAARP site'.

The entire procedure of developing of the idea of HAARP is known to have gone through various processes and there has been the involvement of agencies like the US private sector giant, Raytheon Corporation, the British Aerospace Systems (BAES), Advanced Power Technologies, Inc. (APTI), a subsidiary of Atlantic Richfield Corporation (ARCO). Subsequently, along with the HAARP patents, APTI was sold to E-Systems Inc, in 1994.

Technically, HAARP is a research programme undertaken by the US Air Force. However, various documents (essentially military) directly or indirectly indicate that its main objective is to 'induce ionospheric modifications' with a view to altering weather patterns and disrupting communications and radar. Russian agencies like Duma also claim that the HAARP programme is meant for breaking radio communication lines and equipment installed on spaceships and rockets, provoke serious accidents in electricity networks and in oil and gas pipelines, and could even lead to the negative impact on the mental health of entire regions[40]. Unfortunately, HAARP has been a target of various conspiracy theories. Officially, the US administration had announced that the HAARP programme would be permanently ended by the end of 2014. At present, no authentic information is available in regards to this project.

In order to modify the characteristics of the ionosphere, China and Russia are known to have jointly conducted a series of experiments from a Russian installation called the Sura Ionospheric Heating Facility close to Vasilsursk, east of Moscow. Here the scientists emitted high-frequency radio waves to manipulate the ionosphere, while the China Seismo-Electromagnetic Satellite (CSES) measured the effects on plasma disturbance from orbit. Such exterminations do have potential military applications. The Sura facility is said to have been built in repose to the project HAARP. Some information in regards to the experiments conducted here indicate that their experimentation on ionosphere disturbances affected an area of around 126,000 sq km. In another experiment, ionised gas in the atmosphere increased in heat by 100 degrees Celsius[41].

During 1996, the USAF have outlined their vision for the year 2025[42]. It was visualised then the US aerospace forces can "own the weather" by exploiting emerging technologies and focusing advancement into those technologies to war-fighting applications. The view was that such a capability would offer the warfighter the tools to shape the battle space in ways never before possible. This would provide opportunities to impact

---

40 There are numerous sources are available giving the details of the concept of HAARP. For this work the information has been mainly taken from Michel Chossudovsky, "Weather warfare", *Ecologist*, December 2007, pp.14-15

41 Peter Dockrill, "China and Russia have Run Controversial Experiments that Modified Earth's Atmosphere", 19 Dec 2018, https://www.sciencealert.com/china-and-russia-conducted-controversial-experiments-that-modified-earth-s-atmosphere, accessed on Jan 23, 2022

42 https://archive.org/stream/WeatherAsAForceMultiplier/WeatherAsAForceMultiplier_djvu.txt

operations across the full spectrum of conflict. More than two decades back this vision had outlined a strategy for the use of a future weather-modification system to achieve military objectives rather than to provide a detailed technical road map. The need for technology advancements in five major areas was identified for achieving the stated objectives. These technologies include (1) advanced non-linear modelling techniques (2) computational capability (3) information gathering and transmission (4) a global sensor array and (5) weather intervention techniques. It was then viewed that some interesting wok has already happened in the field of weather modification and there are some intervention tools already available. Hence, the anticipated technology development process is not very difficult to achieve.

The US Air Force document, *AF 2025 Final Report* categorically mentions that various weather manipulation techniques offer the war fighter a wide range of possible options to defeat or coerce an adversary's capabilities. It was viewed that the weather modification would become a part of domestic and international security and states would need to go solo for developing weather weapons. Such weapons could have offensive and defensive applications and even be used for deterrence purposes. The integrated set of military technologies are expected to prove ability to generate precipitation, fog and storms on earth or to modify space weather and the production of artificial weather. At present, nothing much is known about this proposal in open sources. There are various studies underway in the field of meteorology, but no significant project-teams are known to be working on critical aspects of weather modification or development of weather weapons, which could assist in weather warfare.

Weather Warfare: The Future

As per the present trends in warfare, the nature of infrastructural investments found being made by the states, the direction of technology development (both civilian and military) and more importantly, the progress made in the field of science of weather, it is possible to engage in weather warfare, if a state desires. The issue is about the capability versus the intent. At least officially, no state has expressed any intention to follow the weather warfare route. Presently, there are no indications that states are preparing and proposing to engage each other in weather warfare. At the same time, there is a need to take note of activities happening in the field of weather modifications. Particularly, the investments made by China and the results (success) they are getting are worth a debate.

At present, the climate change debate has major global attention and serious efforts are being made to reduce the possible impact of climate change. Many states in the world are regularly facing the wrath from adverse weather events like droughts, floods, hurricanes and tornadoes. Obviously, time could come when the states would feel that 'why they should always succumb to vagaries of nature, when they could possibly use technology to stop this'. All this could boost the research and experimentation in the fields like geo-engineering and weather/space weather modifications. This would lead to a very proactive development of weather control/manipulation technology, which could emerge as dual-use technology. Any such possible developments need to be monitored possibly at the level of the United Nations, for envisaging the future of weather warfare.

Chapter 6

Weather Modification Efforts: China and other States

There are various states having operational programmes to modify the weather. Normally, these programmes include activities undertaken for fog dispersal, enhancement of rain and suppression of hail. Such programmes are conducted mostly at provinces and at the level of municipalities, with central agencies in the loop. For all these years, much research has happened in the arena of weather modification. Notwithstanding such research, still deep distrust exists, both about the exactness of the science and intentions of few states in regards to their significant investments to this field. This chapter presents the details about the investments made by some states to the field of weather modification.

China

It is bit difficult to exactly trace the history of weather modification in China. There are some references indicating that China is possibly experimenting on weather modification techniques since 1950s[1]. In recent times, it is known that the Beijing's Weather Modification Office was opened in 1973. The first project it undertook was to design and test methods for minimising the damage from hailstorms. Also, on an experimental basis the scientists from this office started checking the utility of using liquid nitrogen to disperse the woolly fogs that tend to settle on Beijing's Capital Airport each winter. Almost two decades later since 1990, the office started focusing their efforts on increasing precipitation in dry metropolitan Beijing. It also had weather radars, special aircrafts and a 37-mm anti-aircraft guns positioned around the city to shoot silver iodide

---

1   Elise Misao Hunchuck, Marco Ferrari & Jingru (Cyan) Cheng, "Prologue to the Sky River", https://www.averyreview.com/issues/53/prologue-to-the-sky-river, accessed on Jun 21, 2022

into clouds expected to shower damaging hail on the city and nearby fields. Also, since using aircrafts is too costly, hence the engineers were known to rely on hydrogen balloons rigged with firecrackers on long fuses to carry the pellets of liquid nitrogen and silver iodide into the clouds and disperse them[2].

China is known to have created 'auspicious snow' (RUI XUE) to welcome the year 1997 (snowfall was managed on night of December 31 1996/January 1 1997). In Chinese tradition, the first snow of the new year is deemed a lucky event. The meteorologists in the Beijing office had bombarded liquid nitrogen and silver iodide into clouds drifting over the city. With this they were ensuring to wheedle every last drop of moisture out of the air to ensure that Beijing would have a thicker blanket of snow[3].

The 1997-2007 decade witnessed some rapid and significant advances in the field of weather modification. During this period, more advanced cloud models with bin microphysics[4] and mesoscale models with glaciogenic and hygroscopic cloud seeding processes developed and studied towards understanding of variations of cloud microphysics, dynamics and precipitation processes induced by cloud seeding. Also, some work had happened on identifying new approaches in hail formation mechanisms and possible applications in hail suppression operations. Weather scientists worked towards studying sizes of aerosol, various aspects of precipitating systems and multiscale cloud merging processes. This period also witnessed development and testing of more advanced cloud-seeding tools such as mobile ground based AgI-rocket launching systems and aircraft-based AgI-flares[5]. All this possibly was done towards ensuring that China would

2   "Need More Snow? Beijing Weather Wizards Deliver", Jan 16, 1997, https://www. deseret.com/1997/1/16/19289675/need-more-snow-beijing-weather-wizards-deliver, accessed on Jun 20, 2022

3   "Need More Snow? Beijing Weather Wizards Deliver", Jan 16, 1997, https://www. deseret.com/1997/1/16/19289675/need-more-snow-beijing-weather-wizards-deliver, accessed on Jun 20, 2022

4   Two methods used to represent clouds and precipitation in numerical weather and climate models: bulk and bin microphysics schemes. Bin microphysics schemes are useful to investigate the evolution of size distributions of particles in clouds, bulk microphysics schemes are used in operational weather forecasting. For more on this please refer Hyunho Lee and Jong-Jin Baik, "A Comparative Study of Bin and Bulk Cloud Microphysics Schemes in Simulating a Heavy Precipitation Case", https://www. mdpi.com, accessed on July 31, 2022

5   GUO Xueliang and ZHENG Guoguang, "Advances in Weather Modification from 1997 to 2007 in China", Advances In Atmospheric Sciences, Vol. 26, No. 2, 2009, 240–252

have its options open in regards to weather modification if it is necessitated before the conduct of any major event.

An important facet of China's successful organisation of the 2008 Olympics and smooth conduct of the 60th year celebration during the year 2009 was all about successful management of weather control and modification processes. The rain was predicted during the opening ceremony of the 2008 Olympic Games. Hence, China cleared the skies for the Beijing Olympics by forcing the rain to come early. Though here, weather control was exercised to ensure the smooth conduct of a major event, if employed on a larger scale such 'mastery over weather' would have strategic implications. Now for many years China is found to be suitably manipulating the weather during the conduct of various major events of geopolitical importance in their country. Definitely, this causes concerns for many because there exists a danger of such techniques being used for mischief.

The stories of the 2008 Olympics and 60th year celebrations and weather modification are very fascinating.

For Olympics, the Beijing's Weather Modification Office was tracking the region's weather via satellites, planes, radar, and an IBM p575 supercomputer purchased from Big Blue during 2007. This system was known to execute 9.8 trillion floating point operations per second. Broadly, the area under consideration was of 44,000 square km (17,000 square miles), accurate enough to generate hourly forecasts for each kilometre. Two aircrafts and an array of twenty-one artillery and rocket-launch sites around Beijing were put in service to shoot and spray silver iodide and dry ice into incoming clouds. The idea was to flush the rain out before it makes an approach to reach the stadium. Interestingly, the rain-heavy clouds which were already close to the Olympic stadium (Bird's Nest) were seeded with chemicals to shrink droplets so that rain won't fall until those clouds have passed over. As per Mr Zhang Qian, the head of Beijing's Weather Modification Office, they had used the coolant made from liquid nitrogen to increase the number of droplets while decreasing their average size. As a result, the probability of smaller droplets falling was reduced with a purpose to reduce the precipitation[6].

---

6   Mark Williams Pontin, "Weather Engineering in China", March 25, 2008, https://www. technologyreview.com/s/409794/weather-engineering-in-china/, accessed on Aug 2, 2018

On August 8, 2008, the day of the Olympics opening ceremony, it was reported that the Chinese Weather Modification office had fired a total of 1,104 rain dispersal rockets. These rockets were fired to stop rain clouds approaching the Olympics arena. This operation lasted for eight hours and rockets were launched from 21 different sites. It is probably because of such an 'attack', these rain-bearing clouds precipitated at those locations where they were hovering at the time the rockets were fired at them. Excessive rainfall was in fact witnessed in these areas, with some locales measuring more than 100 millimetres. August is the rainy season in Beijing and the meteorological observatory had predicted rainy weather for the Olympics opening ceremony. Actual humidity around the stadium was touching 90 per cent in a further indication that rains were likely to come.

China had realised that the threat from weather was also there during the 60th year celebrations parade (October 1 2009). A major attraction of the National Day Parade was the aircraft flypast scheduled at 1100 AM. Air Force meteorologists found in the morning hours that clouds were approaching Tiananmen area from the south-west. Between 0730h and 0900h, they launched four 'attacks' on the bank of clouds. To keep skies, clear of cloud and rain, 432 rockets were fired at these clouds. Eyewitnesses stated that a few hours before the start of the parade the weather was extremely gloomy and visibility was poor due to pollution. There were thick clusters of cloud and some mist, and rain appeared imminent. But subsequently, clear weather prevailed and people felt that the clouds had been held back from the square. Probably, the firing of rockets at the clouds made them evaporate or alternately precipitate before reaching the parade ground. Thus, these weather modification experiments allowed the conduct of the parade under clear weather conditions.

Chinese agencies had made a great deal of preparations to thwart any adverse weather approaching the parade ground. They had 48 specialised vehicles ready to throw streams of air to chase away any approaching fog. Efforts were also made to ensure that visibility would remain fine and the surroundings would remain devoid of any mist or haze. Eighteen aircraft were kept ready to sprinkle adequate quantities of dry ice, salt and silver iodide over cloud tops to evaporate them before they start moving in the direction of the parade area.

The success achieved by Chinese meteorologists during the Olympics and during the 60th National Day Parade underlines the importance the Chinese state is paying to artificial weather manipulation. Chinese sources indicate that more than 37,000 people were employed then in weather modification activities nationwide. China has full-fledged weather modification units located in more than 30 provinces and municipalities. Some 30 aircraft have been modified to undertake various weather modification experiments. Approximately 7,000 anti-aircraft guns and 5,000 special rocket launchers are at the service of Chinese meteorologists. In order to have the world's largest artificial weather modification programme, China invests US $63 million a year[7]. It is important to note that all these figures are of 2008 origin and obviously, by this time China has consolidated their infrastructure further. Now for long various cities are facing problems with pollution and visibility during some months in the year. However, just before the commencement of any major international event China is known to ensure that visibility and sky condition increases dramatically. For this China takes various precautions like shutting the polluting industries for few days before the start any submit, controlling vehicular pollution by restricting their movement and artificially 'cleaning' the atmosphere. Various activities related to experimenting with the weather are commonly known and Chinese citizens talk openly about it[8].

All, such investments could allow China to maintain weather of its own choice to a certain extent. Despite the limitations of the science of cloud seeding in creating artificial rainfall or in stopping rainfall, it appears that the Chinese are trying their best to master this art. Further success in this field will have significant relevance to Chinese agriculture. Moreover, weather modification has a military side to it as well.

China's weather modification actions during the October 1, 2009 National Day Parade or earlier during the Olympics or during various other parades held till date[9] did not cause any damage or injury to other states,

---

7   http://www.thelivingmoon.com/45jack_files/03files/Chinese_Weather_Modification. html, accessed on Sep 22, 2018

8   During his visit the China, the author has discussed this issue at informal level with few experts and has also found even the tour guide mentioning proudly about these capabilities while counting China's achievements. The author happened to be in Beijing during the Africa Summit held during September 3-4, 2018. The weather during this period was blue sky. Interestingly, the overall weather conditions in the region were not found supportive for the presence of blue skies in Beijing. A cursory look at the weather conditions in the cities which are between the range of 100 to 200 km from Beijing (cities like Tianjin and Shijiazhuang) indicated that the actual weather was cloudy. People in Beijing call such (modified) weather as 'Summit Blue'.

9   ED Browne, "Cloud Seeding Explained As China Reportedly Controlled Weather Before Political Parade", Dec 07, 2021, https://www.newsweek.com/cloud-seeding-explained-china-control-weather-before-political-parade-centenary-1656823, accessed on Jun 20, 2022

nor were there any militaristic intentions behind them. However, all this indicates that China had slowly started to master this technology and also developed a good infrastructure for the conduct of weather modification activities.

One of the major weather modification activities organised by China, was for the conduct of the 2022 Winter Olympics, which were held at Beijing between 02 and 20 February 2022. Beijing has very limited winter snowfall and there was much dependence on artificial snow for the conduct of these games. Various sources indicate that possibly, the volume of artificial snow used at these games could have been anything between 95 per cent to 99 per cent. However, this is not first of the states depending on artificial snow for the conduct of games. It was first used at the New York 1980 Winter Olympics and since then it has been found almost regularly getting used in these games. Possibly, owing to global warming, the old pattern of snow falling in showing irregular changes. Hence, it is becoming difficult to do much of advance planning (the activities start more than four years before the start of actually games) from weather angle for the organisation of such games. Particularly, almost all across the world mountain weather forecasting during winter season is becoming very tricky. It has been reported that about 80% of the snow used in Sochi, Russia in 2014 was artificial and perhaps it was as high as 98 per cent for the Pyeongchang Games in South Korea in 2018.

Interestingly, as per the International Olympic Committee (IOC), artificial snow is better suited for such games and offers consistent and predictable slope conditions. It also helps to maintain a consistent quality throughout competitions and offers similar conditions for all participants. Modern-day snow machines have an on-board computer system for calculating the most suitable mix of water to produce snow with the similar conditions[10]. The global climate is responsible for an overall increase in temperatures. At present, the warmer temperatures are causing shorter winters and hence, the reduction in participation or unequal spread of precipitation. All this is leading in the reduction of snow presence on ground/mountains. Obviously, this is impacting winter sports significantly.

Human-made snow is much resource-intensive and demands massive amounts of energy and water to produce. If the atmosphere is warmer, then obviously much efforts (and resources) are required to produce and maintain the snow. China had employed Italy-based TechnoAlpin

10 Wanyuan Song, "Beijing Olympics: What's wrong with natural snow?", Feb 18, 2022, https://www.bbc.com/news/60406195, accessed on Jun 25, 2022

to manufacture the snow required to cover the four outdoor event spaces around Beijing. For them the real challenge was that some of the Beijing sites were having temperatures not cold enough to freeze water (possibly, they were around 3 deg Celsius). As per the long-term climatic averages for Beijing, nearly all February days for the past 30 years have been above freezing. With all this climate data at the backdrop, the TechnoAlpin had actually began their work during 2018 itself. The initial phase involved putting logistics in place and it began by shipping a full arsenal of snow guns, fan-driven snow generators and cooling towers to Beijing. These machines also included a new piece of technology meant for the training center for China's athletes: the SnowFactory. For these games around 1.2 million cubic meters of snow was needed to cover roughly 800,000 square meters of competition area. The IOC estimates that around 49 million gallons of water (a day's worth of drinking water for nearly 100 million people) could have been consumed to produce the snow[11].

It is important to note that the artificial snow making also happens for commercial reasons too, like extending ski seasons. As per some estimates[12], the winter sports generate $887 billion in economic revenue and support 7.6 million jobs in the United States alone. These sporting events are important because they could be stressbusters for many. They provide many people with the mental and physical health benefits. The routine training for winter sports athletes limits the places for training and conducting competitions.

Beijing is the first (and only) city that has held both the summer and the winter Olympic Games. The games were held across three zones: Beijing, Yanqing, and Zhangjiakou. Was Beijing most ideally suited for the conduct of winter games? Probably, not. Zhangjiakoua's mountain region, located about 110 miles northwest of Beijing, had hosted one of three outdoor venues for this Olympics. This region doesn't receive much precipitation during the winter months. Obviously, huge efforts were required to be put in for the conduct of the games. The IOC was heavily criticised by athletes and spectators for its decision to host the Winter Olympics in Beijing and adjoining areas, which already receive little precipitation.

---

11 Derek Van Dam, "All the Beijing snow is human-made - a resource-intensive, 'dangerous' trend as planet warms", Feb 5, 2022, https://edition.cnn.com/2022/02/04/weather/artificial-snow-beijing-olympics-climate/index.html, accessed on Jun 25, 2022.

12 Andrew Moore, "Beijing Winter Olympics a Cautionary Climate Tale, Expert Says", February 10, 2022, https://cnr.ncsu.edu/news/2022/02/beijing-winter-olympics-a-cautionary-climate-tale-expert-says/, accessed on Jun 20, 2022

China had various challenges for the conduct of these games from weather perspective. Before TechnoAlpin could install pumps and build more than 40 miles of pipe (costing around US$60 million), Chinese officials were required to plan for delivering required (around one million cubic meters) water to the mountains. For this purpose, various pumping stations were built to carry water from reservoirs miles away[13].

Immediately, one month after the Winter Olympics, Beijing (and the neighbouring Hebei province) also hosted the winter Paralympic Games from 4 to March 13, 2022. It needs to be noted that the creation of artificial snow was an important part of this entire exercise. Technically, it was not about 'modifying' any existing weather system, but was all about artificially creating snow for the purposes of making a pitch/platform/ground for the conduct of sporting events. But the organisers were fully aware that, for making (and sustaining) artificial snow and also for scheduling of various outdoor events, there would be a requirement of monitoring the overall weather conductions more closely. Beyond simple weather observations they also would be required to undertake specific forecasting activities. They were aware that changes in temperature, humidity, visibility and wind conditions could have an impact on event scheduling, athletic performance and course conditions. Hence, to conduct activities like snow-making and snow-storage processes and various other activities they needed accurate high-resolution short-term forecasting and nowcasting facilities. Nowcasting of elements like low-level and surface temperature, humidity and wind was required on regular basis.

Hence, for correctly and timely estimating the behaviour of weather systems and elements over plains and complex mountain areas, for the 2022 Winter Games, a five-part research and development project got undertaken[14]. It has been funded by the National Key Research and Development Programme of China. The focus of the project was to address the forecast challenges and the specialised needs of the various outdoor

---

13 Matthew Futterman and Raymond Zhong, "Beijing Wanted the Winter Olympics. All It Needed Was Snow", Feb 06, 2022, https://www.nytimes.com/2022/02/05/sports/olympics/snow-winter-olympics.html, accessed on Jun 20, 2022

14 All the details about this project explained in subsequent paras please refer Mingxuan Chen et al, "Enhanced Weather Research and Forecasting in Support of the Beijing 2022 Winter Olympic and Paralympic Games", https://public.wmo.int/en/resources/bulletin/enhanced-weather-research-and-forecasting-support-of-beijing-2022-winter-olympic, accessed on Jun 20, 2022 and "China mobilizes meteorological services for Winter Olympics", Feb 04, 2022, https://public.wmo.int/en/media/news/china-mobilizes-meteorological-services-winter-olympics, accessed on Jun 22, 2022

events. The project partners were involving numerous organisations within the China Meteorological Administration (CMA). The project includes five programmes:

> ➤ Enhanced meteorological observations

> ➤ Very short-term forecasting and nowcasting

> ➤ Short- and medium-range prediction

> ➤ Seamless forecasting and early risk warning for key points and events

> ➤ Intelligent meteorological support services

The project added various new state-of-art equipment mainly for the purposes of collecting observations and for understanding the patters. The equipment included automated weather stations (AWSs), HOBO weather stations, X-band dual-polarization Doppler radars, cloud radars, microwave radiometers, microwave wind profilers, Doppler wind lidars, sodars, radio-soundings, satellites, twin-engine research aircraft, etc. In addition, two new S-band Doppler weather radars were also deployed in the mountain area. China's Fengyun satellite too was helping with the meteorological services. Also, the meteorologists are known to have developed high-resolution reanalyses and conceptual models for small-scale weather attributes in the two mountain areas based on multi-sensor observations, high-resolution data assimilation/integration and special numerical simulations (for example, large-eddy simulations and computational fluid dynamics modelling under different winter synoptic conditions).

The purpose behind very short-term forecasting and nowcasting programme was to develop a high-resolution forecast technique for the 0–24-hour period. These will be based on rapid refresh cycling, local data assimilation, improvement of key physics in high-resolution models, integration and blending of multi-source data (observations and forecasts), and downscaling and bias correction of high-resolution numerical weather prediction (NWP) over complex terrain. All this indicates that, China is making very systemic investments towards ensuring that weather does not become an impediment in the conduct of major events in their country and their efforts showcase their capabilities, both for the domestic audience and to the rest of the world in the field of meteorology in general and weather modification in particular.

As it is known that, when various weather modification techniques are used for military gains, then they fall into the category of 'Weather Weapons'. Weather modification techniques could be used for changing the direction of cyclonic storms, create snow storms, flash floods and even forest fires in enemy territory. There are reports that countries like the United States are conducting experiments to control the characteristics of the ionosphere which could allow them to control enemy communications. However, there are significant technological limitations in employing such 'weapons' with precision[15]. At present, there is no direct connect visible in respect of China's investments in weather modification technologies from the point of developing weather weapons. However, some of the ambitious experiments undertaken by China indicate that China is experimenting much in weather modification and geoengineering arenas and the knowledge received and expertise developed would be required to tweak a bit if they decide to develop any weather weapons in the future. Particularly, their neighbours are required to be more cautious as some of the experiments are happening close to their borders and could have an adverse impact on their weather conditions. One such experiment is 'Tianhe' or 'Sky River'.

China is conducting one of the largest and most ambitious weather engineering projects to date over the Tibetan Plateau or the Qinghai-Tibet Plateau region which is often called the water tower of the world and contains the world's third-largest store of ice. This region is the source of most of Asia's significant rivers like the Indus, Ganges, Brahmaputra, Salween, Mekong, Yangtze, and Yellow Rivers. Chinese fear about the possible scarcity of water in future due to climate change and the depletion of glacial reserves[16]. Hence, they are working on water precipitation enhancement technologies.

At present, China is working towards overcoming possible water shortages in future and for that purpose they have conceptualised project Sky River which would be the world's largest weather-control machine[17],

---

15 The entire information above for this case study is based on Ajey Lele, "China's Experiments with Weather Modification: A Cause for Concern", Oct 12, 2009, https://idsa.in/idsastrategiccomments/ChinasExperimentswithWeatherModification_ALele_121009, accessed on Feb 14, 2018

16 Elise Misao Hunchuck, Marco Ferrari & Jingru (Cyan) Cheng, "Prologue to the Sky River", https://www.averyreview.com/issues/53/prologue-to-the-sky-river, accessed on Jun 21, 2022

17 The discussion on this project is based on Trevor Nace "China Is Launching Weather-Control Machines Across An Area The Size Of Alaska", May 10, 2018, https://www.

with the ability to modify the weather in an area similar to the size of Alaska (1.723 million km²). China's craze for doing things on a massive scale is well known (for example, belt and road invite, BRI at one end of spectrum to building of huge airports on the other end) and this is yet another example of the Chinese government working on an unprecedented scale, to undertake weather modification. China's state-owned Aerospace Science and Technology Corporation is executing a plan to send thousands of rain-inducing machines across the Tibetan Plateau to increase rainfall along the region.

This project involves tens of thousands of fuel-burning chambers installed across the Tibetan mountains, with a view to boosting rainfall in the region by up to 10 billion cubic metres annually (the technology was initially developed as part of the Chinese military's weather modification programme). All this is under the plan, which is an extension of a project called Tianhe or 'Sky River' developed by researchers in 2016 at China's Tsinghua University. The initial experimentation in this regard has shown promising results.

The system involves an enormous network of fuel-burning chambers installed high up on the Tibetan mountains. Tens of thousands of chambers will be built at selected locations across the Tibetan plateau to produce rainfall. The purpose is to bring extra rain to a massive area spanning some 1.6 million square kilometres (almost 620,000 square miles). The process involves the chambers burning solid fuel to produce silver iodide, a cloud-seeding agent with a crystalline structure much like ice. As per the design, the chambers stand on steep mountain ridges facing the moist monsoon from South Asia. When winds hit the mountain, they produce an upward draft and sweeps the particles into the clouds to induce rain and snow. This entire effort is expected to increase China's drinking water availability by 7 per cent.

These fuel-burning chambers are also known as cloud-seeding stoves and as per one report by 2018 more than five hundred stoves have been

forbes.com/sites/trevornace/2018/05/10/china-is-launching-a-massive-weather-control-machine-the-size-of-alaska/#48fc8bb63155, accessed on Jun 7, 2018 and Peter Dockrill, "China's 'Sky River' Will Be The Biggest Artificial Rain Experiment Ever", Apr 28, 2018, https://www.sciencealert.com/how-china-s-sky-river-will-be-the-biggest-artificial-rain-experiment-ever-cloud-seeding, accessed on May 2, 2018 and Stephen Chen, "China needs more water. So it's building a rain-making network three times the size of Spain", March 27, 2018, https://www.scmp.com/news/china/society/article/2138866/china-needs-more-water-so-its-building-rain-making-network-three, accessed on Apr 2, 2018

installed for experimental use on the alpine slopes of the Qinghai-Tibet Plateau for a combined area of 110,000 sq km divided into three macro-regions: Sanjiangyuan National Nature Reserve, Qilian Mountains, and the Kunlun Mountains. However, actual locations of the test sites within these three regions are not disclosed. This large network of ground equipment is assisted by a constellation of low Earth orbit satellites, for monitoring and forecasting system that will be able to quantify for cloud seeding. the volume and duration of atmospheric water transport—that activate the stoves when favourable meteorological conditions are met. The LEO satellite platform aims to enhance the sensing capabilities of the current and future Fengyun-4 family of geostationary Chinese meteorological satellites. Also, there are plans to have new satellite systems for the purpose of undertaking the ecological monitoring of the region[18].

This project has raised major global concerns globally, in regards to China's actual intentions and thus China needs to clear suspicions that have been aroused by its weather modification actions.

All in all, China proposes to massively expand its weather-modification programme. They are keen to cover half the country in artificial rain and snow by 2025. The government has announced that they are planning to expand its weather-control project, which creates artificial rain and snow, by fivefold. The Chines State Council has announced that the project aims to cover 2.1 million square miles (about 56% of China's entire surface area) to meet the 2025 deadline. The State Council envisages that by 2035, project will be at a worldwide advanced level and would help lessen disasters like drought and hail and facilitate emergency responses to forest or grassland fires[19].

Weather Modification: Global Footprint

Today, apart from China some countries like Russia and the US are conducting research on weather modification too. There are reports stating that Russian government had spent about US$1.3 million to prevent rain on May 1, 2016, a public holiday, known locally as International Labour

---

18 Elise Misao Hunchuck, Marco Ferrari & Jingru (Cyan) Cheng, "Prologue to the Sky River", https://www.averyreview.com/issues/53/prologue-to-the-sky-river, accessed on Jun 21, 2022

19 Bill Bostock, "China is massively expanding its weather-modification program, saying it will be able to cover half the country in artificial rain and snow by 2025", Dec 4, 2020, https://www.businessinsider.in/science/news/china-is-massively-expanding-its-weather-modification-program-saying-it-will-be-able-to-cover-half-the-country-in-artificial-rain-and-snow-by-2025/articleshow/79568008.cms, accessed on Jun 20, 2022

Day. A single contractor was hired by the Russian government and he employed cloud seeding technique by launching various chemicals into clouds to cause precipitation earlier than expected. The basic idea behind all these experiments is to force the rain out in certain places at certain times, leaving other areas dry[20].

A Russian firm called the Climate Global Control Trading Company was contracted by the Pakistani government to artificially create rain over the drought-hit parts of Baluchistan. This company has a good track record and has already assisted states like UAE and Iran. Interestingly, in the case of Pakistan the conventional technique of cloud seeding of spreading silver iodide, dry ice, or calcium chloride in the atmosphere was not followed. The technique used in Pakistan is known as electromagnetic distribution/ electromagnetic shifting. In this case, small amounts of electromagnetic energy are used to adjust the path of clouds, causing them to travel over areas where rain is most needed[21].

Russia is also known to have a very advanced programme for weather modification. In 1986, Russian scientists had deployed cloud-seeding measures to prevent radioactive rain from Chernobyl from reaching Moscow, and in 2000 they cleared clouds before an anniversary ceremony commemorating the end of World War II. It was China's then president, Jiang Zemin, who had witnessed the results first-hand in 2000 and decided to emulate the same idea back home[22].

The members of a 1964 US delegation to the Soviet Union estimated that their programme was two or three times as large as that of the US. In addition to an extensive hail suppression effort, the Russians are reported to be active in the areas of artificially induced precipitation and airport fog dissipation[23].

---

20 David Nield, "Russia Spent Millions on 'Cloud Seeding' Tech to Prevent Rain on Its Public Holiday", May 4, 2016, https://www.sciencealert.com/russia-spends-millions-on-weather-tech-to-try-and-stop-it-raining-on-bank-holiday, accessed on Aug 23, 2018

21 Ahmad Ahsan, "The business of rainmaking", Jun26, 2018, https://www.thenews.com.pk/print/333672-the-business-of-rainmaking, accessed on July 5, 2018

22 Mark Williams Pontin, "Weather Engineering in China", March 25, 2008, https://www.technologyreview.com/s/409794/weather-engineering-in-china/, accessed on Aug 2, 2018

23 James N. Corbridge, Jr. and Raphael J. Mosesi, "Weather Modification: Law And Administration", Natural Resources Journal, Vol 8, No 2, Apr 1968, p. 212

Forest fires are not new to Russia. The year 2020 was a very difficult year. It was a period of an unusually hot winter and spring, which led to extreme temperatures in remote Siberian towns. By June 17, Verkhoyansk, a town located in the Arctic region of Siberia, recorded a reading of more than 38° Celsius, the highest temperature ever documented north of the Arctic Circle. As per some estimates, the fires had burnt more than 20.9 million hectares of land in Russia, and 10.9 million hectares of forest, since the start of 2020. Russian agencies had reported that firefighters had used cloud seeding techniques for rain creation so as to bring down rain over wildfires raging in Siberia. Planes were used to fire chemicals into the clouds above fires in northern, remote parts of the Krasnoyarsk and Irkutsk regions of Siberia[24].

Interestingly, weather modification happening in the US, presently could be placed in an 'average' category. Certain committees appointed by the US government were of the view that, "weather modification should be viewed as a fundamental and legitimate element of atmospheric and environmental science. Owing to the growing demand for fresh water, the increasing levels of damage and loss of life resulting from severe weather, the undertaking of operational activities without the guidance of a careful scientific foundation, and the reality of inadvertent atmospheric changes, the scientific community now has the opportunity, challenge, and responsibility to assess the potential efficacy and value of intentional weather modification technologies"[25]. In the US, the National Oceanic and Atmospheric Administration (NOAA) keeps records of weather modification projects. NOAA on its own does not perform research on weather modification. There have been various serious attempts during the year 2005 to establish a Weather Modification Operations and Research Board, and have a national weather modification policy. However, neither were made into law.

The US is known to be working on cloud seeding experiments to increase precipitation in areas experiencing drought and to reduce the size of hailstones that form in thunderstorms. As per a WMO report (2014)

---

24 Elizabeth Claire Alberts, "Photos show scale of massive fires tearing through Siberian forests", July 23, 2020, https://news.mongabay.com/2020/07/photos-show-scale-of-massive-fires-tearing-through-siberian-forests/ and "Russia seeds clouds in Siberia to douse raging wildfires", Jul 10, 2020, https://www.reuters.com/article/us-russia-fires-siberia-idUSKBN24B1JT, accessed on Jun 26, 2022

25 http://www.nationalacademies.org/OCGA/109Session1/testimonies/OCGA_151007, accessed on May, 12, 2018

there are 39 active weather modifications (cloud seeding) experiments happening in the US.

On some occasions, the US agencies have been accused of intentionally tampering with weather in Russia. The year 2019 was the warmest winter ever experienced by Russia in 133 years with Moscow recording 5.6 degrees Celsius temperature during the month of December. Meteorologists attributed Russia's warm temperatures to an unusual front coming in off the Atlantic. However, some Russian lawmakers had argued that it was owing to the climate weapon used by the US[26]. Such claims were not backed by any scientific reasoning and appear politically motivated.

India is regularly undertaking rain enhancement operations. Such operations have helped increase rainfall in rain-deficient areas like Andhra Pradesh and Maharashtra.

In Thailand, the enlightened and far-sighted role played by His Highness King Bhumibol has been instrumental in the development of Thailand's excellent record of successful operations to boost rainfall in water basins and agricultural areas.

A major research programme for rain enhancement has been undertaken by the UAE. The programme's objectives include the development of techniques to improve the efficiency and predictive capabilities of targeted cloud seeding operations. The budget for this programme is around US $5 million[27].

---

26 K Thor Jensen, "Russian Lawmaker Blames U.S. 'Climate Weapon' for Moscow's Warm Winter", Jan 15, 2021, https://www.newsweek.com/russian-lawmaker-blames-climate-weapon-warm-winter-1482371, accessed on Jun25, 2022

27 http://www.uaerep.ae/en/app/rain-enhancement/16, accessed on Aug 28, 2018

Chapter 7

Space Weather and Space Warfare

S implistically, space weather could be viewed as the natural phenomena happening in the space environment between the sun and Earth. Space is not a vacuum but a dynamic environment consisting of electromagnetic and charged particles that impact the sun's activities. Observation and forecasting of space weather is required for various purposes. Occasionally, space weather can impact the weather on earth. It can also impact the systems placed by humans in space, like orbiting satellites and communication nods. It may have impact on human activities in space, like the astronauts staying in space stations or limited period human space missions. For some time now, five domains of warfare are getting discussed (land, air, maritime, space and cyber) and space is known as the forth domain/dimension of warfare. Obviously, knowledge of space weather would be important for this fourth domain of warfare. Also, from the perspective of climate change, some investigation is underway in regards to the possible impact of space weather on long-term climatic conditions. This research would also assist the militaries.

The main focus of this chapter is to understand the relevance of space weather from the perspective of space warfare. For developing the context for the discussion, the chapter discusses important aspects of space weather and features of space warfare.

Space Weather

Typically, space weather represents the activity on the Sun's surface, which ends up creating a typical weather. The Sun is far away from the earth, around 150 million km, still it has been observed that the space weather can affect earth and the rest of the solar system. At its worst, such weather can even damage satellites and also source electrical blackouts on earth.

The Sun is always spewing gas and particles into space. This stream of particles is known as the solar wind. The gas and particles come From the Sun's hot outer atmosphere, termed the corona, gas and particles emerge. They charged with electricity and the solar wind carries these particles toward earth with a speed of approximately a million miles per hour. Fortunately, the earth has an area of magnetic force activity, called a magnetic field. It is also surrounded by a jacket of gases, called an atmosphere. Earth's magnetic field and atmosphere actually makes a tough shield and protects the earth from the bulk of the solar wind blast. Sometimes these charged particles slip past earth's shield and hit the atmosphere and earth observer's glowing light, which is termed as auroras.

Occasionally, magnetic activity within the Sun causes intense solar storms and ends up making the solar wind much stronger which at times can be dangerous. During these storms explosions called solar flares break out which end up sending tons of energy zooming through space at the speed of light. These flares sometimes, emanate huge solar eruptions called coronal mass ejections (CME). All these extra radiations on occasion cause damage to satellites. This leads to impacting communications and navigation services. Also, this can disrupt electricity providing power grids. The radiation from solar storms can also be dangerous for astronauts in space.

The planet earth is surrounded in the solar wind which is a variable of plasma and is made up of fast-flowing electrons and protons, a few heavier ions, the interplanetary magnetic field, and radiation. The solar wind originates from the outer atmosphere of the sun and takes two to three days to reach the earth's atmosphere. Apart from Solar flares activities like sunspots or coronal mass ejections (CME) do happen on the sun's surface and cause disturbances in the solar wind. When such disturbances reach earth, a lot of energy and momentum can be exchanged between the solar wind and the earth's geomagnetic field. All this leads to disturbances in magnetic field and this phenomenon gets referred as geomagnetic storms.

Unfortunately, various technologies which have been great innovations for society as well as for the armed forces do get adversely impacted by the space weather. For example, geomagnetic storms can induce currents in pipelines or the transmission lines of the power grid. This could lead to pipelines suffering accelerated corrosion and overloading the power grid. This impacts the transformer performance leading to electric outages. There is a possibility of aircrafts flying in higher altitudes getting exposed to increased radiation and impacting the health of crew and passengers.

Satellites are particularly sensitive to harsh conditions since increase in radiation can damage their electronics. This could lead to making satellites inoperative and disturb navigation (GPS) and satellite communication on the earth. The degree of difficulty depends on the severity of space weather. It needs to be remembered that the ionosphere itself is part of space weather.

The major victim of quirks in space weather is a satellite. Space weather can impact satellite operations in different ways. Solar EUV (Solar Extreme Ultraviolet) and Joule heating during geomagnetic storms ends up heating the atmosphere and increasing drag on satellites in LEO (low Earth orbit) and can cause uncontrolled re-entry. For, higher orbits, the most important space weather hazard is high energy charged particles. Cosmic rays and SEPs (Solar Energetic Particle) can pierce electronic components. They cause ionisation in insulating layers triggering current leakages and eventually leading to the corruption of memory circuits. Owing such possible challenges, during satellite manufacturing phase itself, fault-tolerant software and duplicate circuits are incorporated, but a major SEP event can cause a challenging environment with many malfunctions in a short space of time. While SEP events also cause damage in electronic components and this may result in a degradation of solar array power over the lifetime of the satellite. High energy (MeV, million electron volts) electrons in the earth's radiation belts pose a major risk of internal satellite charging. Radiation belt electrons can penetrate the outer skin of the spacecraft and damage cables and ungrounded conductors. All this eventually leads to causing permanent damage to the dielectric and component failure, causing uncontrolled behaviour of the spacecraft[1].

There could be a domino effect of disruptions in HF radio communication or making GPS signals unreliable. Indirect consequences and failures from space weather events can come from the dependence of many systems on accurate timing using GPS signals, say cell phone service requires accurate timing for synchronisation. Particularly, data traffic and the Internet depend on accurate timing. Luckily, the space weather related events are very few. However, you require a timely space weather forecast so that some preventative measures could be implemented.

---

1   The above discussion is based various web sources like https://www.nasa.gov/mission_pages/sunearth/spaceweather/index.html, and https://www.sciencedirect.com/topics/earth-and-planetary-sciences/extreme-ultraviolet-radiation and few others, accessed on Jun 23, 2022 and R. B. Horne, "Space weather impacts on satellites and forecasting the Earth's electron radiation belts with SPACECAST", *Space Weather*, Vol. 11, 169–186.

Long before GPS, geomagnetic storms sparked off by solar activity interacting with the Earth's magnetosphere were causing difficulties for navigators. As early as 1806, the explorer and nature researcher Alexander von Humboldt (1769-1859)[2] described the erratic behaviour of his compass during an auroral event. There has been some interesting investigation[3] carried out about how space weather may have affected the navigation and communication of the Titanic in the run up to the disaster, and the subsequent rescue operation. RMS Titanic was a British passenger liner, which sank in the North Atlantic Ocean on April 15 1912 after striking an iceberg. Titanic hitting iceberg was possibility owning to the erratic compass performance. The available evidence suggest that the space weather and related geomagnetic storms affected several aspects of the Titanic tragedy: collision with the iceberg, navigation errors, communication failures and the rescue operation. On the night of April 14-15, 1912, several ships in the north Atlantic had reported communication problems. At the time of the disaster, the skies were clear, the sea was calm and there was no moon. There have been several sightings of the aurora borealis, indicating geomagnetic disturbance. were reported. The sunspot cycle was near the minimum in 1912, and reports from the British Antarctic Expedition on a fateful night were compatible with a coronal hole event on the sun[4]. The author has not been able to check the veracity of this story. The incidence has been mentioned over here has an anecdote.

Forecasting space weather is difficult, but some active work is happening in that direction and efforts are being made to understand the science behind space weather forecasting. Predicting activities on and around the sun (and their severity) well in advance could be key to the success of space weather forecasting. The real challenge for the forecaster is to predict the type of the event (say flare or CME) likely to happen. Such prediction could give more clarity about the intensity of the event. The science behind space weather is very complex and is still an emerging field

---

2   His lengthy Latin American journey from 1799 to 1804 was celebrated as the second scientific discovery of South America.

3   Mila Zinkova, "A possible role of space weather in the events surrounding the Titanic disaster", August 04, 2020, https://rmets.onlinelibrary.wiley.com/doi/10.1002/wea.3817, accessed on May 19, 2021

4   Peter Lynch, "Was space weather the cause of the Titanic disaster?", Apr 1, 2021, https://www.irishtimes.com/news/science/was-space-weather-the-cause-of-the-titanic-disaster-1.4518921, accessed on May 19, 2021

of research. Much research is under progress to observe and understand the solar-terrestrial interaction, the 'space weather'[5].

At present, space weather forecasts are issued at regular intervals during 24 h and 365 days, by the Space Weather Prediction Center (SWPC), previously known as the Space Environment Center (until 2007). This is a laboratory and service center of the US National Weather Service, part of the National Oceanic and Atmospheric Administration (NOAA). The NASA Advanced Composition Explorer (ACE) satellite enables SWPC to give advance warning of geomagnetic storms. Also, NASA's Solar Terrestrial Relations Observatory (STEREO) mission enhances SWPC forecasts by providing off-Sun-Earth-line measurements of the in-situ solar wind, interplanetary magnetic field, and energetic particle environment, in addition to coronal and heliospheric imagery. There are satellites to collect data from the sun, from the solar wind, and from geospace. These observations are processed in real time to refine predictions and to make forecasts. For instance, NASA's Solar and Heliospheric Observatory (SOHO) observes coronal mass ejections. Other spacecraft, like the Solar Dynamics Observatory (SDO) and NOAA's Geostationary Operational Environmental Satellite (GOES) R-series, monitor the Sun and detect solar storms and changes in the solar wind. In addition, NASA's Advanced Composition Explorer (ACE) collects and analyses particles of solar, interplanetary, interstellar and galactic origins. This data contributes towards understanding of the Sun, its interaction with Earth, and the evolution of the solar system. The location of ACE is at the L1, the Lagrange point between the Earth and the Sun, about 1,500,000 km forward of Earth. It gives one hour advance warning about of the arrival of damaging space weather events at Earth.

The research of space weather is of recent origin and mainly (both from scientific and infrastructure point of view) the US is found to have taken a lead and also few other state players like India are found involved into it. Also, there have been some international programmes, which were put in place like the CAWSES (Climate and Weather of the Sun–Earth System) sponsored by SCOSTEP (Scientific Committee on Solar–Terrestrial Physics) was in operation during 2006–2013 with an aim to enhance the understanding of the Sun–Earth environment and its impacts on society

---

5   This section is based on https://spaceplace.nasa.gov/spaceweather/en/, accessed on July 10, 2022 and Lummerzheim, D. (2014). Space Weather. In A. J. Hund (Ed.), Antarctica and the Arctic Circle: A Geographic Encyclopedia of the Earth's Polar Regions. Santa Barbara, CA: ABC-CLIO. Retrieved from http://ebooks.abc-clio.com/reader.aspx?isbn=9781610693936&id=A4091C-5552, accessed on July 12, 2022

and life. The Indian counterpart of CAWSES, sponsored by ISRO (Indian space research organisation), named CAWSES-INDIA, worked towards bringing various Indian institutes and universities under one umbrella and promote space weather research in the country. The CAWSES launched with a specific purpose ended during 2013–2014. This was followed by a programme called, Variability of the Sun and Its Terrestrial Impact (VarSITI) which was also sponsored by SCOSTEP (2014–2018). This programme focused on the relevant peculiar solar activity and its consequences on the earth. Next in line, is the programme called the PREdictability of the Solar–Terrestrial Coupling (SCOSTEP-PRESTO) programme. This four-year programme (2020-2024) aims to address the predictability of space weather events on two folds: one, prediction of events at the Sun, in the heliosphere and in the earth's magnetosphere, ionosphere and atmosphere at timescales from seconds to days and months and secondly, prediction of sub-seasonal to decadal and centennial variability in the Sun–Earth system[6].

For space weather observations, only spacecraft and space-based instruments are not sufficient. There is a requirement to establish a network of ground-based systems, including solar observatories (optical and radio), magnetometers, neutron monitors, and ionospheric monitors. Such networks would provide data crucial for monitoring space weather impacts, for validating and calibrating in situ satellite measurements, and for providing input to forecasting[7].

On May 26, 2021 an institute called the Institute for Solar-Terrestrial Physics at the German Aerospace Center (DLR) to study space weather and conduct research to enable scientists to better understand and predict its effects was inaugurated. This institute has been established with a view that our high-tech society is in great need of protection from any ill effects of space weather and we need to invest more in this field to avoid any possible economic damages. In this institute, the researchers would

---

6   In addition to the earlier mentioned sources the discussion is based on Singh, Ashok K., Asheesh Bhargawa, Devendraa Siingh, and Ram P. Singh. 2021. "Physics of Space Weather Phenomena: A Review" *GEOSCIENCES* 11, no. 7: 286. https://doi.org/10.3390/geosciences11070286 and https://stereo.gsfc.nasa.gov/ and https://www.swpc.noaa.gov/products/solar-terrestrial-relations-observatory-stereo and https://solarsystem.nasa.gov/missions/ace/in-depth/ and https://www.swpc.noaa.gov/products/ace-real-time-solar-wind, accessed on July 12, 2022

7   National Academies of Sciences, Engineering, and Medicine 2021. Planning the Future Space Weather Operations and Research Infrastructure: Proceedings of a Workshop. Washington, DC: The National Academies Press. https://doi.org/10.17226/26128, p.4

be focusing on the magnetosphere-ionosphere-thermosphere (MIT) system. This system relates to regions of earth's atmosphere with special properties and interactions that are influenced by solar storms. A better understanding of the complex interrelations here will help safeguard the negative consequences of space weather by doing early prediction[8].

China and Russia have jointly established a space weather centre to provide services for aviation operators around the world. This centre became operational during November 2021. It monitors space weather events including solar activities. The centre provides space weather services for global aviation users, including making advisory products, surveying global users' demands and responding to users' queries. The International Civil Aviation Organization (ICAO) has approved this fourth global space weather centre. The other three are run by an Australian, Canadian, French and Japanese consortium; a European consortium; and the United States[9].

Apart from solar flares and CMEs, activities like Sunspot are known to impact the weather on earth. Actually, sunspots were first observed by Galileo in the early 1600's. These spots are the dark areas on the solar surface (a moderate-sized sunspot is as large as the Earth), contain strong (shifting) magnetic fields. It has been observed that, the sunspots form and dissipate over periods of days or weeks. They are known to occur after strong magnetic fields emerge through the solar surface and allow the area to cool slightly, say from 6000 °C to about 4200 °C. This relative cold could be seen as a dark spot in contrast with the Sun. Scientists over last three centuries have observed that the average number of sunspots has regularly waxed and waned in an 11-year sunspot cycle[10]. Certain amount of earth weather prediction is possible based on the assessment of the sunspot cycle. There has been a certain correlation about the Indian Monsoon and sunspot cycle performance. Indian Monsoon is known to be strong during the peaks in 11-year solar cycle.

Solar Storms occur, when a Sun emits large bursts of energy in form of solar flares and coronal mass ejections. There is a possibility of damaging of satellite during a major solar storm. During October 2003,

8 "Reliable space weather forecasting", May 31, 2021, https://www.spacedaily.com/reports/Reliable_space_weather_forecasting_999.html, accessed on Jun 08, 2021

9 "Sino-Russian center for space weather monitoring operational", Nov 18, 2021, https://www.spacedaily.com/reports/Sino_Russian_center_for_space_weather_monitoring_operational_999.html, accessed on Nov 22, 2021

10 "A Profile of Space Weather", https://www.swpc.noaa.gov/sites/default/files/images/u33/primer_2010_new.pdf, accessed on July 12, 2022

satellite controllers had lost track of hundreds of spacecraft for days after a major solar storm had hit Earth. Luckily, no direct collision was reported. But, now with the increase in the number of satellites and continuously increasing number of debris orbiting the planet, the probability of satellite collisions owing to big solar storms has increased. This uncertainty is because of changes in density of earth's thermosphere, the upper layer of the atmosphere at n altitudes of 100 to 600 km. Thin gasses at those altitudes interact with particles emitted by the sun in coronal mass ejections (CMEs) and this leads to heating up of the thermosphere and makes it swell. This leads to the denser gases from lower altitudes move to higher altitudes, where satellites suddenly experience stronger drag that changes their speed and pulls them toward earth[11]. There are some known cases of satellites sinking. All in all, it is important to track the solar storms, which may not be happening very routinely, but when they happen, then they could be dangerous for the health of operational satellites.

One of the famous incidences of solar storms impact is the Sept 1&2, 1859 incidence. These two days witnessed telegraph systems around the world failing catastrophically. The telegraph operators reported receiving electrical shocks and telegraph paper catching fire. However, they were able to run the equipment with batteries disconnected. The evenings of these days witnessed the northern lights, which were seen as far south as Colombia. Typically, these lights are only visible at higher latitudes, in northern Canada, Scandinavia and Siberia. This is famous as the Carrington Event, was a massive geomagnetic storm. The Carrington Event of 1859 is the largest recorded account of a geomagnetic storm, but it is not an isolated event and few other similar incidences have taken place. A geomagnetic storm three times smaller than the Carrington Event occurred in Quebec, Canada, in March 1989. It caused the Hydro-Quebec electrical grid to collapse. Transformers were damaged in New Jersey and tripped the grid's circuit breakers. This outage led to five million people being without power for nine hours[12].

It is very important that the study on solar storms and other aspects of space weather should continue and continuous monitoring of the situation in space should happen. Under a highly volatile military situation, there is a

11 Tereza Pultarova, "Satellites can get lost in major solar storms and it could take weeks to find them", July 26, 2022, https://www.space.com/satellites-lost-after-solar-storms-for-weeks, accessed on July 27, 2022

12 David Wallace, "A large solar storm could knock out the power grid and the inter-net", Mar 19, 2022, https://www.spacedaily.com/reports/A_large_solar_storm_could_knock_out_the_power_grid_and_the_internet_999.html, Mar 22, 2022

possibility of humans misreading the impacts of geomagnetic disturbances as an effect of possible enemy attack. On May 23, 1967, when the Cold War was at its peak, surveillance radars on far-northern parts of the globe (northern Alaska, Greenland, and the UK) abruptly and mysteriously got jammed. These radars were designed to detect incoming Soviet nuclear missiles. Obviously, first reaction from the US military commanders was that, the jammed radars might be owing an attack by the enemies and high alert was ordered. They authorised nuclear armed aircraft to take to the skies. Luckily, before this to happen, an unlikely set of heroes – the space-weather forecasters – emerged to save the day. They suggested that that the jamming was not done by the adversary, but the effects of a powerful solar flare had jammed the radars[13]. Their knowledge of the sun averted a possible all-out nuclear war. During Feb 2022, around forty high-speed internet satellites launched by company SpaceX were knocked out of orbit by a geomagnetic storm soon after launch.

Human interests in space are not restricted towards only exploring the space till geostationary orbit (36,000 km above the earth's surface). In fact, just within few years after the beginning of space era (1957) the Soviets successfully attempting the first lunar flyby during Jan 1959 and their mission Luna 1 became the first artificial satellite in heliocentric orbit (an orbit around the barycenter of the Solar System). More missions in this programme during the same year achieved putting first artificial object on the moon (first lunar impact) and taking first images of another celestial body taken from the space. While NASA's Mariner 2, made its closest approach to the planet Venus on December 14, 1962, flying at a distance of 34,854 km from Venus, a planet which is about 61 million km distant when it is nearest to the earth. Mariner 2 was the first spacecraft to get close to another planet and successfully fulfilling the mission objectives.   The data carried by Mariner 2 presented that, temperatures across Venus were more or less uniform and that the planet in general was a hothouse. It also discovered that the planet is under high pressure and that the entire Venus is shrouded in a dense cloud layer above the surface[14]. Human ingenuity reached its peak when the United States' Apollo 11 undertook the first crewed mission to land on the Moon, on July 20 1969. During all these and the subsequent planetary missions the emphasis has always been (beyond

13 "A 1967 solar storm nearly caused a nuclear war", August 3, 2021, https://earthsky.org/human-world/1967-solar-storm-nearly-caused-a-nuclear-war/, accessed on Feb 18, 2022

14 A S Ganesh, "The first successful interplanetary mission", Dec 13, 2020, https://www.thehindu.com/children/the-first-successful-interplanetary-mission/article33250265.ece, accessed on July 16, 2022

technology demonstration) towards understating the atmosphere and weather situation at different planets. During last six decades or so good amount of information has been collected about the weather situation of the earth's planetary system (solar system). The modern-day missions to other planets do take in to account the weather aspects. It needs to be noted that each planet has its own weather and some attempts are even been made to predict the weather situations (NASA's Space Weather Prediction Center) on them and in the near vicinity. For all these years, various states have shown main interests towards undertaking missions to Moon and Mars. There have also been NASA missions like Voyager 1: mission to Jupiter and Saturn and Voyager 2: mission to Jupiter, Saturn, Uranus, Neptune, and beyond. However, since the main theme of this chapter is to contextualise space weather and space warfare, following paras provide some basic details about the weather of Moon and Mars mainly because there are only two places, where there is a possibility of establishment of human colonies in coming few decades.

The closest companion to the Earth in the vastness of space, is the Moon, which is at a distance of 384,400 km from the earth. It is fundamentally linked to Earth's very existence, with lunar tempos embedded in the cycles of life on Earth. The effects of the Moon's actions upon Earth are yet to be understood fully. The most obvious effect the Moon on the Earth is the occurrence of ocean tides. It is important to note that a world without tides would have very different weather systems. Tides are one factor that influences the movement of ocean currents, which eventually play an important role in occurrence of weather[15].

For generations, people have observed the Moon for signs of changes in the weather. There is a famous saying that the *Pale Moon rains. Red Moon blows. White Moon neither rains nor snows.* It is a proven fact that the Moon does affect the earth's climate and weather patterns in several subtle ways. However, it is often said that there is no atmosphere on the Moon. But some recent studies indicate that Earth's Moon does indeed have some atmosphere consisting of some unusual gases, including sodium and potassium, which are not found in the atmospheres of Earth, Mars or Venus. It has miniscule amount of air when compared to earth's atmosphere[16]. The average temperature on the Moon (at the equator and

---

15 Katherine Latham, "The subtle influence of the Moon on Earth's weather", August 24, 2021, https://www.bbc.com/future/article/20210820-the-subtle-influence-of-the-moon-on-earths-weather, accessed on July 16, 2022

16 Marshall Shepherd, "Does Our Moon Have Weather?", Jul 18, 2019, https://

mid latitudes) varies from -183 degrees Celsius, at night, to 106 degrees Celsius during the day. It has been observed that over the course of a full lunar day and night, the temperature on the Moon can vary wildly, from around +200 to -200 degrees Celsius. For astronauts to survive this huge temperature variation special space suits are made[17].

Mars is the fourth planet from the Sun and the second smallest planet (Mercury is the smallest) in the Solar System. The planet is recognised by the name Red Planet. The reddish appearance of the planet because of the iron oxide present on its surface has become the basis for this name. There is a reasonable idea about the climate over the Mars owing to various observations been made available for the number of Martian missions (since 1960 many missions have taken place). However, scientists are yet to conclusively establish the theory, which has been pushed by few scientific groups, that the climate on Mars 3.5 billion years ago was similar to that of early earth: warm and wet. The seasons in southern hemisphere of Mars are more extreme, while in the northern hemisphere, they are less extreme. Presently, the Mars atmosphere is very thin, the temperature is very cold. The current climate changes drastically during the year. It has seasons similar to the Earth's due the tilt of its axis. But because its orbit around the Sun is elliptical, the distance from the Sun varies about by 20 % depending on where it is in its annual orbit. Mars is at greater distance from the Sun in comparison to the Earth (average distances 150 million km vs. 228 million km) and this has got the implications for the temperatures on these planets. Also, the low temperature of Mars is a result of the presence of large amount of carbon dioxide, which radiates away the energy that reaches the planet from the Sun. The average Mars temperature is around -60 deg C (very at different locations like poles and equators and catering for the seasonal variations, they are around in the range between -125 and +20 deg C). Barometric pressure varies at each landing site on a semi-annual basis. The spacecrafts which have reached Mars undertaken pressure observations show the readings as low as 6.8 millibars and as high as 9.0 millibars. Mars has a very thin atmosphere about 100 times thinner

---

www.forbes.com/sites/marshallshepherd/2019/07/18/does-our-moon-have-weather/?sh=152f900245b2, accessed on July 16, 2022

17 Jonathan O'Callaghan, "How did lunar astronauts survive the extreme temperatures on the Moon?", Nov 19, 2012, https://www.spaceanswers.com/space-exploration/how-did-lunar-astronauts-survive-the-extreme-temperatures-on-the-moon/, accessed on July 16, 2022 Jonathan O'Callaghan, "How did lunar astronauts survive the extreme temperatures on the Moon?", Nov 19, 2012, https://www.spaceanswers.com/space-exploration/how-did-lunar-astronauts-survive-the-extreme-temperatures-on-the-moon/, accessed on July 16, 2022

than Earth's and is incapable of easily supporting life. The composition of its atmosphere: Carbon dioxide is 95.32 per cent. While Nitrogen is 2.7 per cent and Oxygen is hardly 0.13 per cent[18].

In regards to the planetary system all this knowledge of weather is important form the point of view of futuristic missions. There is a possibility the humans colonising some planets in future and all efforts should be made towards exploring more about the weather of planets in our solar systems. At present, it would be premature to speak of the security angle in this regard, but in distant future, if such issue emerges, then this could become an important backgrounder.

Space Warfare

On earth, land, air and sea have been the areas of conflict for many centuries. Human are doing space gazing for time immemorial. However, space emerged as an area of interest (possibly also of influence) during 1957, when the Soviet Union launched the first artificial satellite called Sputnik. That was the period of intense Cold War rivalry amongst the US and Soviets. The success of Soviet Union fed fears in the minds of the US political and military leadership. It was a period, when some unannounced technology superiority race was happening amongst these major power blocks and with the launch of Sputnik the US realised that they have fallen back in this race. The public perception in the US, about them lagging behind in the technology race was so high that they felt the echoes of the Japanese attack on Pearl Harbor (December 7, 1941), in this technology demonstration by the Soviets. There was a view that now the Soviets have mastered the technology to launch ballistic missiles armed with nuclear weapons at the US[19]. Hence, it could be argued that the domain of space has been politicised since inception and has played a major role towards escalating the tensions in the Cold War period. It has also led to increase in the arms race and put a 'germ' for the possibility of space arms race too.

The launch of first satellite had strong strategic connotations, but over last six decades, the space technology has emerged as a major saviour for the humankind. This technology has singlehandedly improved human life in multiple ways. The unique feature of space technology is that, it is an inherently dual-use technology and since early sixties, it has been used very effectively for military requirements too. The strength of space

---

18 Ajey Lele, *Mission Mars*, Springer: London, 2014, pp.21-23.

19 Elizabeth Howell, "Sputnik: The Space Race's Opening Shot", September 30, 2020, https://www.space.com/17563-sputnik.html, accessed on July 13, 2022

technologies for meteorological observations is well-known and the US had launched the world's first meteorological satellite TIROS-1 on April 1, 1960. The weather information is one of the basic necessities for the armed forces too, both during wartime and peacetime and as early as 1962, the US department of defence had established Defence Meteorological Satellite Program (DMSP). For long, defence forces all across the world are regularly using satellites for the purposes of weather information, reconnaissance/intelligence gathering, navigation and communications.

The 1991 Gulf War (Operation Desert Storm) witnessed for a first time a major role played by space technology in a military conflict. This war often gets labelled as the first space war. This war witnessed space technology affecting multiple areas of airland operations. The air offensive played a very crucial role towards the allied force getting a quick success in this war. The air offensive had used stealth bombers, cruise missiles and laser-guided 'smart' bombs. The main targets were communications networks, weapons plants and oil refineries. Various satellite systems were put in use for the purposes of gathering timely weather information, undertaking reconnaissance operations for gathering intelligence and for communication purposes. The major gamechanger in this war was the efficient use of GPS satellite architecture (before it was even fully developed) by the US air force.

The allied forces had systematically prepared for this war. The main focus was to have accurate maps of region for effective planning of operations. Multi-Spectral Imaging (MIS) was an excellent tool for tactical planning. LANDSAT and the French SPOT imaging satellites were used for creating updated area maps, which were more precise, provided broader coverage and helped the military leadership towards planning tactical operations. Personnel in the field received almost dedicated 24-hour service from various satellite systems[20].

Subsequently, in various wars, space technology is found getting used with some success. Since early 1990s, much of development has happened in various domains of outer space. Technology has evolved significantly and now there has been an increasing dependence on space technologies for various purposes including strategic requirements. Post 1991 Gulf War,

---

20 Gulf war inputs are from Larry Greenemeier, "GPS and the World's First Space War", February 8, 2016, https://www.scientificamerican.com/article/gps-and-the-world-s-first-space-war/, and Sharon Watkins Lang, "SMDC History: 25 years since first 'Space War'", January 20, 2016, https://www.army.mil/article/161173/smdc_history_25_years_since_first_space_war, accessed on July 14, 2022

in conflicts like Afghanistan the US forces were much dependent on GPS. So far since 1991, in various conflicts, GPS has played an important role towards helping ground troops, pilots and marines in finding locations, moving ground equipment in correct direction, identifying targets in the battlefield and routing guns, artillery and missiles correctly on to the targets. GPS also helps to hit the targets accurately, which are otherwise not visible owing to bad weather conditions.

Today, the world is witnessing the use of the state-of-art weapon systems. Most of the modern weapon systems and weapon platforms are GPS based. Owing all this, there is a realisation that somehow if the GPS gets compromised, then in all probability the US forces and many other forces, which are depending on GPS or other sat nav systems (Russia has their own nav sat network called GLONASS, while the Chinese network is Biedou) would become toothless. Obviously, GPS is one of the most vulnerable targets. Theoretically, for targeting GPS few specific options could be there: attack the ground infrastructure, destroy few GPS satellites or jam the GPS satellites. It is difficult to destroy any operational satellite, but not impossible. During 2007, China undertook an anti-satellite test (ASAT) to destroyed their own aging weather satellite by using kinetic kill vehicle (KKV) technology. For this purpose, a missile from the ground was fired towards a satellite. This missile had no warhead other than a metal portion, which impacted the satellite and owing to the kinetic energy produced, the satellite got fragmented into number of small pieces. With this test, China demonstrated to the rest of the world their capabilities towards destroying adversary satellites, if need arises. This China's unproved action has led to the talk of Space Warfare. Other major powers in the world like the US (2008), India (2019) and Russia (2021) have also demonstrated their ASAT capabilities. All these demonstrations of capabilities have happened on the satellite targets, which are in a low earth orbit (LEO). The GPS satellites are mostly in the MEO (medium earth orbit). Reaching those hights for KKV is a challenging task. There are some indications that China may (not confirmed[21]) have the capacity even to reach the geo-stationary orbit (GEO; 36,000 km above the earth's surface). In the 21st century, the idea of space warfare has taken a root and many states have started establishing specific agencies to cater for the military aspects of the space. Particularly, the US has taken a major leap and gone ahead and established a separate defence vertical called the US Space Force.

---

21 B Weeden, "Chine Direct Assent Anti-satellite Testing", May 2022, https://swfound.org/media/207376/swf-chinese-da-asat-may-2022.pdf, accessed on July 31, 2022

As witnessed during the Gulf War and some other wars, that the satellite technologies help militaries in a big way. This aspect of space technologies getting used for weather information, intelligence gathering, communications and navigation has increasing acceptability amongst the nation-states and this is known as the militarisation of space and it is not breaching any global rules, treaty mechanisms or norms in respect of the conduct of activities in the outer space. But, to intentionally jam or destroy space assets or ground infrastructure of adversary state or private actor by using space-based systems or ground-based systems amounts to the weaponisation of space and no country in the world is in (officially) favour of this. Broadly, space weapons could constitute of intentionally developed technologies capable of targeting space assets or ground infrastructure. The current focus of states is not directed (at least overly) towards developing space weapons. But there is some interest to develop counter-space technologies, possibly, as some form of deterrence mechanism. Following are some important categories[22] of counter-space technologies:

> **Kinetic Physical**: Technology intended to create permanent and irreversible destruction of a satellite or to ground support infrastructure through force of impact with an object or a warhead. Such technology includes direct-ascent anti-satellite (DA-ASAT) missiles and co-orbital systems. The co-orbital systems are satellites placed on similar orbits and can be directed to intercept or interfere by means of a close orbital rendezvous.

> **Non-Kinetic Physical**: Technology meant to create interference or temporary damage and physical impact on space systems without physical contact. This category includes electromagnetic pulses or directed energy (laser beams or microwave bombardments) technologies.

> **Electronic**: Technology that uses radio frequency energy to interfere with or jam the communications to or from satellites but not cause permanent physical damage.

> **Cyber**: Technology that uses software and network techniques to compromise, control, interfere or destroy computer systems that are linked to satellite operations.

In principle, various states including ASAT power states argue that there is a need to prevent the transformation of outer space into a

---

22 "Counterspace Capabilities", Aug 2018, https://www.unidir.org/files/medias/pdfs/coun-terspace-capabilities-backgrounder-eng-0-771.pdf, accessed on Feb 24, 2021

battlefield. But, some of them mainly the states like China and Russia are found continuing to conduct testing of various technologies to improve theircounter-space capabilities. The US is also known to have a very active counter-space R & D programme.

At present, there is much concern about the development of Chinese and Russian counter-space weapons. It is expected that these states have the ability to use jammers, ground-based lasers, and ground/space-based kinetic weapons. They can also mount attacks against ground facilities that support space operations, or are in a position to nuclear detonation in space. Realising the possible impact of the Chinese and Russian counter-space capabilities on the US security, some detailed assessments have been carried out by the experts[23].

It is not the purpose over here to get into all intricate details about the counter-space programmes of various states. But it needs to be mentioned that states like China are known to be developing direct ascent anti-satellite (DA-ASAT) capabilities, either as dedicated counter-space systems or as midcourse missile defence systems that could provide counter-space capabilities. They are testing these technologies since 2005. They have proven capabilities for attacking the targets in the low earth orbit (LEO) and are also developing (even possibly succeeded) kinetic kill capabilities, both for medium earth orbit (MEO) and geo orbit (GEO). They probably have developed sophisticated capabilities for jamming or spoofing space-based positioning, navigation, and timing (PNT) capabilities. There are indications that Chinese military PNT jammers are being deployed on islands in the South China Sea. They are also possibly developing directed energy weapons (DEW) for counter-space use. China is known to be developing a sophisticated network of ground-based optical telescopes and radars for detecting, tracking, and characterising space objects as part of its space situational awareness (SSA) capabilities. Like the US and Russia, several of the Chinese SSA radars also serve missile warning functions[24].

---

23 Brian Weeden and Victoria Samson (eds) Global Counterspace Capabilities:An Open Source Assessment, April 2020, , accessed on Jun 12, 2020 and "U.S. Counterspace Capabilities Versus Chinese Space Systems (Ch 9)", The U.S.-China Military Scorecard: Forces, Geography, and the Evolving Balance of Power, 1996–2017, Rand Cooperation, 2015, pp 227-244, available at Heginbotham, Eric, et al. The U.S.-China Military Scorecard: Forces, Geography, and the Evolving Balance of Power, 1996–2017. RAND Corporation, 2015, and https://www.nationaldefensemagazine.org/articles/2020/8/21/us-space-command-hints-at-new-capabilities-to- accessed on Feb 24, 2021

24 http://www.parabolicarc.com/2020/04/21/a-summary-of-chinas-counterspace-capabilities/, accessed on Feb 25, 2021

There are ideas like an 'inspector satellite' which is capable of diagnosing the technical condition of the other satellite from the closest possible distance[25]. There is a possibility that such satellite could be misused for military purposes.

There are various challenges in the domain of space and the most important challenge is that of the space debris. This debris is harmful to the health of satellites if it comes in its way. There are various technologies which are presently been worked on, for the purposes of space debris removal. These technologies/techniques could be considered as dual-use systems which could be misused for harming the space assets of the advisory. Also, agencies are working towards developing technologies for on-orbit servicing of satellites. Such technologies also have possibility of misuse. Ideas of development of space weapons to hit the targets in the space or on ground are being discussed more at academic level presently. But there exists a possibility that some state may make some progress in that direction in future. Such ideas include the possibility of developing space mines, energy weapons, laser weapons and concepts like 'rods from god' which are essentially tungsten rods dropped from space towards the targets on earth (such rods are projected to cause impact equivalent to nuclear attack). At present, space tourism has just begun happing and it is difficult the trace the trajectory for its future. However, it would be important for the states to ensure that the privet sector is not getting manipulated for conducting some covert activities. It is expected in coming years few states (and private players) would try to establish their own space stations. Apart from the International Space Station (ISS), China is establishing its space station called Tiangong and is expected to make it operational by the end of 2022.

In common lexicon, space or outer space gets referred to the outer atmosphere. While there is concept called Deep Space, which normally is associated with the region, where planets are there. But, for some this is an area of space beyond the terrestrial planets (part lying beyond the earth-moon system). There is also a view that anything beyond 1 lakh km from the earth should be considered as deep space. Presently, planetary missions are finding the increasing attention of the states and private agencies. Already, missions to Moon and Mars have taken place and more missions are in the offering. The focus in future would be towards undertaking human missions to these planets. There are also some missions planned

---

25 Todd Harrison et al, "Space threat assessment 2021", Marc 31, 2021, https://www.csis. org/analysis/space-threat-assessment-2021, accessed on Mar 22, 2022

for other planets like Venus. There has been a fear expressed by NASA that China National Space Administration, may be planning a 'takeover' of the Moon as part of its military space programme (China has denied that)[26]. Presently, it would be bit untimely to make any specific comment about the strategic aspects of planetary missions and missions in deep space. Would space warfare or more so the power-positioning would reach those hights? Presently, such idea appears to be an extremely technologically challenging proposition. But it is difficult to predict what may happen after some decades hence.

Legal Aspects[27]

International law classifies outer space as a 'Global Common,' meaning outside any country's national jurisdiction and hence to be governed only by international legislation. The high oceans, Antarctica, and cyberspace are examples of 'Global Common'. International law, together with the Charter of the United Nations, applies to outer space and celestial bodies, which are free for exploration and use by all states in conformity with international law.

Activities in space are regulated by the United Nations Outer Space Treaty (OST) of 1967. Actually, this treaty came into being with a limited mandate of banning testing of weapons of mass destruction (WMD) in the outer space. However, this treaty has various useful provisions. As per Article II of the treaty, 'Outer space, including the moon and other celestial bodies, is not subject to national appropriation by claim of sovereignty, by means of use or occupation, or by any other means.' While, Article IV of OST prohibits the 'establishment of military bases, installations and fortifications, and testing of any type of weapons and the conduct of military manoeuvres on celestial bodies. It also binds the nation-states from 'placing in orbit around the earth any objects carrying nuclear weapons or any other kinds of weapons of mass destruction, or install such weapons

---

26 "China rejects NASA accusation it will take over the moon", July 04, 2022 https://www.reuters.com/lifestyle/science/china-rejects-nasa-accusation-it-will-take-over-moon-2022-07-04/, accessed on July 06, 2022

27 Govind Bhattacharjee, "Weapons in Space~I", May 13, 2022, https://www.thestatesman.com/opinion/weapons-in-spacei-1503071313.html and "Space Law Treaties and Principles", https://www.unoosa.org/oosa/en/ourwork/spacelaw/treaties.html and Benjamin Silverstein and Ankit Panda, "Space Is a Great Commons. It's Time to Treat It as Such", Mar 09, 2021, https://carnegieendowment.org/2021/03/09/space-is-great-commons.-it-s-time-to-treat-it-as-such-pub-84018, and Ajey Lele, "India needs to avoid Moon Trap", Oct 11, 2021, https://www.financialexpress.com/lifestyle/science/india-needs-to-moon-trap/2347744/,accessed on July 17, 2022

on celestial bodies, or station such weapons in outer space in any other manner'. The responsibility for this lies with the United Nations Office for Outer Space Affairs (UNOOSA). However, this agency lacks the necessary legal authority or even the institutional capacity to enforce it effectively.

Another agreement in 1979, the Moon Agreement, similarly forbids the use of the moon for military purposes or its weaponisation, but this treaty has been ratified by only handful of states and the major space powers are not a part of this mechanism. Apart from OST and Moon agreement, there are three other treaty mechanisms and they all together deal with issues such as the non-appropriation of outer space by any one country. These mechanisms include the Rescue Agreement which deals with the return of astronauts and the return of objects launched into Outer Space, while the Liability Convention is about the liability for damage caused by space objects and lastly the Registration Convention, which is about the registration of objects launched into outer space.

International governance in space is a need of the hour. Much needs to be done in that direction. At present, there is an absence of effective enforcement mechanism. Naturally, states are found putting their own national interests over the interests of the global commence.

A classic case for the states putting their own agenda and neglecting the idea of global commence, is the US Commercial Space Launch Competitiveness Act (singed by President Obama on November 25, 2015). As per this act, the US agencies (private players) have commercial property rights in resources extracted from extra-terrestrial bodies by them. States like Luxembourg and the UAE are also having similar act. All these regulations permit their space industry to undertake the extraction of minerals from extra-terrestrial bodies. Such regulations are in conflict with Article II of the Outer Space Treaty (OST), which the US and many countries are signatories. More so, all this is contradictory to the notion that Moon and other celestial bodies are the Common Heritage to Mankind (CHM).

In future, 'space resources mining' is anticipated to emerge as one of the most important issues of global contention. The mining of asteroids (and other planets) is about controlling a vast source of wealth consisting of rare earth elements and precious metals. There is an asteroid named 16 Psyche, which is known to have gold and other minerals worth $700 quintillion (a number equal to 1 followed by 18 zeros). The Moon has abundant deposits of Helium-3, while Earth has almost none. This isotope could provide safer nuclear energy in a fusion reactor. Also, it is a climate friendly energy source, since it is not radioactive and would not produce dangerous waste products. As per some predictions, a big cargo aircraft load of Helium-3 could cater for the global energy needs for around ten years. Obviously, there is a necessity for having a globally accepted mechanism on the management of space resources. In future (after few decades) this could emerge as a major area for confrontation. History is replete with examples of wars fought for resources. Hence, there exists a possibility of war for space resources and one important feature of any such war would obviously be a space warfare.

General Discussion

At present, space warfare is more of a concept. Luckily, till date no state has attempted to engage into space warfare. Also, there have been no covert attempts to do some act, which could be classified as an act involving space warfare (unlike cyber warfare). But since some states have already demonstrated their ASAT capabilities and some continue testing counter-space technologies, the possibility of space warfare falls into the realm of reality for the future.

Theoretically, the expanse of space warfare is vast. It could be about assets in space getting targeted by ground-based weapons (both kinetic or non-kinetic) or space-based weapons being used for destroying space systems or space-based weapons attacking ground targets or even attacks on ground infrastructure meant for space systems. In a holistic sense, it could be said that even for space warfare, except the possibility wars in space conducted by using space-based weapons, the knowledge of weather both from earth and space would be required. Much is known about the earth weather (in relative sense), however there is need to know more about how the space weather could impact various human derived military actions in space and in case of an actual space war, what space weather inputs would assist.

Interestingly, many phenomena associated with space weather occur within the Earth's magnetosphere and upper atmosphere. Geomagnetic storms can be accompanied by enhancements in the radiation belts and complex changes in the ionosphere and thermosphere.

The present understating about the effects of space weather is restricted to aspects like the occurrence of geomagnetic storms increases the probability of an astronaut being hit by a damaging particle (could even lead to cancer). Also, there are chances of impact of harmful radiation on high-flying airplanes (flying in upper atmosphere) and those flying over the North Pole. While most of spacecraft in Earth orbit operate partly or entirely within the radiation belts and hence during periods of intense space weather, sensitive electronics would get affected. There are also adverse impacts on radio-frequency signals[28]. Now, is such a limited understanding about the space weather, sufficient for addressing space warfare related challenges? The answer could be both, yes and no. Yes, because now we know, which aspects of space weather are dangerous. This backgrounder is useful for further research. No, because space warfare is much beyond safety of humans, satellites and communication lines. It is going to be an offensive act and would require more specific and timely space weather inputs.

Presently, it is really difficult to quantify the possible exact nature of space warfare and possible requirements of the space weather to fight and win such a war. One should not do an oversimplistic comparison of space warfare with other forms of warfare like land, air or sea warfare. It is highly unlikely that space warfare would be an all-out warfare, where warring states would openly start destroying each other's satellites. Modern-day life is much dependent on satellites and every country has satellites which has significant utility for civilian purposes. Actually, damage to such systems could result in to major economic damages and an increase in social tensions. Obviously, the states would like to avoid it. Hence, it is unlikely (would be foolish) that they to get in the business of random satellite 'killing' only for military gains.

As of January 1, 2022 data there are total 4,852 active artificial satellites orbiting the Earth. Amongst them, the US has 2,944 satellites, China has 499 and there are 169 satellites with Russia[29]. Mostly around 75% of total number of satellites are in the low earth orbit (LEO). Technically, killing a satellite in the LEO is a doble proposal and hence in principle they all are lucrative targets. However, killing hundreds of satellites during a conflict looks to be highly unlikely. States when attacked in space, may opt for options like diplomacy, undertaking jamming activities, threatening adversary satellite/s by positioning some other satellite in its close proximity, trying to grab a satellite with a robotic arm or go for a kinetic attack on one or two most important military satellites of the enemy. At the same time,

28 https://www.nasa.gov/mission_pages/rbsp/science/rbsp-spaceweather-human.html, accessed on July 17, 2022

29 https://www.statista.com/statistics/264472/number-of-satellites-in-orbit-by-operating-country/, accessed on July 17, 2022

the aggressor country is likely to undertake some cost-benefit assessment, before going for a kinetic (KKV) attack on the adversary satellite, from harmful debris generation point of view too. This debris put all satellites in danger. Also, there should be a realisation that, physical destruction of satellite would amount to raising the ante and the aggressor state should be prepared for a heavy backlash.

Under such circumstances, how the military space meteorologists should prepare themselves from space weather point of view, so as the state can effectively address the challenge of space warfare or prepare itself for unleashing space warfare? Here there is a need for the military leadership of the state, which proposes to enter the arena of space warfare to first decide for itself the nature of missions it proposes to undertake and the nature of weaponry likely to be used for such missions. Also, there would be a requirement to delineate the likely strategic and tactical gains of entering this domain of warfare and possible enemy reactions. Military meteorologists should be briefed about the nature of operations and expected weather information for effective conduct of such operations. All this should be done during peacetime, so as the meteorologists could equip themselves for providing timely weather inputs and forecasts, both during planning stage and also for the conduct of actual operations.

Space Warfare over other planets or in deep space is too futuristic of an idea. However, human presence over Moon and Mars in near future appears be a conceivable idea. It needs to be noted that human presence is not going to be a necessity for space warfare. There could be warfare amongst two (or more) robotic systems too. The military space meteorologists need to focus more about collecting data, developing models for better understating the nature of weather in the deep space. Basically, as and when (and if) the need occurs for a state, the knowledge about the weather in LEO, MEO and GEO orbits is much essential and serious efforts should be made to increase the observation base and developing various modelling techniques for forecasting. Planetary weather is one area where much more is required to be done and this is time to establish structures for real-time observation platforms on various planets and development of deep space forecasting models.

Chapter 8

Geoengineering, Environmental and Legal Aspects

The focus of this book has been to understand the relevance of weather for warfare. In a sense, the entire story told so far is fine focussed. Warfare is a huge construct, but weather is even bigger. It becomes a narrow concept, when we try to understand it only at the backdrop of warfare. Theoretically, the idea of 'construct', gets referred as hypothetical construct or psychological construct. All sciences are known to be built on systems of constructs and their interrelations. The natural sciences use constructs such as gravity, temperature, phylogenetic dominance, tectonic pressure, and global warming[1]. Some aspects of global warming are expected to have major concerns for the security, it is more about the war by the nature against humanity. Unfortunately, it is happening owing some misallocations by the humans (some decades back) about use and management of natural resources. For some time now the climate change debate is getting much traction since the adverse impact of climate change is becoming much visible.

Occasionally, the terminologies like global warning and climate change are found getting used together. However, global warming is about the rise in global temperatures owing mainly to the increasing concentrations of greenhouse gases in the atmosphere, while climate change raises the aspects like the increasing changes in the measures of climate over a long period of time including precipitation, temperature, and wind patterns[2]. Also, there is a practice of using the terms: weather and climate interchangeably. The difference between weather and climate

---

1   https://www.britannica.com/science/construct, accessed on July 18, 2022

2   What is the difference between global warming and climate change? | U.S. Geological Survey (usgs.gov), accessed on July 18, 2022

is a measure of time. Weather is what conditions of the atmosphere are over a short period of time, and climate is how the atmosphere performs over relatively long periods of time[3]. From the warfare perspective, it could be said that both the knowledge of climate and weather is important, broadly climate information gets used for strategic planning and weather information is important for the conduct of tactical operations.

In the near future, climate aspects are expected to leave a major impact, both on national and global security. The UN Secretary-General António Guterres in a meeting during Feb 2021, had told the UN Security Council that climate change is a 'crisis multiplier' and would have profound implications for international peace and stability. Also, in the same meeting, one of the influential voices, Sir David Attenborough, an English broadcaster, biologist, natural historian and author, called climate change "the biggest threat to security that modern humans have ever faced"[4].

There are major concerns in regards to climate crisis today, globally. Climate science is an umbrella term referring to scientific disciplines studying various aspects of the Earth's climate[5]. One chapter in this book has also addressed the issue of space weather. Broadly, it could be said that the book at the background of warfare has addressed the issues related to environment, climate, weather (including space weather) and some aspects terrain. Still there are some specific aspects of meteorology and terrain sciences, which merits attention. Probably, these facets many not have a direct connection with the battlefield, but still, they are important because they have direct or indirect association with warfare and weather, both. The book has so far discussed the role of weather in the warfare, but there is also another important issue that needs some discussion and that is, the role of warfare on weather/climate. As well, it is important to have a brief look at the legal aspects and treaty mechanisms/norms, which govern the science of environment. In earlier chapters some mention the aspects of geoengineering have been made in passing, however it is important to look at it more closely. This is because climate engineering methods, which can cause significant intervention in the Earth's climate system, could also

---

3   https://www.nasa.gov/mission_pages/noaa-n/climate/climate_weather.html, accessed on July 18, 2022

4   Climate Change 'Biggest Threat Modern Humans Have Ever Faced', World-Renowned Naturalist Tells Security Council, Calls for Greater Global Cooperation | UN Press, Feb 23, 2021, accessed on July10, 2022

5   https://iep.utm.edu/philosophy-of-climate-science/,accessed on July 18, 2022

be partially manipulated for warfare purposes. This chapter debates briefly on all these three important aspects.

Geoengineering

Geoengineering is the considered as a large-scale intervention in the Earth's natural systems to counteract climate change. The inkling is to have a set of emerging technologies to manipulate the environment and partly offset some of the impacts of climate change. For some time now, there various ideas have been floated to the arrest the earth's temperature. They include mimicking the power of volcanoes, using sea as a mirror and painting cities white[6].

Solar Radiation Management (SRM) or Solar Geoengineering, hear idea is to reflect a small proportion of the Sun's energy back into space. SRM is like a reflective shield, artificially providing regional or global cooling. There are various ideas which have been floated to achieve SRM. At ground and sea level, SRM suggestions have included using gigantic pumps to introduce microbubbles into reservoirs or other bodies of still water, the genetic engineering of crops to make leaves shinier, and the spreading of reflective films on the ocean's surface or on vulnerable ice flows. Specifically some proposed techniques include Albedo enhancement, Space Reflectors and Stratospheric aerosols. For albedo modification, there are suggestions like sulphate aerosol spraying. Here, the purpose is to spray sulphur dioxide or sulphuric acid into the stratosphere (upper atmosphere) to form tiny particles that reflect an extra 1 to 3 per cent of incoming solar radiation back into space. This would help in cooling the planet. Basically, this process amounts to installing a radiative shield between the Earth and the Sun and regulate the temperature of the planet.

There is another broad idea called the Greenhouse Gas Removal (GGR) or Carbon Geoengineering. GGR techniques objective is to remove carbon dioxide or other greenhouse gases from the atmosphere, directly countering the increased greenhouse effect and ocean acidification. Such techniques would be required to be implemented on a global scale to have a significant impact on greenhouse gas levels in the atmosphere. Suggested techniques comprise ideas like Afforestation (global-scale tree planting effort), Biochar which involves 'Charring' biomass and burying it so that its carbon is locked up in the soil. Some more techniques are Bio-energy with carbon capture and sequestration, Ambient Air Capture (remove carbon

---

6   https://www.dw.com/en/solar-geoengineering-global-warming-cooler-planet/a-58051069, accessed on July 19, 2022

dioxide directly from ambient air), Ocean Fertilisation for drawing down carbon dioxide from the atmosphere, Ocean Alkalinity Enhancement and Enhanced Weathering[7].

Space-based Geoengineering involves some very interesting theoretically possibilities, but technically challenging ideas to implement on ground (in space). Such ideas involve methods for reducing the amount of sunlight that hits the Earth. The purpose over here is to reduce global temperatures to pre-industrial/pre-fossil fuel levels. The suggested approaches include deployment of objects in space that can block or reflect sunlight away from the planet and for these purposes sunshades, reflectors or mirrors, and clouds of sun blocking particles could be used. Also, there are ideas like manufacturing self-replicating robotic 3D printers to produce the components required to build assemblies of solar-powered spacecraft that could be positioned as a solar shield constellation[8].

The ideas of geoengineering look very attractive on paper, though there could be number of risks associated with it. First, there is no guarantee about the effectiveness of these interventions. Secondly, climate systems are very complicated. It is difficult to draw firm conclusions about the consequences of undertaking such a radical intervention. The chemistry of the upper atmosphere, including the ozone layer is very complicated and yet not completely understood. Thirdly, no country in isolation can conduct such experiments. There would be requirement of global arrangement for undertaking such experimentation. Fourthly, those who have technology would dominate the discourse and there could be groupings of haves and have-nots, politically difficult to manage.

Military planners identify climate change as a 'threat multiplier'. States have integrated the changing climate aspects in the military planning and logistical activities. It is expected that the climate change would create political instability in near future. In the same context, there have been talks about water wars, food wars, and energy wars. There are some possible scenarios, which actually indicate how precarious the situation could emerge, if such scenarios comes out to be true. One such scenario could

---

7   For the entire discussion please refer https://geoengineering.environment.harvard. edu/geoengineering#:~:text=Geoengineering%20is%20conventionally%20split%20 into,albedo%20modification%2C%20or%20sunlight%20reflectionaccessed on July 18, 2022 https://www.wilsoncenter.org/article/solar-radiation-management

8   https://geoengineering.global/space-based-geoengineering   /#:~:text=Space% 2D based% 20geoengineering%20approaches%20consist,clouds%20of%20sun%20block-ing%20particles, accessed on July23, 2022

be, China facing with a catastrophic drought in the north of the country. Under such situation they may decide to air spray sulphur dioxide so as to achieve rapid cooling. But this may lead to affect the monsoon rains, which is a lifeline for India and Pakistan. This could lead to bringing on famine in these regions. Imagine the security challenges emerging owing to intentional change of weather patterns, when all the three states involved are nuclear weapon states[9].

There could be various uncertainties regarding the consequences of geoengineering of any type. It could be difficult to prejudge the precise impact of geoengineering solutions. At the same time, there is a risk that such techniques could be utilised for hostile purposes. They could be weaponised – strategically manipulated or used to alter the environmental conditions in a given area for military purposes[10]. It is important that experiments associated with geoengineering should be allowed to be performed under international consensus, else there exists a danger that such techniques be used covertly for military purposes.

Role of Warfare on Weather and Climate

There is a growing narrative arguing that the climate crisis is a national security threat that demands military investments. Globally, militaries are known to play a major role in a disaster management. Many of the recent disasters have been the natural disasters, mainly owing to climate change and armed forces have come to assistance to handle such disasters on various occasions. The importance of armed forces towards handling the challenges of climate change just cannot be overlooked. But unfortunately, in spite being a saviour during climate crisis at one hand, the armed forces are also known as the destroyers of environment too. This is because, wars are known to cause a major damage to the environment.

There are various reasons that why wars add up to climate crisis. The militaries consume massive amounts of fossil fuels, which contributes directly to global warming. Another reason for environmental degradation is that various bombing operations and other methods of modern warfare directly harm wildlife and biodiversity. The collateral damage during any

---

9   Clive Hamilton, "Could geoengineering cause a climate war?", June 05, 2019, https://www.sciencefocus.com/planet-earth/could-geoengineering-cause-a-climate-war/, accessed on July 20, 2022

10 Gabriela Kolpak, "From ENMOD to geoengineering: the environment as a weapon of war", April 7, 2020, https://ceobs.org/from-enmod-to-geoengineering-the-environment-as-a-weapon-of-war/, accessed on July 18, 2022

major conflict can even eradicate up to 90 per cent of large animals in an area. More so pollution from war contaminates bodies of water, soil, and air, making areas uninhabitable.

Based on various research findings some interesting statistics is available in respect of the damage the US military alone possibly must have caused to the environment. Researchers have found that the US military is one of the largest climate polluters in history, consuming more liquid fuels and emitting more CO2e (carbon-dioxide equivalent) than most countries. Some statistics shows that, if the US military is hypothetically considered as a nation-state, then it would be the 47th largest emitter of GHG in the world, if only taking into account the emission from fuel usage. The infrastructure of the US department of defence (USDoD) is huge and spread across in many countries in the world, they have nearly 800 bases worldwide. The USDoD has around 566,000 buildings and they account for almost 40% of its fossil fuel use. As per some estimates, the US and allied forces, have fired more than 337,000 bombs and missiles on other countries over the past 20 years. The jets carrying those weapons possibly have burn through 4.28 gallons of gasoline per mile, with each detonation releasing additional greenhouse gas emissions, and extinguishing natural carbon sinks like soil, vegetation, and trees. The 'War on Terror' has possibly released 1.2 billion metric tons of greenhouse gases into the atmosphere, which alone has more of a warming effect on the planet than the annual emissions of 257 million cars[11]. It is expected that the wars fought in various other theatres also could have caused the damage to environment.

Gulf war (1991), apart from showcasing various modern technologies also ended up showcasing the adverse impact tactics during the war on the environment. As the US led force commenced the intense air war against Iraq in January 1991, Saddam Hussein responded differently, not by using air force or ground forces, but by crating environmental obstacles. He had put in fire Kuwaiti oil wells, refineries, and storage tanks. The purpose was to create huge number of blazes and black smoke to confuse the aggressor's ground forces & air forces and mainly obstruct the air campaign. By February 1991, the Pentagon reported that over 590 Kuwaiti wells and facilities were on fire, and scientists had stated that the result would be an episode of pollution that is unprecedented in history. Saddam Hussein's

---

11 Joe McCarthy, "How War Impacts Climate Change and the Environment", April 7, 2022, https://www.globalcitizen.org/en/content/how-war-impacts-the-environment-and-climate-change/, accessed on Apr 12, 2022 and "U.S. military consumes more hydrocarbons than most countries -- massive hidden impact on climate", June 20, 2019, https://www.sciencedaily.com/releases/2019/06/190620100005.htm, accessed on July 20, 2022

environmental warfare also happened in form of, intentional oil spills. On January 22, 1991, two Iraqi tankers in the northern Gulf began to release oil into international waters and three other intentional spills followed[12].

There are some direct and indirect sources of emissions during and after conflicts. The emission trends during conflicts are typically a function of how and where conflicts are fought (location of warzone) and the intensity of the conflict. Normally, in low intensity conflict the firepower used is limited and there is restricted damage to the infrastructure. The emissions come in two forms: direct and indirect emissions. During any war, mostly the first targets are oil production, storage or transportation infrastructure. In various wars during recent times mainly from 1991 Gulf war onwards to the wars in Colombia, Libya and Syria it has been observed that the consistent bombardment leads to fires and spills, which in turn generate emissions. There have been various cases of oil installations coming under massive attack. It has been assessed that the 1991 Gulf War's oil fires led to more than 2% of global fossil fuel CO2 emissions that year, with distant and long-lasting consequences. Forest cover and vegetation are other main victims of wars. During conflicts Vietnam, Cambodia and Laos is known to have lost the forest cover, with between 14 to 44 %. Even during the 2020 Nagorno-Karabakh conflict (territorial conflict between Armenia and Azerbaijan) forest was burnt owing drone warfare[13]. Also, there are other examples like crops been attacked in north east Syria.

Indirect emissions are difficult to quantify. Emissions from damaged infrastructure, the loss of vegetation, migration and delivering humanitarian aid could amount to indirect emissions. Mostly, there are fuel shortages during conflicts. This leads to people turning to more harmful and less efficient alternatives. Say in case of Syria, there is a crisis of artisanal oil refining[14], with little understanding of how the highly polluting practice contributes to emissions. In African region, at conflict prone area and at places like DRC, Yemen, South Sudan similar challenges do occur[15].

---

12 Ross, Marc A. (1992) "Environmental Warfare and the Persian Gulf War: Possible Remedies to Combat Intentional Destruction of the Environment," Penn State International Law Review: Vol. 10: No. 3, Article 7. P. 520.

13 "Report: Investigating the environmental dimensions of the 2020 Nagorno-Karabakh conflict", February, 2022, https://ceobs.org/investigating-the-environmental-dimensions-of-the-nagorno-karabakh-conflict/, accessed on May 24, 2022

14 Artisanal refining of crude oil comprises the treating of illegally tapped crude oil in bushes (forests) using local technology, resources and skills.

15 Eoghan Darbyshire, "How does war contribute to climate change?", June 14, 2021, https://ceobs.org/how-does-war-contribute-to-climate-change/, May 23, 2022

Russia-Ukraine war (2022) is expected have some disastrous consequences for the environmental safety of the region. The war has put Ukraine's ecosystems under threat from direct military action, which risks destroying landscapes, exacerbating deforestation and increasing the risk of forest fires. The conflict has render farmers unable to harvest the crop and risks a potential food crisis. More so, this invasion has raised concerns about the safety of Ukraine's nuclear facilities, its industrialised eastern regions and its vital role in global food supply chains. It is predicted that, owing to the long-drawn war, the risk of ecological fallout is high[16]. Ukraine war has already had a huge impact on wheat crop and food exports.

As discussed above, it is essentially the conventional nature of warfare, which is having serious impacts on the environment. All recent wars (mostly conventional in nature) indicate that, wars do impact climate adversely. One another form of warfare that needs some discussion in regards to the possible challenges for the environment (and humans) and that is the Nuclear Warfare.

Second World War, is the only occasion in the history, where the nuclear weapons were used. Subsequently, the idea of nuclear deterrence has taken a root and nuclear weapon states generally believe that these are more political weapons than the military weapons. However, this does not guarantee that the states would not use them in future. Particularly, no assurances can be given in case of states like North Korea, which is a pariah state with a recluse and autocratic political leadership, about their nuclear controls. Also, nuclear policies of Iran have always been a concern. More importantly, during Russia-Ukraine War (2022), the offensive nuclear posturing taken by Russia was very surprising. In addition to all this states like Pakistan are arguing in favour of tactical nuclear weapons as usable weapons. Under such circumstances it is important to apricate that what could be the possible environmental challenges of any unfortunate nuclear catastrophe.

If the state gets attacked by the nuclear weapons, then along with loss of human life and destruction of property, there would be a sever and long-term impact on the climate of the area, where the nuclear attack has taken place. Similarly, for the nearby vicinity, there would be major problems of nuclear radiations. There is a significant amount of literature available

---

16 Genevieve Kotarska and Lauren Young, "Green Insecurity: The Environmental Costs of War in Ukraine", April 25, 2022, https://rusi.org/explore-our-research/publications/commentary/green-insecurity-environmental-costs-war-ukraine, accessed on July 20, 2022

discussing how any possible nuclear war would affect the climate in long-term and weather conditions in short-term. Particularly, during the Cold War period much of metathetical modelling had happened to guess the possible short term and long-term impact of nuclear attacks. Much of work during these days did happen mostly for the extratropical region and there were some major projections about the possibility of nuclear winter.

During eighties, important research was done in regards to the lasting effects of nuclear war on the environment and people. However, possibly with the Cold War underway, the disastrous predictions done by such studies were undermined, so as not to attract much public attention. The idea was not to allow building of any public pressure to ban nuclear weapons. The projections by scientific community like the 'nuclear winter' were questioned by the authorities. This slowed the further research on this subject. The focus during the Cold War period, was to argue that the nuclear war would have short-term effects on the environment, however that was only partially true. The subsequent research in this field based on the actual inputs from locations like Hiroshima, Nagasaki and Chernobyl does indicate that there are long-term impacts of radiation spread and even the Fukushima reports second that.

In recent times, scientists have broadly worked on two to three possible scenarios like the conflicts involving North Korea-US, India-Pakistan and US-Russia. There are some projections, which indicate that North Korea is still not in the position to reach the continental US and hence the nuclear conflict could remain limited to the Korean peninsula alone. There are different studies available on this subject. There could be long-term climate change consequences, if a regional nuclear war with North Korea breaks out. In context of India-Pakistan, the focus is on the possibility of a small-scale nuclear war. While the larger scenario is a full-scale strategic war between the US and Russia or now owing to 2022 Ukraine conflict, it could even be NATO and Russia.

Various research findings conclude that any nuclear war would kick up huge amounts off soot into the upper atmosphere. Here it would counteract with the greenhouse effect and create a period of rapid cooling known as nuclear winter. The strategic targeting in case of smaller nuclear forces would possibly be big cities. This would lead to major firestorms spreading across urban and industrial spaces. The prevailing wind conditions would play its own role towards spreading the fire in a particular direction. All this would kick significant amount of soot into the air, on the scale of a couple of million tons. This soot would reach into the upper stratosphere, where it would reflect and absorb sunlight, and thus block the light from reaching the surface of the Earth. However, such impact could be regional depending on the strength of the blast. For the region there is a possibility of decrease in the average yearly rainfall amounts.

Some the recent more accurate models than the Cold War period, indicate that the original estimates of global cooling as a result of nuclear war needs a relook. The old models projected that the global average temperatures would decrease quite a bit initially and that the soot would remain in the upper atmosphere for a couple years at most. But, the present-day simulations indicate that the Earth's average temperature would actually decrease further than initially estimated and that the soot would remain in the upper stratosphere for significantly longer period, than actually predicted. As per new estimates, the average global temperature is likely to decrease by about 1.25 degrees Celsius on average for the first few years and that the soot would remain in the upper stratosphere for at least a decade, with temperatures still about half a degree Celsius below average at the end of that decade. Likewise, there is a possibility of some of the global temperature averages getting affected too (all depends on the nature of blast). All this would impact the weather patterns and there is a possibility of crops failing in the affected areas. There would be colossal disastrous results in case of a major war between the US/NATO-Russia[17]. There are different predications available for such scenario, but all will depend on the actual number of the nuclear weapons (and the yield) used in the conflict. Simplistically, a major nuclear war would lead to larger catastrophe and hence irreversible damage to environment.

All in all, there has been a great concern about the possible impact of war on environment, be it conventional war or nuclear war or any other form of warfare.

Actually, since the great wars (WW I and WW II) period onwards, environment has been the most silent sufferer of the doings of the war. For some time now, there has been a feeling that counting war casualties

---

17 For the entire discussion on nuclear issues please refer Andrew Freedman, "Nuclear war with North Korea 'would be suicidal', climate experts warn", August 9, 2017, https://mashable.com/article/north-korea-nuclear-war-climate-change-winter, accessed on May 14, 2022 and Sarah Van Hoesen, "Science of Environmental Effects of Nuclear War", Artifacts Journal, Issue 17, Sumner 2019, https://artifactsjournal.missouri.edu/2019/06/science-of-environmental-effects-of-nuclear-war/, accessed on July 21, 2022 and Yonglong Lu et al, "Monitoring long-term ecological impacts from release of Fukushima radiation water into ocean", Geography and Sustainability, Volume 2, Issue 2, June 2021, pp. 95-98.

in terms of dead and wounded soldiers and civilians, destroyed cities and livelihoods is not sufficient and there is a need to appreciate the environmental damage during the wars too. The United Nations Environment Programme (UNEP) has found that over the last 60 years, at least 40 percent of all internal conflicts have been connected to the exploitation of natural resources, from timber, diamonds, gold and oil to scarce resources such as fertile land and water. Conflicts involving natural resources have also been found to be twice as likely to relapse.

The United Nations since 1999 is known to be monitoring and assessing the damages caused to the environment due to the armed conflicts. On 5 November 2001, the UN General Assembly has declared that 6 November of each year would be observed as the International Day for Preventing the Exploitation of the Environment in War and Armed Conflict (A/RES/56/4). While on 27 May 2016, the UN Environment Assembly adopted resolution UNEP/EA.2/Res.15, which recognizes the role of healthy ecosystems and sustainably managed resources in reducing the risk of armed conflict, and reaffirmed its strong commitment to the full implementation of the Sustainable Development Goals listed in General Assembly resolution 70/1, entitled 'Transforming our world: the 2030 Agenda for Sustainable Development'[18].

Legal Structures

The ENMOD (environmental modification) Convention is the only international treaty that specifically addresses the means of methods of environmental warfare. This United Nations Convention came into force on October 5, 1978. It was approved in 1976 by UN General Assembly resolution 31/72 in response to international concern over the use of military tactics to manipulate and damage the environment. At that point in time, attention on the weaponisation of the environment had increased after the US had use of weather modification techniques (cloud seeding and Agent Orange herbicide) in the Vietnam War[19].

This convention prohibits states from 'engaging in military or any other hostile use of environmental modification techniques having widespread, long-lasting or severe effects as the means of destruction, damage or injury

---

18 https://www.un.org/en/observances/environment-in-war-protection-day, accessed on Jun 17, 2022

19 Gabriela Kolpak, "From ENMOD to geoengineering: the environment as a weapon of war", April 7, 2020, https://ceobs.org/from-enmod-to-geoengineering-the-environment-as-a-weapon-of-war/, accessed on July 18, 2022

to any other State Party'. Many countries including India, Pakistan and the US are signatories to this Convention. But China is not.

The ENMOD defines Environmental modification technique (EMT) as any technique for changing – through the deliberate manipulation of natural processes – the dynamics, composition or structure of the earth, including its biota, lithosphere, hydrosphere and atmosphere, or of outer space (article II)[20].

This environmental treaty mechanism[21] has its own limitations too. In a sense, it could be viewed as only an agreement on paper. As such it would be very difficult to claim that a particular weather event has occurred as a result of covert weather modification experimentations. Also, the Convention has no authority to enforce any punishment.

At the state level, the US appears to be a one country, which has felt the need to have legal provisions to address the issues related to the weather modification. They have been systematically thinking of evolving legal structures to address the issues of weather modification since the 1940s (this is not to forget that, they are the only country, which has actually used weather weapons in warfare). During the 1940s, commercial application of the weather modification technology, commercial rainmaking had begun (was in nascent state), but the industry involvement also brought with it, the legal complexities. The state regulations did commence during the 1950s. The scientific community was particularly very keen to have legal support from the state and hence the need for a law was getting projected. During 1960s, there have been few legal cases in the US, involving issues related to weather modification. As a result, by the 1960s-70s, two-thirds of the states in the US had passed weather modification laws[22].

The following are the Weather Modification Reporting Laws in the US[23]:

---

20 https://www.un.org/disarmament/enmod/, accessed on July 21, 2022

21 For various details about the negotiations on the ENMOD treaty please refer: Lawrence Juda, "Negotiating a Treaty on Environmental Modification Warfare: The Convention on Environmental Warfare and its Impact Upon Arms Control Negotiations", *International Organization*, Vol. 32, No. 4 (Autumn, 1978), pp. 975-991

22 Ray Jay Davis, "Four Decades of American Weather Modification Law", J. Reuben Clark Law School, Brigham Young University, Utah, pp.102-106 and James N. Corbridge, Jr. and Raphael J. Moses, "Weather Modification: Law and Administration", Natural Resources Journal, Vol. 8, No. 2 (April 1968), pp. 207-235

23 http://uscode.house.gov/view.xhtml?path=/prelim@title15/chapter9A& edition= prelim, accessed on Sep 23, 2018

➢ Weather Modification Reporting Act of 1972-Public Law 92-205 "AN ACT To provide for the reporting of weather modification activities to the Federal Government"15 CFR Part 908-"Maintaining Records and Submitting Reports on Weather Modification Activities"

➢ National Weather Modification Policy Act of 1976-Public Law 94-490 "AN ACT To authorize and direct the Secretary of Commerce to develop a national policy on weather modification, and for other purposes"15 U.S. Code Chapter 9A-"Weather Modification Activities or Attempts; Reporting Requirement"

During 1975, the US and Canada entered into an agreement under the aegis of the UN for exchange of information on weather modification activity.

Epilogue

The science of meteorology entails study of the physics and chemistry of the earth's atmosphere. The main focus of the science of meteorology is on the lower parts of the atmosphere, primarily the troposphere, where most weather takes place. For many years, scientists are trying to decode the behaviour of the weather and are also attempting to predict its future trajectory. They have received a significant amount of success in this regard. However, there is still no guarantee that the prediction about the weather will always come true.

For last few decades, the science of meteorology is getting benefited from the availability huge volume of data, almost in real-time. This has become possible, due to increase in number of observational platforms. The present-day of global weather observational platforms are fitted with state-of-art sensors and are supported by constellations of weather and other remote sensing satellites delivering weather imagery. All this is assisting much towards improving the quality of observations and now weather information is also available from remote locations. This data (current weather conditions) is improving the accuracy of numerical weather prediction (NWP) forecasts which use mathematical models of the atmosphere and oceans to predict the weather. But, there are still some challenges, which are mainly associated with scientific interpretations like lack of very clear understanding of the nature of the interaction between atmospheric and land surface processes, full understating of the hydrological cycle, the dynamics of deep convection, the role of the tropopause in atmospheric dynamics and some other factors. Also, around 8% of recent global climate change can be attributed to solar variability, but the mechanisms coupling solar variability to the earth's climate system remain poorly understood[1].

---

1   https://www.frontiersin.org/articles/10.3389/feart.2013.00001/full, accessed on July 25, 2022 and Goswami B N (1996). "The challenge of weather prediction". *Resonance*, Vol 2, pp. 8-15.

Military meteorologists are known to be predicting the battlefield weather since the World War periods. The nature of battlefield has evolved over a period of time. In the 21st century, military meteorologists are required also to focus on urban climate more seriously since now battles also fought in cities. They are required to focus more on micrometeorology owing to the scales involved. Overall, it could be said that the modern-day military meteorologists are far better equipped with availability of wider and more accurate observational base and various IT tools for undertaking climate and weather modelling. But at the same, they are required to factor in new factors like: the challenges owing quickly changing nature of warfare, addition of new fighting platforms and weapon systems and vagaries in weather systems and patterns owing climate change, while apricating the future of weather.

This work argues that, in the 21st century, armed forces need to look at weather information, not only as one of the essentials to be factored in before the start of any military operation, but as a tool helping them to decide on overall conduct of operations and also a factor towards identifying the choice of fighting platform and weapon system, so as to derive maximum benefit either from good weather or adverse weather conditions. Modern-day wars could happen in different shapes and sizes. Now, the medium in which wars happen has even reached to the outer space. At the same time, the aspects like avoiding collateral damage have become the key in the modern-day warfighting. Obviously, military meteorologists are required to be more accurate and also are required to establish special units to cater for requirements like space weather forecasting.

Modern-day weapon systems are making rapid progress. Various new weapons are getting designed and developed for army, navy and air forces. There are standoff weapons which may be launched from a distance adequate to allow aggressor to evade any defensive fire from the target area. Typically, they are used against land and sea-based targets during an operation and they comprise of cruise missiles, glide bombs and short-range ballistic missiles. Also, there are precision guided munitions (PGMs), which travel in air on its own for considerable amount of distance and time. In recent times, major innovations have happened in the field of self-propelled artillery. Ukraine-Russia war has witnessed the Ukraine forces receiving ten self-propelled artillery systems and loitering munitions (suicide drones) which are supposed to be the most modern systems. Hypersonic missiles, which travel more than five times the speed of sound, have already been battle tested by Russia on Ukrainian targets.

There are reports that some defence manufacturers have succeeded in reducing the size of directed energy weapon system and this pod could be mounted on a fighter aircraft for firing. Such laser weapons can help shooting down incoming anti-aircraft missiles. Maritime forces are also known to be getting equipped with all-electric, high-energy laser weapons. In addition, some states have started arguing that tactical nuclear weapons could emerge as usable weapons (?).Presently, focus has increased towards developing autonomous weapons and quantum technology-based weapons. All this indicates that the modern warfare is growing beyond the conventional ways of war fighting where a weapon delivery platform would simply deliver a bomb on the target. Military meteorological services are mostly designed to the 'conventional' requirements. But, in the era of Industry 4.0, smart weapons are becoming the key for warfighting. Now, military meteorologists are required to forecast weather and atmospheric conditions, not only for the operations of platforms (like air craft, tank, ship or submarine), but also for weapons.

There are three case studies presented in this book, which discuss the role of weather in some of the recent conflicts. They have been presented to appreciate that, how the weather could have been a disabler or an enabler during the conduct of these military operations. These studies indicate that weather plays a vital role, both during strategic and tactical phases of warfare. These studies also indirectly indicate that the projections made by defence industry, that 'the modern technologies make all-weather warfighting feasible', are only partially true and weather continuous to remain a hazard.

It is important to note that these case studies are carried out based on open-source information and hence they are very broad-based. Military organizations are required to undertake detailed and multi-faceted studies based on the actual data available with them like performance of platforms, say aircrafts, ships or submarines in a specific battle. For example, in regards to understating the effectiveness of air power in bad weather, some specific studies should be carried out based on the statistics like: how many sorties were undertaken, how many returned back since they were unable to approach the target due to bad weather, were munitions delivered accurately on the targets, were any weather related problems faced in the landing/dropping zones, which aviation weather hazards were more problematic, were specific mission related weather forecasts issued during planning stage, were the weather related challenges highlighted or the bad weather occurred all of a sudden, what was the accuracy factor of mission forecasts and various other related accepts. Best on such inputs a detailed audit of existing military meteorological setups and their performance during actual operations could be undertaken for suggesting further improvements.

Intentional tampering of weather for the purposes of military gains is not a new idea. The technology to control or modify the weather is available for many years. Operation Popeye (1967-72) has proved beyond doubt that weather warfare is a reality. However, post-Vietnam War, no major incidents of the state manipulating the weather for military gains have come to light. At present, various new developments happening in the field of science and technology are directly getting reflected in to the war doctrines of the states. Ideas like cyber warfare, space warfare have already taken roots in the global security architecture. The globally followed war practices in the ICT era, like network centricity is all about using modern technologies. On similar lines, there is a possibility that meteorological manipulation could be viewed by some states as a new form of meteorological science driven warfare.

Weather modification is a dual-use technique, it would be extremely difficult to identify the real intentions of any state undertaking such experimentations. At the same time, modern-day technologies offer various options for surveillance and intelligence-gathering. In future, there could be a requirement of establishing an agency for Weather Situational Awareness (WSA), which could contentiously keep on tracing all weather modification experiments in real time. For this purpose, a network of satellites, radars, reconnaissance aircraft and human intelligence would be required to be put in place for gathering information about various weather modification-related activities. Conceptualization and management of project is possible under the aegis of UN or as a major multilateral agenda. Such efforts could also help to dismiss any possible conspiracy theories.

There are claims that the ambitious project by the US, the HAARP system, is put on backburner. However, there are also some reports that a fully operational HAARP system is already in place. Theoretically, the capability of this system could be said to dwarf various existing conventional and strategic weapons systems. It looks unlikely that the US would allow such significant technological and financial investments to wither away. Possibly, they are waiting for correct 'environment' to induct such systems in their defence architecture.

The Chinese investments in weather modification and their continuous experiments with these techniques from the 2008 Olympics, the 60th National Day Parade, 2018 Africa Summit to the conduct of Winter Olympics in the year 2022, gives them adequate experience to become more proficient in the business of weather modification. There is no guarantee that China would desist from using weather modification techniques in conflict situations to gain a military advantage. Even during peace time, such techniques could be used to create artificial drought or floods to affect the economy of the adversary. In particular, states bordering China need to be careful. Weather knows no political borders and weather patterns in a neighbouring state can be affected even by conducting experiments on one's own territory.

There is a danger form the projects like the China's Sky River, which are meant to produce rainfall over a vast area. The science of artificial cloud making still remains an incomplete science. Scientists are not totally confident that experiments like Sky River would make rain happen only on the identified zones. If such experiments divert the rain belt unknowingly to the adjoining parts (say Indian region) then that may lead to creation artificial floods. Hence, apart from scientific implications, there are major geostrategic implications of such projects. As such India has major concerns in regards to China's proposal to build a massive dam (hydel project) over the Brahmaputra River (for China, Yarlung Tsangpo). India wants Beijing to ensure that the interests of lower riparian states are not harmed. Any uncontrolled weather modification in China would cause harm to India being a lower riparian state.

During the last few decades, China has made exceptional progress in the field of supercomputing. They are known to have more than 200 such machines, which fall in the list of worlds' fastest 500 supercomputers. Present-day weather forecasting depends much on such machines. Weather modifications have great dependency on computational science. China appears to have a major edge in this regard. Also, it is important to note that China is making good progress in the field of quantum technologies. Major breakthroughs in quantum computing and quantum communications could go a long way towards assisting China's weather modification programme. There is a need for global powers to peruse China to sign and ratify the ENMOD Convention.

At present, the nature of damage and destruction the world is witnessing owing to typhoons/hurricanes in phenomenal. Also, drought conditions and high temperatures are leading to devastating forest fires.

Since states like China, Japan and the US are one the main sufferers from such natural calamities. There is a possibility that some of these states could argue for the need for manipulation of major weather systems to save humanity. Under such circumstances, there could be attempts, say to break (or weaken) a dangerous storm/hurricane in the high seas or divert the storm approaching the coast. The time has come for the UN and other multilateral agencies to become proactive in regards to such possibilities and add the issue of weather modification on their agenda.

Presently, the world could be said to be passing through a state of transition. Energy, food, water, minerals are considered to be the possible future interstate security flashpoints. The adverse impact of intentional modification of weather by one state on its neighbour could also emerge as interstate security flashpoint in the future.

Currently, on the global stage, very minimal legal provisions are available to address various challenges associated with the modification of weather. It may be difficult to address any act of intentional tampering of weather by using existing edifices of international law. All these years, policy makers and legal community appear to have provided less attention towards legal issues related to weather. This needs to change, because the threat may become more real in years to come.

Today, it would be difficult to say with certitude about the prospects of weather warfare for the future. Much will depend upon the technological, physical, social, economic and geostrategic settings. Weather warfare is much different than any other form of warfare. But, at the same time, the capabilities developed by a few states in the arena of weather modifications should become a cause of concern. Hence, there is a need for reckoning issues related to weather modification, in the 21st century's security discourse.

Modern-day military conflicts indicate that wars could be, both short period and long period wars. Defence forces need to remain prepared to fight under variable climatic conditions prevailing during different seasons. The terrain conditions for the troops could be very challenging like the presence of desserts, snowclad mountains or thickly vegetated jungles. The weather would have an impact (peacetime and wartime) on every type of military operation; be it special forces operations, conventional operations, nuclear operations or operations in the outer space. For all these years, the subject of meteorology is been studied as a scientific discipline, and required weather information was shared as and when required for warfighting purposes. However, particularly since 1990s, the nature of warfare is found continuously evolving. Weather information is found playing a crucial role towards directing various military actions. Military planners need to take in account various nuances of weather in correct strategic context. Weather information needs to be fed, both for the operations of military platforms and as well as for weapon's autonomous travel. Beyond conventional warfare, new turfs like weather warfare, space warfare are found deliberated on. Hence, in modern-day military architecture, there is a need to factor in applicability of science of meteorology at the strategic realm.

Index

A

Al-Qaeda 118

American War for Independence 53

Andronicus 15

Anti-Submarine Warfare (ASW) 89

Argonne National Laboratory 145

Aristotle 12, 13, 17, 49

Artificial rainfall 144

Askesian Society 21

Atlantic Richfield Corporation 159

B

Battle of Agincourt 50

Battle of Leipzig 56

Battle of Waterloo 55, 56

Belarus 128, 129, 130

Bering Straits 155

Black Sea 58, 129, 130, 131

British Aerospace Systems 159

British Royal Navy 22, 62

C

Carl von Clausewitz 10, 80

Carrington Event 185

Chernobyl 175, 208

China Meteorological Administration 171

China Seismo-Electromagnetic Satellite 160

Civil War 16, 53, 54, 71, 143

Climate Engineering 141

Close Air Support (CAS) 85

Cloud Ionisers 146

Cloud Seeding 146, 167, 175

Cold War 2, 3, 6, 7, 42, 43, 68, 69, 70, 71, 74, 154, 155, 186, 189, 208, 209

Crimean Peninsula 127, 129

Crimean War 57

Cyber warfare 139

D

Daniel Gabriel Fahrenheit 15

Défense Advanced Research Projects Agency 159

E

Edmund Halley 18

ENMOD Convention 217

Environmental Science Services Administration 43

European Centre for Medium-Range Weather Forecasting 39

European Space Agency 39

European Union 10

F

Falklands War (1982) 71

G

Galilei Galileo 18

General Electric Research Laboratory 144, 154

Genghis Khan 52

Global Climate Observing System 43

Gulf War 1991 3, 10, 71, 72, 73, 74, 99, 101, 102, 150, 190, 192, 206

H

Hakata Bay 52

Hannibal 51, 148

High-frequency Active Auroral Research Program 159

High-frequency Active Auroral Research Program (HAARP) 159, 160, 216

Hiroshima 68, 95, 208

Hitler 58, 59, 61, 135, 148

Hybrid Warfare 81

I

India Meteorological Department (IMD) 46, 47

India-Pakistan War (1971) 71

Intergovernmental Oceanographic Commission 94, 147

Intergovernmental Panel on Climate Change 43

Intermediate-Range Nuclear Forces Treaty (INF) 71

International Civil Aviation Organization 93, 184

International Meteorological Organization 22, 40

International Space Station 194

International Telecommunication Union 94

Ionospheric Heater 146

Iraq War 2003 74, 99, 102

Islamic State of Iraq and Syria 117

J

Johannes Kepler 18

Joint Direct Attack Munitions 99

K

Kandahar 119, 122, 125

Korean War (1950-1953) 71, 123

Kunduz 126, 127

L

Landing Craft Air Cushion 91

Laser-guided bombs 107

Lebanon War (1982-1985) 71

Low Altitude Navigation Targeting
     Infrared for Night (LANTIRN)
     73

Luck of Kokura 67

M

Macedonian army 50

Madden-Julian Oscillation 35

Maritime Operations 87

Martyrdom Operatives Battalion.
     See Katibat al-Istishadiin

Mazar-e-Sharif 119

Meteorological Society of Mannheim
     21, 40

Metropolitan Meteorological Experi-
     ment 145

Mongol invasion 148

Mosaic Warfare 81

Mosul Campaign 117

Mullah Umar 119

N

Nagasaki 67, 68, 95, 208

Napoleon Bonaparte 54, 56, 57

Napoleonic wars 143

National Hurricane Research Project
     153

National Oceanic and Atmospheric
     Administration 17, 43, 176, 182

National Weather Service 17, 30, 31,
     38, 44, 182

Neolithic Revolution 14

Network Centric Warfare 81

Niemen River 55

Non-contact Warfare 81

Normandy Landings 65

North Atlantic Treaty Organization
     10, 39, 128, 208, 209

Northern Alliance 119

North Korea 95, 207, 208, 209

Nuclear Warfare 81, 95, 207

O

Ocean Fertilisation 203

Office of Marine & Aviation Opera-
     tions 44

Office of Oceanic and Atmospheric
     Research 44

Operation Anaconda 119, 127

Operation Barbarossa 58, 135, 148

Operation Desert Storm 71, 72, 190

Operation Overlord 65

Operation Popeye 155, 156, 158, 216

Operation Typhoon 58, 59

Organisation for Economic Co-opera-
     tion and Development 39

Osama bin Laden 118, 124

P

Paralympic Games 170

Persian Gulf 72, 73, 99, 103, 104, 106, 109, 206

Project Cirrus 144, 151, 152, 153

Project Stormfury 153

R

Rhone River 51

S

Sabine Island 64

Saddam Hussein 71, 99, 101, 205

Salang Pass 126

Search and Rescue (SAR) 85

Second Punic War 50, 51

Second World War 2, 7, 23, 29, 37, 52, 58, 60, 78, 82, 83, 145, 207

Shang Dynasty 50

Solar and Heliospheric Observatory 182

Solar Dynamics Observatory 182

Solar Radiation Management 202

Solar System 186, 188

Solar Terrestrial Relations Observatory 182

Space warfare 139

Space Weather v, 141, 178, 180, 182, 183, 184, 187

Stratospheric Aerosol Injection 146

Syrian War 74

T

Tectonic Weapons 151

Television Infrared Observation Satellite 42

Theophrastus 13

Tomahawk land-attack cruise missile 96

Trojan War 2

Types of Warfare 81

Asymmetric Warfare 81

Conventional Warfare 81, 82

Cyber Warfare 81

Nuclear Warfare/WMD Warfare 81

Space Warfare v, 81, 178, 189, 191, 199

U

Ukraine-Russia War 127

United Nations Educational, Scientific and Cultural Organization 147

United Nations Environment Programme 43, 210

United Nations Office for Outer Space Affairs 196

Unmanned aerial vehicles (UAVs) 85, 107, 111, 127

Urban Warfare 101, 113

V

Vietnam War (1955-1975) 71

W

Wakhan Corridor 121

Weapons of mass destruction (WMDs)
82, 99, 195

Weather Warfare 142, 144, 150, 151,
153, 154, 156, 157, 161

Weather Weapons 150, 172

World Climate Research Programme
43

World Meteorological Organization
22, 32, 40, 94

Y

Yom Kippur War (1973) 71